MW01612147

# CONTEMPORARY ISSUES *in* PERMANENCY PLANNING

GERALD P. MALLON AND BOGART R. LEASHORE, EDITORS

CWLA PRESS
WASHINGTON, DC

The Child Welfare League of America and the journal *Child Welfare* gratefully acknowledge The Hite Foundation for its generous support of this book.

CWLA Press is an imprint of the Child Welfare League of America. The Child Welfare League of America is the nation's oldest and largest membership-based child welfare organization. We are committed to engaging people everywhere in promoting the well-being of children, youth, and their families, and protecting every child from harm.

CHILD WELFARE LEAGUE OF AMERICA, INC.
HEADQUARTERS
440 First Street, NW, Third Floor, Washington, DC 20001-2085
E-mail: books@cwla.org

CURRENT PRINTING (last digit)
10 9 8 7 6 5 4 3 2 1

Printed in Canada
Cover design by James Melvin
Text design by Julie Pignataro
ISBN # 0–87868-859-5

# Contents

# PREFACE

S ince 1980, with passage of the Adoption Assistance and Child Welfare Act [P.L. 96-272], and again reinforced in the Adoption and Safe Families Act of 1997 (ASFA), permanency planning has served as the broad casework and legal practice umbrella for the provision of the continuum of child welfare services. Permanency planning involves a mix of family-centered, child-focused, and culturally relevant philosophies, program components, and practice strategies designed to help children and youth live in families that offer continuity of relationships with nurturing parents or caregivers and the opportunity to establish lifetime relationships (Maluccio & Fein, 1993).

The process of permanency planning is intended to safely limit entry into placement and limit the time children and youth spend in care, because it is widely acknowledged that separation, loss, and unresolved grief, as well as the uncertain and long-term nature of the foster care experience, can have a negative effect on children's overall sense of belonging, identity formation, and emotional well-being (Greenblatt & Day, 2000; Sudia, 1986). Thus, planning for children's permanency as well as their safety and developmental well-being should begin when a family first comes in contact with the child welfare agency—with families actively included in individualized case planning, service delivery, and decisionmaking about where their child will grow up. Permanency planning requires that case-by-case assessments and interventions balance the time needed for a family to change with a child's need for continuity of relationships, secure attachments, and the ability to tolerate separation and loss.

An array of permanency outcomes should be considered as desirable for children, beginning with consideration of the benefits of keeping children and youth at home safely with their parents or relatives to prevent the trauma of unnecessary separation and placement. For children and youth who cannot remain with their families and for whom placement in family foster care or group care settings is temporarily necessary, family reunification efforts are, in most cases, the preferred permanency option whenever they can be done safely. When children and youth cannot return home within the time frame of 12 to 15 months established by federal law, alternative permanency options should be pursued including adoption by relatives, foster parents, or a new family; legal guardianship with relatives, foster parents, or another caring adult; and in special circumstances, another planned alternative living arrangement with relatives, foster parents, or in a small community-based group or residential setting, each with attention to lifetime family connections that can be nurtured and preserved.

Permanency planning balances the rights and needs of children, youth, and parents with the harm that can be brought by the passage of time and delays in decisionmaking. Although there is no one correct outcome for achieving permanency for all children and youth, the challenge is to arrive at the best permanency outcome in a timely manner that offers the greatest measure of emotional and legal permanency for every child or youth.

Permanency planning involves a mix of family-centered casework and legal strategies designed to ensure that children and youth have safe, caring, stable, and lifelong families in which to grow up. According to the National Resource Center for Foster Care and Permanency Planning at the Hunter College School of Social Work (1999), these strategies include the following:

- Targeted and appropriate efforts to protect safety, achieve permanence, and strengthen families' and children's well-being.

- Early intervention and prevention with reasonable efforts to prevent unnecessary out-of-home care when safety can be ensured.
- Safety as a paramount concern throughout the life of the case, with aggravated circumstances identified when reasonable efforts to preserve or reunify families may not be required.
- Appropriate, least restrictive, out-of-home placements within family, culture, and community, with comprehensive family and child assessments, written case plans, goal-oriented practice, and concurrent permanency plans encouraged.
- Reasonable efforts to reunify families and maintain family connections and continuity in children's relationships when safety can be ensured.
- Reasonable efforts to find alternative permanency options outside of the child welfare system when children cannot return to parents, through adoption, legal guardianship, or in special circumstances, another planned, alternative, permanent living arrangement.
- Filing of the termination of parental rights petition at 15 months after placement when this is in best interests of the child and when exceptions do not apply.
- Collaborative case activity, which includes partnerships among birthparents, foster parents, agency staff, court and legal staff, and community service providers.
- Frequent and quality parent-child visitation.
- Timely case reviews, permanency hearings, and decisionmaking about where children will grow up, based on children's sense of time.

In addition, children, youth, and family service practitioners who are responsive to the fulfilling the promise of permanency are aware of the need to include the following elements in their practice:

- Family-centered and strengths- or needs-based practice.
- Service delivery that is community based.
- Cultural competency and respect for diversity.
- Open and inclusive practice, with full disclosure to parents.
- Nonadversarial approaches to problem solving and service delivery.
- Concurrent rather than sequential consideration of all permanency options.

Although the articles presented in this special issue do not address the full range of permanency planning issues (no special issue could do that), many prominent themes have been included. Because the majority of these articles are written by academics, the reader will also see reflected in them a broad range of opinions and perspectives specifically about permanency planning and, in some cases, about child welfare in general. These multiple perspectives do not always conform to the viewpoints of the National Resource Center for Foster Care and Permanency Planning (NRCFCPP), or to those of the Children's Bureau at the Administration for Children and Families at the U.S. Department of Health and Human Services. Members of the academy are free to exercise their right to academic freedom and, as such, colleagues were free to and in fact expected to challenge, critique, or commend practices, policies, and perspectives as they pertained to permanency planning. We are sure, however, that these multiple perspectives make a valuable contribution to the professional literature and in fact promote excellence in child welfare practice.

This special issue represents the first attempt by *Child Welfare* to comprehensively examine and investigate the meaning and experiences of permanency planning for children and youth in out-of-home care settings. As an early contribution to a wider inquiry, we hope that it will expand over the next few decades and stimulate further discussion by practitioners, policymakers, and scholars in the field of children, youth, and family services.

We extend our appreciation to those colleagues who contributed to this volume, and we are grateful also to our good colleague, Sarah Greenblatt, former Director of the NRCFCPP and current Director of the Casey Center for Effective Child Welfare Practice at Casey Family Services in Shelton, Connecticut, who contributed to the initial stages of this volume. We also thank The Hite Foundation for its support of this special issue.

Gerald P. Mallon, DSW
Associate Professor and Director, NRCFCPP
Hunter College School of Social Work, New York

Bogart R. Leashore, PhD
Dean, Hunter College School of Social Work, New York

## References

Greenblatt, S. B., & Day, P. (2000). *Renewing our commitment to permanency for children—Wingspread conference summary report*. Washington, DC: CWLA Press.

Maluccio, A. N., & Fein, E. (1993). Permanency planning: A redefinition. *Child Welfare, 62*(3), 195-201.

National Resource Center for Foster Care and Permanency Planning at the Hunter College School of Social Work. (1999). *Handouts on concurrent permanency planning*. New York: Author.

Sudia, C. (1986). Preventing out-of-home placement of children: The first step to permanency planning. *Children Today, 15*(6), 4.

# Chapter 1

# Older Children in Preadoptive Homes: Issues Before Termination of Parental Rights

*Susan B. Edelstein, Dorli Burge, and Jill Waterman*

In many jurisdictions, after the end of reunification services to birthparents, but before termination of parental rights, children are placed with parents who are licensed as foster parents but are committed to adopting the child. Using case examples, this article discusses the emotional and psychological difficulties often encountered by children and their prospective adoptive parents when birthparent visitation takes place and legal uncertainties exist. In addition, this article offers clinical and policy recommendations to help both the children and families in these situations as well as the professionals who work with them.

*Susan B. Edelstein, MSW, LCSW, is Director of TIES (Training, Intervention, Education, and Services) for Adoption, University of California at Los Angeles (UCLA) Center for Healthier Children, Families, and Communities; and Adjunct Assistant Professor, UCLA Department of Pediatrics. Dorli Burge, PhD, is Chief Psychologist, TIES for Adoption; and Associate Clinical Professor, UCLA Psychology Department. Jill Waterman, PhD, is Mental Health Coordinator, TIES for Adoption; Coordinator, UCLA Psychology Clinic; and Adjunct Professor of psychology at UCLA. The au-*

In many jurisdictions, once a court ends reunification services to birthparents, children who are not already living with caregivers committed to adopting them are moved to foster-adoptive parents instead of waiting until termination of parental rights (TPR). These applicants have an approved adoption home study and a foster care license. In this way, the court can be reasonably assured that the child will be adopted and not become a "legal orphan." The children can experience earlier permanency than if they had to wait until TPR occurs and appeals are completed. This approach, although clearly beneficial in some ways, may present special challenges for children beyond toddlerhood and their new prospective adoptive families. This article explores the similarity and dissimilarity of this approach to foster-adoptive placement and concurrent planning. The emotional and psychological difficulties encountered by the children and their prospective adoptive parents as they deal with legal uncertainties that can arise are discussed. Clinical and policy recommendations are offered to help both children and families as well as the professionals who work with them in these situations.

## Literature Review

During the past 30 years, legislators and child welfare professionals have attempted to develop sound and creative legislation and practice approaches to providing the earliest possible permanency for children in foster care. Two approaches have been foster-adoptive programs and concurrent planning.

The Federal Adoption Assistance and Child Welfare Act of 1980 highlighted permanency and continuity of relationships for

*thors wish to thank the staff of TIES for Adoption for their clinical contributions to the material presented; the Los Angeles juvenile court dependency judicial officers; and Randee Schuster Motzkin, Research Attorney, juvenile court, for their consultation on this topic; the adoption division social workers who are challenged daily by these issues; and the parents and children who share their struggles and joys with us and from whom we continually learn and draw inspiration.*

children in informing case planning and practice (Lutz, 2001). The Adoption and Safe Families Act of 1997 (ASFA) went further by requiring states to achieve permanent placements for children in shorter time frames and by identifying what outcomes constitute successful permanency for children. ASFA also supports concurrent planning, the practice that allows social workers to simultaneously plan for more than one possible outcome. Section 103 instructs states to "concurrently...identify, recruit, process, and approve a qualified family for an adoption" while filing a TPR petition, and Section 201 encourages "programs that place children into preadoptive families without waiting for TPR."

*Foster-adoptive programs*, developed in the 1970s, are defined as programs that place children with approved or prospective adoptive families, on a foster care basis, before the children are free for adoption. In these situations, the foster-adoptive families have a desire to be adoptive parents, and the children have a high likelihood of being adopted. The practice developed out of the child welfare field's concern that children not experience multiple placements and that a permanent plan for young children be made at the earliest possible time, rather than having to wait until TPR has occurred. The foster-adoptive parents commit to providing foster care for as long as the child requires this service and to assisting the child in navigating through the realities of foster care, including visits with birthparents. These same parents agree to adopt the child if and when parental rights are terminated. These programs are basically foster care with the potential for, but not certainty of, adoption. The focus is to stabilize the child's life. This goal may not necessarily meet the foster parents' desire to adopt a child (Gardiner, 1987; Gill & Amadio, 1983; Mica & Vosler, 1990).

Concurrent planning—with its emphasis on the use of permanent planning families who are carefully recruited, trained, and supported in working with and mentoring the birthparents—began as an extension of the foster care-adoption model (Gill & Amadio, 1983; Katz, 1999). This approach was designed for the very young child whose family's chronic problems (often neglect associated with poverty and drug or alcohol abuse) left the child languishing in out-of-home care (Katz & Robinson, 1991). *Concurrent planning* is defined as "working toward family reunification while, at the same time, developing an alternative permanency plan" (Katz, Robinson, & Spoonemore, 1994). With concurrent planning, a greater possibility exists for the children's return to birthfamilies (Gill & Amadio, 1983; Lutz, 2001) than with the foster-adoptive programs. The components of concurrent planning are intensive, focused outreach and services to birthfamilies; early searches for relatives; and frequent, consistent, safe visits between children and birthparents to mend relationships and promote attachment.

Documented benefits of concurrent planning include:

1. Shortening the length of time in care for the child by full disclosure with birthparents about the detrimental effects of out-of-home care on children, the urgency of reunification, and the agency's concurrent plan to prevent the child from remaining in out-of-home care;
2. Enhanced comfort with communication between birthparents and caregivers because the foster parents are helped to collaborate with the birthparents;
3. Greater likelihood of relinquishments, as well as continuity of relationships for the child, because the foster parents will keep in touch with a child reunified with birthparents or the foster parents will permit an open adoption; and
4. Using permanency planning families who assume the major risks of uncertainty of placement outcome for the child instead of the child's bearing the risk (Katz et al., 1994; Lutz, 2001).

In many jurisdictions, concurrent planning, as described in the literature, has not yet been fully instituted for all children whose prognosis for family reunification is poor. It is difficult to find families who are willing and ready to perform the dual function of facilitating family reunification as well as adoption, and it is challenging for struggling, understaffed agencies to implement such vigorous and demanding programs. However, because legally free children are not readily available, many families, recruited as adoptive parents and whose primary desire is to be adoptive parents, are willing to stretch their preferences and accept a child who is not yet legally free because this situation creates a higher probability of being matched with a child. Usually, their understanding is that the children are likely to be adopted, because reunification services have ceased. Placing the children in these homes before TPR is similar in some ways to the foster-adoptive placement and the concurrent planning programs described above. The children involved have a poor prognosis for reunification, the foster parents are approved and committed to adopt if adoption is feasible, and the child is placed with them before a TPR petition is filed. In accordance with ASFA, the child can experience permanency earlier than if placement were delayed until TPR. This approach differs, however, from foster-adoptive placement and concurrent planning programs described in the literature. In this approach, the child is placed with the prospective adoptive family very late in the dependency court process, usually after reunification services have been ordered to cease. In many instances, the child has not lived with the birthparent for a year or longer. The family has no commitment to fostering for as long as is necessary, to working toward family reunification, to facilitating visitation, and to mentoring the birthparent. In many instances, these parents have no prior experience with foster parenting or parenting in general. They have obtained their license as a foster parent just to be able to accept the placement of a child they hope to adopt.

This article is based on the clinical experience of staff of the University of California, Los Angeles (UCLA) TIES (Training, Intervention, Education, and Services) for Adoption, an interagency, interdisciplinary collaborative project of the UCLA Department of Pediatrics, the UCLA Psychology Department, the Los Angeles County

Departments of Children and Family Services and Mental Health, and private foundations. Project staff support the adoption of children with special needs by providing services before, during the transition to, and after adoptive placement of the children from the foster care system. In our work with prospective adoptive parents, we facilitate empathy for the struggles of the birthparents, so the adoptive parents will be able to communicate with the children about their birthparents in a more constructive way. Children served by TIES for Adoption are extremely high risk because of multiple placements, prenatal substance exposure, and abuse and neglect. Many have been separated from their birthfamilies for many months or years. This article resulted from observations of the emotional difficulties exhibited by and problems encountered by the children as well as their new parents.

## Vignettes

The following vignettes illustrate the dilemmas raised when older children are placed in foster-adoptive families before parental rights are terminated and the stresses associated with the process. The vignettes are composites of many cases; details are disguised to preserve confidentiality.

### Vignette 1

Two sisters, Elizabeth (age 7) and Suzanne (age 6), were placed with the Smiths, foster-adoptive parents who were expecting to adopt the girls. They had previously adopted a boy, and that placement and adoption process had gone smoothly. At the first court hearing after placement, the Smiths learned that the birthmother was contesting the children's placement in their home, and the birthmother confronted the Smiths. For their own safety, they had to be escorted from court by security. Subsequently, the Smiths have attended numerous court hearings, because the birthfamily challenges the plan for adoption and has requested increased visitation. The family experiences chronic emotional turmoil and exhaustion from the ongoing stress surrounding court proceedings. Now and then, the foster-adoptive parents question their ability to continue this process.

The girls were removed from their birthparents at ages 4 and 3, respectively, because of parental drug abuse, neglect, and domestic abuse. Elizabeth and Suzanne continued to have regular visits with their birthmother as part of a reunification plan. Before placement with the Smiths, the girls had five placements. Their behavior became increasingly problematic, including tantrums, defiance, aggression, enuresis, and encopresis. Several allegations were made of their physical abuse in foster care. Regular visits with the birthmother continue. At times, she instructs the girls to act out so that they will be sent back to her. She tells the girls to keep these conversations secret. The girls are confused, ambivalent, and secretive about their visits with their mother. Behavioral problems and symptoms of stress increase in the children after visits with their birthfamily and around court dates. The legal limbo of the case continues.

### Vignette 2

Jason, age 6 1/2, was placed with Sandra, a foster-adoptive mother, who knew his previous foster mother. She requested to adopt Jason once a TPR hearing was set. The birthparents had weekly, unmonitored, four-hour visits with Jason before his current placement. He had been removed from his birthparents at age 3 because of neglect. Jason reported that his parents lived in the park. He was placed in six foster homes and one group home before his current placement. Usually, he was moved at the foster parents' request due to his acting-out behavior. The TPR hearing was continued three times over the last year, and Jason continues to have sporadic visits with his birthmother. Jason has insisted that "the judge is going to let me choose who I want to live with," despite repeated clarifications to the contrary. He has felt consistently torn between his foster-adoptive mother and his birthmother. One week he reports that he wants to live with

Sandra; the next week he wants to live with his birthmother. The birthmother has repeatedly told Jason to tell the judge that he wants to live with her. She has suggested that Jason not listen to Sandra so that Sandra won't want him anymore. Jason is showing increased anxiety and acting-out behaviors around the visits, and he seems preoccupied with where he will live.

## Parents' Emotional Reactions

### Shock and Anger

We have seen foster-adoptive parents go through a range of emotions as they experience the vagaries of the child welfare and legal system. Often, the emergence of legal complications, resumption of visitation with the birthfamily, and threats to the adoption plan are initially met with shock, disappointment, and anger. Almost all the parents participating in TIES for Adoption applied to the local child welfare agency for adoption. They know that they have to go through a period of being a foster-adoptive parent, but their intent is to adopt the child placed in their home. These parents frequently report that they were not prepared for the possibility that the adoption would not go forward, and they experience a sense of betrayal. It is often difficult to know whether the parents (who enter the system with the expressed intent to adopt) have not been fully informed about the possibilities of legal complications, or whether they were reassured that legal challenges by the birthparents or relatives usually do not succeed, or whether they were not emotionally able to take in the information at a time when they were extremely eager to welcome a child into their family. Clearly, they have intense reactions when legal challenges or unexpected visitations occur.

### Helplessness and Depression

Along with anger, some parents experience a profound sense of helplessness. In many cases, they do not have any legal standing in the courtroom, even though they have become extremely invested in the child. They may not know about the possibility of seeking de facto parenting status, or they may have been advised against it, or they may not feel comfortable with revealing their identity in a courtroom in the presence of the birthfamily. Often, the parents experience a sense of suddenly not having any voice or power in a system that they had perceived to be on their side. This sense of lack of efficacy can be deeply disturbing and can have a negative effect on their parenting, especially when the child has special needs and requires effortful and creative parenting strategies. In some cases, parents become depressed because of their experience of helplessness and loss of control. Depression, of course, can impair the quality of parenting (Gelfand & Teti, 1990).

### Attitudes Toward the Child's Birthfamily

One task of the adoptive parent is to be sensitive and empathic to the issues of the birthparents and their struggles. Such a stance is vital for the adoptive parents' ability to talk to the children about their birthparents openly and supportively as questions about the children's history and background emerge. When visitation with the birthfamily is resumed after the child is in the preadoptive home, the prospective adoptive parents may feel profoundly threatened in their new role, especially when the possibility of visitation was not anticipated.

Often, the prospect of the child's adoption mobilizes the birthparents and stimulates their wish to reclaim the child. When birthparents communicate to their children, during visitation, that they are working at getting them back or that now they are getting their life together, the children may return from the visit and tell the adoptive parents that they are going home. This statement may stimulate adoptive parents' feelings of anger and resentment toward the birthfamily for undermining the current placement. Feelings of competition with the birthparents, common for adoptive parents, may be heightened (Akhtar & Kramer, 2000).

Another common scenario is when children return from a visit with birthparents saying that they are going to "act bad" so they will be sent back to their birthfamily. In some cases, a desperate birthparent may actually encourage the child to act out. Understandably, this behavior can create further resentment in the prospective adoptive parent, who may have struggled with working at controlling the child's behavior.

In some instances, foster-adoptive parents who initially felt willing and able to work toward an open adoption become increasingly angry and hostile toward the birthparents. Negative feelings may escalate further if, during court appearances, confrontations occur between the birthparents and the prospective adoptive parents. In several cases, prospective adoptive parents had to be escorted out of the courtrooms for their own protection. In these situations, the foster-adoptive parents may feel threatened about having future contact with birthparents or relatives.

Clearly, these concerns and fears are not conducive to positive communication with the children about their birthfamily. In addition, positive communication between foster parents and birthparents, as well as continuity of relationships for the child, become less likely. Escalating conflict and negative feelings between the potential adoptive parent and birthrelative may also jeopardize the placement over the long term. Some reports suggest that disrupted placements are more likely when the child maintains contact with someone opposed to the adoption (Festinger, 1990).

When the adoptive parents develop hostility toward the birthfamily, these feelings may erupt during conflict with the children. The foster-adoptive parent may tell the children that they are acting terribly "just like their birthparents." Negative consequences may result, both in the quality of the parent-child relationship and in the child's self-esteem. Carrying negative and hostile feelings about the birthrelatives can lead to fears and self-fulfilling negative fantasies that the children will be difficult, destructive, and unmanageable as they get older, like their parent or other birthrelative. The adoptive parents may become more inclined to attribute any behavioral disturbances to the child's genetic endowment and view the child as doomed to failure and evil (Akhtar & Kramer, 2000).

## Attachment Issues

Many adoptive parents have had to deal with complex issues of loss related to infertility or a life course that differed from what was expected and hoped for (for single parents). In addition, they are mourning the loss of the fantasized, ideal adopted child. Welcoming a child into the family is an act of hope for the future and represents the beginning of a new family. The time period surrounding the initial placement in an adoptive family is a time of great vulnerability but also an opportunity for growth and change. Although the adoptive parents may have been informed about possible legal complications, they inevitably and appropriately focus on creating a family with and for the child. The possibility of the adoption's not being realized is likely to create powerful fears about experiencing further loss.

Adoptive parents have repeatedly described their surprise at the intensity of their emotions both about birthparent visitation and court dates. They want to feel fully connected, attached, and entitled to the child, but they also find themselves holding back to protect themselves against potential loss. At the same time, they may feel guilty about holding back, because they know the child needs a wholehearted commitment from them. The adoptive parents may experience complex and conflicted feelings around promising children a permanent home, because they know that reunification with the birthparent is possible, although unlikely. The foster-adoptive parents often see that the children need a sense of permanency to facilitate the development of trust. They realize they would be lying to the children and would be criticized by the system if they promise the children permanency. Thus, parents can feel like frauds. If uncertainty and limbo persist, this experience can eventually contribute to distancing from the child, which can jeopardize the quality and permanency of the placement.

As the adoptive parents become close to the child, they may develop strong feelings of protectiveness and want to shield the child from any further experience of pain and trauma. This feeling is an important aspect of parental attachment to the child (Cassidy, 1999; George & Solomon, 1999). The fear that the child may experience another disruption in her or his life—and that they might contribute to such a traumatic experience—becomes profoundly disturbing in the context of the developing attachment. In addition, out of this protectiveness, the adoptive parents may develop angry feelings toward the birthparents who, perhaps because of substance abuse or difficult life circumstances, were not able to care adequately for their child and/or may have subjected the child to abuse or neglect. They may see the birthfamily's efforts to reclaim the child as evidence that they do not really care about the child's well-being, just as they had not cared about the child's well-being in the past.

## Issues Related to Court Dates

Court dates are usually highly stressful for the families. Many complex emotional issues and reactions surface around these times. Foster-adoptive parents struggle with what to tell the children about court dates. The adults want to protect the children (and themselves) from uncertainty. Inevitably, the children sense the tension in the household. Often, they react with acting-out behavior. Near court dates, foster-adoptive parents may feel that they do not have the emotional resources to cope. To protect themselves from possible loss, and because of their emotional depletion, they may talk about letting the children go back into the system, so their birthrelatives can reclaim them.

*Family Issues*

Marital stress can increase when two foster-adoptive parents cope in different ways with the uncertainties of the placement and each feels unsupported by the other. Such stress, in turn, can affect children negatively. In addition, extended family may not be supportive and may take the stance of "I told you that you were just taking on a lot of trouble." This viewpoint can lead to increased emotional isolation of the prospective adoptive parents.

As the foster-adoptive parents and the birthfamily go through the process of legal uncertainty, cope with resumed visitation, and struggle with a range of emotions, the children have their own complex reactions. These may be intensified because many of the children have experienced multiple disrupted attachments.

## Clinical Issues for the Children

*The Burden of Keeping Secrets*

In trying to cope with the needs of both the adoptive parents and the birthparent, the children may find themselves having to compartmentalize and keep secrets. Information shared or requests made by the birthparent may need to be kept from the adoptive parent, because of either the birthparent's explicit statements or the child's perceived need. For example, as in the case of Jason in Vignette 2, the birthmother may say that the child should be bad with the foster-adoptive mother so that she will not want him to live with her. Compartmentalization may be the most adaptive response in some of these situations, but it may come at great emotional cost to the child. Possible costs include wariness and a decrease in spontaneity, constricted emotional expression, and withdrawal.

Young children are not good at keeping secrets, as parents will attest. A need for secrecy can put a great strain on the child's coping capacity. The child may also feel torn between the need to keep secrets and the need to tell the truth. Children may be forced to lie to maintain the secret information. In many ways, this need to keep separate information or requests made by two sets of parents parallels the situation faced by children in a contentious divorce (Garrity & Baris, 1994; Johnston, 1994; Wolchik & Karoly, 1988). For some children in foster-adoptive placements, the stakes may be even higher, given that children know from experience that relationships with caregivers may come to an abrupt end. The children may be wary of saying something they are not supposed to say. They may fear losing either the birthparents, with whom they have the longest history, or the new parent who offers a sense of security and stability. Similar to divorce, as well, is the subtle (or not-so-subtle) undermining of the other parents to which the child may be subjected by the adults. For example, statements such as "She obviously doesn't know how to fix your hair so it looks cute," or "You had a fast food hamburger and fries? That's not a healthy meal," reinforce the child's tendency to feel that information about what occurred on a visit or in the new home must not be shared.

In addition, the need to keep secrets may affect the children's ability to engage fully with the adoptive parents. Being wary of not saying something they are not supposed to say significantly interferes with forging a new intimate bond with the foster-adoptive parents. A similar phenomenon may occur with the therapist. If keeping secrets seems vital to the child, the child will be prevented from openly exploring in therapy the full range of feelings about two sets of parents. The treatment room then cannot become a place of safety, support, and refuge that children need to explore their complex feelings.

### Increased Anxiety and Acting Out Around Visits

When children visit with their birthmothers or birthfathers after placement in a foster-adoptive home, the visits often become highly emotionally charged. For a variety of reasons, children may show behavioral escalation of aggression, temper tantrums, and emotional distress prior to the visits. First, the child may need to pull away from the fragile bonds starting to develop with the adoptive parents to be ready and available to interact with the birthparent. In fact, the child may be overtly rejecting of the foster-adoptive parent. Second, the anxiety and stress of the adoptive parent about the visit may be apparent to the child and even contagious. Third, the child may experience a great deal of worry about whether the birthparent will keep the meeting appointment. Feelings of abandonment and anger are likely if the parent does not come.

After the visits, the child faces another painful transition back to the foster-adoptive home. The child may have difficulty leaving the birthparent, may be very aggressive upon return, and may express wishes to live with the birthparent. Even for mature new parents, it is very difficult to cope when they feel rejection from the child. The children often face the added burden of guilt when they feel they have upset one or both sets of parents. The ways in which the upset caused by the visits manifests itself are myriad. For example, with the Smiths' two girls, one child suppresses all emotion, withdraws, and tries to be perfect after the visits; the other girl has tantrums, nightmares, and daytime enuresis. Both girls experience poor self-esteem that seems to worsen after visits. In contrast, Jason throws things, has extended tantrums and falls screaming on the floor, and shows aggressive and oppositional behavior in school after visits.

As the relationship between the foster-adoptive parent and the child deepens over time, the child may dread the birthparent visits and experience a great deal of distress before such visits. For example, a child repeatedly stated that he did not want to see his birthmother, but visits continued until he climbed a tree when he was due to go. He refused to come down, threatening to kill himself if forced to visit.

### Need to Take Care of Parent Figures

Children may experience a strong wish to be reunited with their birthparents but be very concerned about hurting the feelings of the foster-adoptive parents who provide a much-needed sense of safety and security. Conversely, the children may become increasingly close to the adoptive parents over time and not want to be with birthparents who may have been inconsistent. However, the children may be very concerned about the effect of these feelings on the parents. These dynamics increase the risk of a child becoming "parentified" and feeling responsible for the adults' emotional well-being. This feeling is a problem for many children because of previous circumstances.

### Loyalty Conflicts and Impossible Choices

Children may feel they are put in the position of making an impossible choice between an old attachment bond and the new experience of safety and consistency in a foster-adoptive home. Experiencing overt or subtle pressure from both sets of parents, many children feel caught in the middle, much like children of divorce (Garrity & Barris, 1994; Teyber, 1992). They may care deeply for both parenting figures and want to please and be with both. These feelings cause strong loyalty conflicts that may intensify as the birthparent increases contact for fear of losing the child and as the child's relationship with the new foster-adoptive parents deepens. The children may feel they have to make a choice about who will be their parents. This sense of responsibility can be both frightening and overwhelming. Although the child does not make the decision in most cases, some children cling to the belief that they can choose. This belief helps them feel as if they have some control over their lives in the face of much change, transition, and chaos.

---

## Recommendations Regarding Legal and Systems Issues

*1. Foster-adoptive parents need detailed information about the degree of uncertainty and legal risk in a potential placement.*

A. Attorneys and/or social workers should make it clear that adoption is not a legal certainty. The possibility that unanticipated developments may delay legal procedures for months or years should be discussed. Prospective adoptive parents should be made aware that, although birthparents may not have visited for many months, they may start visiting again when they are faced with TPR and adoption of their child.

B.  Written material, in addition to verbal clarifications, should be provided to foster-adoptive parents about the complex legal process leading to reunification, TPR, adoption, and the appeal process.

C.  Foster-adoptive parents might be advised to consider obtaining independent legal consultation in complex cases.

*2. Use of guardians ad litem and/or dispute resolution mechanisms to represent the interests of the child should be considered in highly volatile situations.*

*3. Judicial officers need to consider whether the child's emotional well-being may be harmed by visits with birthparents under certain circumstances.*

If the birthparents are contesting a placement at a time when prospective adoptive parents are trying to integrate a child into their family, the chances are great that an older child will be caught in the middle before, during, and after visitation. Issues to be considered in decisions about visitation include the child's placement history and emotional status, as well as the birthparents' impulsivity and cooperation.

*4. Trained monitors in accessible, neutral settings should be available to monitor parental visits, intervene if indicated, and report back to the court.*

## Recommendations for Social Service and Mental Health Professionals

*1. Professionals should give special preparation and support to foster-adoptive parents who choose to take an older child whose parents' rights have not been terminated.*

A.  The expectations of parents who enter the system primarily to adopt are usually different from the expectations of more traditional foster parents. These foster-adoptive parents require much advance preparation, as well as assistance, about legal uncertainty before TPR so that they are able to respond to the child's needs, instead of only to their own need to adopt the child (Gill & Amadio, 1983).

B.  A child's social workers and attorneys should provide to the foster-adoptive parents full information, in writing, about the background, strengths, and vulnerabilities of the child. Then the parents can decide whether they can fully and permanently integrate the child into their family. These tasks cannot be done without full disclosure. Technically, the foster-adoptive parents may not be entitled to this information, but they cannot make an informed decision without it (Barth & Berry, 1988; Edelstein, Howard, Tyler, Waldinger, & Moore, 1995; Edelstein, Waterman, Burge, McCarty, & Prusak, 2000; Gill & Amadio, 1983; Lutz, 2001; Rosenthal & Groze, 1992).

C.  Foster-adoptive parents should receive anticipatory guidance to learn ways of explaining the foster-adoptive status to the child. Thus, they can proceed with integrating the child into their lives, while acknowledging realistically that they cannot yet promise to be the child's "forever family" (Gill & Amadio, 1983). For example, parents may be advised to say something like, "We love you very much and hope you will be able to stay with us always. It will be up to the judge to decide where you will live. This is a confusing time for everyone."

D.  To mitigate their feelings of isolation and anxiety, foster-adoptive parents benefit from attending support groups and/or from meeting individually with other parents who have had similar experiences.

*2. Heightened tensions and negative feelings between birthparents and foster-adoptive parents during this critical period—when reunification services are stopped but TPR has not occurred—should be acknowledged and interpreted.*

Visits and court appearances may be the only contacts the new foster-adoptive parents have with the child's birthparents. The feelings generated may be communicated to the child and may have a negative effect on the child's emerging sense of identity (Gill & Amadio, 1983). Complex feelings arising at this time may also decrease the receptivity of the foster-adoptive parents to future contacts with the birthparents.

*3. All parties involved need therapeutic supports as they deal with the possibility of losing their child to another family.*

Birthparents, relatives, and foster-adoptive parents each need support to enable them to act in the child's best interest. In addition, if the child is reunified with the birthfamily or that possibility seems likely, foster-adoptive parents may experience a more intense grieving process, burnout, and anger, compared to the feelings of traditional foster parents, because of their dashed hopes of adoption (Edelstein, 1981; Edelstein, Burge, & Waterman, 2001; Lee & Hull, 1983). These therapeutic supports are most crucial around visitation and court hearings.

*4. Preschool and school-aged children need their own therapists to help them deal with conflicting loyalties, confusing feelings, and opposing demands.*

Children cannot feel free to share conflicting feelings about their parent figures if they share the therapist with either set of parents. For their sense of safety and emotional security, they need to have a therapist who is theirs alone.

*5. A critical need exists for studies of concurrent planning and foster-adoptive placements.*

Specifically, data are needed on which children are being served by which approaches, which approaches lead to increased and stable permanency and under what conditions, what challenges can emerge during this process, what possible remedies address the challenges, and what risks and benefits pertain to the child.◆

# References

Akhtar, S., & Kramer, S. (2000). *Thicker than blood: Bonds of fantasy and reality in adoption.* Northvale, NJ: Jason Aronson.

Barth, R. P., & Berry, M. (1988). *Adoption and disruption: Rates, risks and response.* Hawthorne, NY: Aldine de Gruyter.

Cassidy, J. (1999). The nature of the child's ties. In J. Cassidy & P. R. Shaver (Eds.), *Handbook of attachment* (pp. 3–20). New York: Guilford.

Edelstein, S. B. (1981). When foster children leave: Helping parents to grieve. *Child Welfare, 60,* 467–473.

Edelstein, S. B., Burge, D., & Waterman, J. (2001). Helping foster parents cope with separation loss and grief. *Child Welfare, 80,* 5–25.

Edelstein, S. B., with Howard, J., Tyler, R., Waldinger, G., & Moore, A. (1995*). Children with prenatal alcohol and/or other drug exposure: Weighing the risks of adoption.* Washington, DC: Child Welfare League of America.

Edelstein, S. B., Waterman, J., Burge, D., McCarty, C., & Prusak, J. (2000). T.I.E.S. for Adoption: A model to support the adoption of children who were prenatally exposed to alcohol and/or other drugs. In R. P. Barth, D. M. Brodzinsky, & M. Freundlich (Eds.), *Adoption and prenatal alcohol and drug exposure: Research, practice, and policy* (pp. 115–145). Washington, DC: Child Welfare League of America.

Festinger, T. (1990). Adoption disruption: Rates and correlates. In D. M. Brodzinsky & M. D. Schechter (Eds.), *The psychology of adoption* (pp. 201–220). New York: Oxford University Press.

Gardiner, E. A. (1987). *The Fost-Adopt program: A review of the literature.* Washington, DC: Child Welfare League of America.

Garrity, C. B., & Baris, M. A. (1994). *Caught in the middle: Protecting the children of high-conflict divorce.* New York: Lexington Books.

Gelfand, D. M., & Teti, D. M. (1990). The effects of maternal depression on children. *Clinical Psychology Review, 10,* 329–353.

George, C., & Solomon, J. (1999). Attachment and caregiving: The caregiving behavioral system. In J. Cassidy & P. R. Shaver (Eds.), *Handbook of attachment* (pp. 649–670). New York: Guilford.

Gill, M. M., & Amadio, C. M. (1983). Social work and law in a foster care/adoption program. *Child Welfare, 62,* 455–467.

Johnston, J. R. (1994). High-conflict divorce. *Children and Divorce: The Future of Children, 4,* 165–182.

Katz, L. (1999). Concurrent planning: Benefits and pitfalls. *Child Welfare, 78,* 71–87.

Katz, L., & Robinson, C. (1991). Foster care drift: A risk assessment matrix. *Child Welfare, 70,* 347–358.

Katz, L., Robinson, C., & Spoonemore, N. (1994). *Concurrent planning: From permanency planning to permanency action.* Seattle, WA: Lutheran Social Services of Washington and Idaho.

Lee, R. E., & Hull, R. K. (1983). Legal, casework, and ethical issues in "risk adoption." *Child Welfare, 62,* 450–454.

Lutz, L. L. (2001). *Concurrent planning: Tools for permanency, survey of selected sites.* New York: National Resource Center for Foster Care and Permanency Planning at the Hunter College School of Social Work of the City University of New York.

Mica, M. D., & Vosler, N. R. (1990). Foster-adoptive programs in public social service agencies: Toward flexible family resources. *Child Welfare, 69,* 433–446.

Rosenthal, J. A., & Groze, V. K. (1992). *Special needs adoption: A study of intact families.* New York: Praeger.

Teyber, E. (1992). *Helping children cope with divorce.* San Francisco: Jossey-Bass.

Wolchik, S. A., & Karoly, P. (Eds.). (1988). *Children of divorce: Empirical perspectives on adjustment.* New York: Gardner.

Chapter 2

# Getting Home on Time: Predicting Timely Permanence for Young Children

*Cathryn C. Potter and Susan Klein-Rothschild*

The timelines of the Adoption and Safe Families Act (ASFA) (P.L. 105-89) require increased attention to the timing of permanent placement, regardless of the type of placement outcome. This study examines the multivariate predictors of timely permanence for children served by Colorado's Expedited Permanency Planning (EPP) project. EPP has used an intensive concurrent planning model aimed at reaching permanency within 12 months of initial placement for children aged 6 and younger. The EPP requirement that children be living in the permanent home by 12 months postplacement is more stringent than the technical ASFA requirements. This article uses qualitative interviews with child welfare and court personnel to identify critical barriers to and supports for effective permanency planning.

*Cathryn C. Potter is Associate Professor at the University of Denver School of Social Work, Institute for Families. Susan Klein-Rothschild is Director of Child Welfare Services for Clark County, Nevada.*

T he growing body of research on child welfare placement outcomes focuses primarily on factors associated individually with reunification, adoption, or kinship care. The timelines of the Adoption and Safe Families Act (ASFA) (P.L. 105-89) require increased attention to the timing of permanent placement, regardless of the type of placement outcome. Since 1994, Colorado's Expedited Permanency Planning (EPP) project has used an intensive concurrent planning model aimed at reaching permanency within 12 months of initial placement for children aged 6 and younger. The EPP requirement that children be living in the permanent home by 12 months postplacement is more stringent than the technical ASFA requirements. Examination of the ability to meet this timeline offers an opportunity to ask an important question: "Who gets home on time?" This study examines the multivariate predictors of timely permanence for children served by EPP. In addition, qualitative interviews with child welfare and court personnel identify critical barriers to and supports for effective permanency planning.

## Factors Associated with Child Welfare Case Outcomes

Previous studies examining predictors of placement outcomes focus on three points in time:

- Placement patterns at entry to care, with specific focus on factors associated with kinship care (Beeman, Kim, & Bullerdick, 2000; Grogan-Kaylor, 2000b; Rittner, 1995; Scannapieco, Hegar, & McAlpine, 1997; Zuravin & DePanfilis, 1997);
- Factors associated with placement outcomes at exit from care (McMurtry & Lie, 1992), specifically with adoption (Barth, 1997; Barth, Courtney, & Berry, 1994) and reunification (Courtney, 1994; Nugent, Carpenter, & Parks, 1993); and
- Factors associated with return to foster care following adoption (Barth, Berry, Yoshiakami, Goodfield, & Carson, 1988; Barth et al., 1986) or reunification (Courtney, 1995; Festinger, 1996).

These studies approach the question of prediction of case outcomes using differing statistical techniques, sampling approaches, and independent variables. Nevertheless, some patterns emerge across studies.

Although some studies have found that race/ethnicity is not a predictor of entry to foster care (Lindsey, 1991, 1992; Zuravin & DePanfilis, 1997), once children are in care, race/ethnicity is a predictor of placement outcome in almost all studies. Children of color are more likely to be placed in kinship care at the point of entry into substitute care (Beeman et al., 2000; Rittner, 1995). Specifically, African American children are the most likely to move to kinship homes (Scannapieco et al., 1997). African American children are half as likely to be reunified as Caucasian children are (Barth, 1997; McMurtry & Lie, 1992; Wells & Guo, 1999). This trend is the same whether African American children are served in kinship or non-kinship foster homes (Courtney, 1994). African American children who do reunify are more likely to return to care than Caucasian children are (Courtney, 1995; Wells & Guo, 1999). Similarly, African American children are less likely to exit foster care to adoption than Caucasian children are (Barth et al., 1994). Some studies have also found that Latino children have slower rates of reunification in some localities (Courtney, 1994; Davis, Landsverk, & Newton, 1997). The most consistent race/ ethnicity predictor, however, is being African American, and these effects are uniformly in the direction of decreased permanence.

The age of the child is a predictor of placement outcome, sometimes in interaction with other factors. For example, infants are more likely to exit foster care to adoption (Barth, 1997; Barth et al., 1994). McMurtry and Lie (1992) estimated that each year of increase in age reduces the odds of adoption by 22%. Similarly, each year of increase in age for children who do exit to adoption increases the odds of adoption disruption by 32% (Barth et al., 1988). For children in kinship care, age interacts with being Latino to decrease the likelihood of reunification for young Latino children (Courtney, 1994). For children served in non-kinship homes, young children and adolescents are least likely to be reunified, whereas children ages 7 through 12 are least likely to have disrupted adoptive placements (Courtney, 1995). Wells and Guo (1999) found that age is not related to reunification, but that older children are more likely to re-enter care after reunification.

Children with disabilities and those with emotional or behavioral problems are at increased risk for negative placement outcomes. Children with health problems are less likely to be reunified (Courtney, 1994; McMurtry & Lie, 1992; Wells & Guo, 1999) and more likely to return to care if reunified (Courtney, 1995). They are also less likely to exit foster care to adoption (McMurtry & Lie, 1992). Children with behavioral problems are more likely to have disrupted adoptive placements (Barth et al., 1988; Barth et al., 1986).

Other factors have been associated with specific placement outcomes but have been examined less closely in multiple studies. Parental visiting patterns are associated with reunification, that is, more visiting has a positive effect (McMurtry & Lie, 1992). Children with siblings in care are less likely to exit to adoption (McMurtry & Lie, 1992) and less likely to exit to reunification (Grogan-Kaylor, 2000a). Poor children are more likely to have disrupted adoptive homes (Barth et al., 1994) and to re-enter foster care after reunification with their families (Courtney, 1995). Poor children placed in kinship care are less likely to be reunified (Courtney, 1994), however when they are reunified, they are no more likely to return to care than other children are (Courtney, 1995).

Most research focuses on characteristics of children and families, especially those data readily available in large state administrative data systems. Consequently, fewer service factors have been examined. When children are reunified after a short (less than three month) stay in out-of-home care, they are more likely to return to care (Courtney, 1995). This result may indicate that insufficient intervention has taken place to affect the reasons for placement. For children exiting to adoption, residing in a planned foster-adopt home decreases the time to adoption (Barth et al.,

1988). Barth and colleagues (1986) found that increased face-to-face time with a child welfare worker serves to decrease the odds of adoption disruption. Having a more experienced child welfare worker increases the odds of a successful reunification (Festinger, 1996). Engaging in family therapy and successfully completing planned services increase the probability of family reunification (Nugent et al., 1993). Better parenting skills, stronger levels of social support, and parental participation in community organizations are predictors of successful reunification, whereas having more unmet service needs predicts reunification failure (Festinger, 1996).

Clearly, some characteristics of children and families are commonly found to predict placement outcomes. Being an African American child reduces the odds of permanence. Similarly, being older and having an emotional or physical disability decrease a child's chances of permanence. Parental visiting patterns and poverty may also affect placement outcomes. Service characteristics have been less closely examined, but having a higher intensity of services, completing services successfully, and working with an experienced child welfare worker seem to increase the odds of good placement outcomes.

## ASFA

ASFA made several changes to federal requirements for permanency planning. Specifically, the permanency hearing for children in out-of-home care must now take place within 12 months of initial placement. At this hearing, there must be a decision about whether and when a child will be returned home, a termination petition filed, legal guardianship pursued, or another specific alternate permanent plan implemented. Petitions for termination of parental rights (TPR) should be filed for children who have been in care for the last 12 consecutive months (or for 15 of the past 22 months) unless agency policy exempts children being cared for by relatives, the agency documents compelling reasons why TPR is not in the child's best interests, or the parents were not provided with services meeting the reasonable efforts standard. Although reasonable efforts toward reunification are still required, ASFA does set forth exceptions to this requirement and permits concurrent planning, an approach in which family reunification and adoption planning are pursued simultaneously.

## Colorado's EPP Initiative

In 1994, Colorado passed legislation establishing the EPP program (CRS 19-1-102). The project serves families with at least one child age 6 or younger at the time of entry into foster care and requires that children served by EPP be living in a permanent home by 12 months following placement. The legislation calls for a number of changes to promote timely permanent placements for children, including:

- Accelerating the pace of court hearings including adjudication, disposition, and permanency planning hearings;
- Early provision of services to the parents and children;
- Discouraging delays or continuances in judicial proceedings;
- Discouraging transfers of judicial proceedings across jurisdictions; and
- Permitting TPR for a number of reasons, including incarceration of the parent for more than 36 months, a lack of visiting with the child by the parent, and a lack of adequate improvement in the areas leading to the out-of home placement of the children.

A concurrent planning model is used that emphasizes the use of foster-adopt homes, simultaneous planning for reunification and adoption/guardianship, and intensive services to families.

Concurrent planning is an approach to working with the families of children in care that emphasizes the need to maximize the intensity of family service and the focus on children's need for permanence. The approach entails a dual focus, with the child welfare worker focusing simultaneously on reunification and the development of permanent alternatives. This approach relies on foster care or kin providers who can provide a permanent home if reunification is not possible. Intervention with birthfamilies and with foster and kin providers emphasizes full disclosure to all parties, a firm timeline, vigorous visiting plans, and clear, behaviorally oriented expectations (Katz, 1999). The approach requires a commitment to the child's sense of permanence and to the suspension of judgment about the ultimate nature of that permanence until the outcomes of intensive intervention plans can unfold.

Evaluation efforts are few and have primarily focused on the percentage of children residing in an intended permanent home within 12 months (Katz, 1999; Kelly & Taylor, 1999; Schene, 1998). Evaluation of Colorado's EPP program indicates that a significant majority of children age 6 and younger are placed in a permanent home within 12 months of the original placement (82% for children served in the fifth year) (Kelly & Taylor, 1999). To improve this success rate, child welfare managers sought a more detailed understanding of cases that did not reach permanence on time.

Because EPP timelines are similar to those required under ASFA, and because EPP has been operational in Colorado since 1994, the program presents an opportunity to examine factors associated with meeting ASFA timelines. Although most children served by EPP reside in an intended permanent home at 12 months postplacement, some do not. To learn more about the children being served in EPP, the Department of Human Services and the Judicial Department initiated an independent evaluation to identify factors that distinguish those children who achieved permanency within 12 months (successful cases) from those children who did not (unsuccessful cases). The goal was to use this information to inform child welfare workers and managers as they seek to improve EPP programs.

The specific goals of the independent evaluation were:
- To identify the characteristics or factors associated with the permanent placement of children younger than the age of 7 within 12 months of initial out-of-home placement,
- To interview key informants in EPP counties regarding the supports and barriers to effective implementation of EPP, and
- To make recommendations for strategies aimed at increasing timely permanence for children.

## Quantitative Method and Results

The quantitative study focused on children who entered out-of-home placement in a county providing EPP services between July 1, 1997, and June 30, 1998. During this time, a total of 366 children younger than 6 years of age and their siblings had an original out-of-home placement made by a county department with an expedited permanency program. Of the 366 children, 297 achieved permanency and 69 children did not achieve permanency within 12 months. All children who did not achieve permanency were sampled, as well as a random sample of 69 successful cases. As an intensive review of case records moved forward, it was soon noted that many cases had been inaccurately reported as unsuccessful and that some children were considerably older than 7. The final sample consisted of 125 children younger than the age of 7, 79 successful cases (63.2%), and 46 unsuccessful cases (36.8%).

A trained researcher read all case files using a standardized data gathering tool. The tool was used to record data on 47 factors in four domains: child characteristics, family characteristics, caseworker/agency actions, and court/judicial actions. Table 1 describes the sample relative to selected factors. Of children in the sample, 90% eventually achieved a permanent placement, although only 63.2% did so within 12 months. (Note that this

## TABLE 1
### Characteristics of Expedited Permanency Planning (EPP) Sample Cases

| Variable | % | n | X | Range | SD |
|---|---|---|---|---|---|
| *Permanence* | | | | | |
| Timely permanence | 63.2 | 79 | | | |
| *Type of Eventual Permanent Placement* | | | | | |
| Reunification | 29.6 | 37 | | | |
| Relative placement | 22.4 | 28 | | | |
| Adoption | 38.4 | 48 | | | |
| None | 9.6 | 12 | | | |
| *Child Characteristics* | | | | | |
| Age at placement | | | 2.26 | 1.9-6.98 | 1.92 |
| Male | 52 | 65 | | | |
| Ethnicity | | | | | |
| Hispanic | 22.4 | 28 | | | |
| African American | 13.6 | 17 | | | |
| Other ethnicity | 5.6 | 7 | | | |
| White | 58.4 | 73 | | | |
| Title IV-E eligible | 59.2 | 74 | | | |
| Type of maltreatment[a] | | | | | |
| Physical abuse | 18.4 | 23 | | | |
| Sexual abuse | 4.8 | 6 | | | |
| Emotional abuse | 7.2 | 9 | | | |
| Physical neglect | 76.8 | 96 | | | |
| Medical neglect | 10.4 | 13 | | | |
| Emotional or behavioral problem | 28.0 | 35 | | | |
| Medical condition | 27.2 | 34 | | | |
| Previous placement | 7.2 | 9 | | | |
| *Parental Characteristics* | | | | | |
| Family structure | | | | | |
| Two parents | 31.2 | 39 | | | |
| Single mother | 46.4 | 58 | | | |
| Single father | 2.4 | 3 | | | |
| Parent and other | 18.4 | 23 | | | |
| Number of siblings | 1.63 | 0-6 | 1.51 | | |
| Mother's problems[a] | 2.88 | 0-6 | 1.33 | | |
| Mental health | 51.2 | 64 | | | |
| Developmental disability | 8.8 | 11 | | | |

## TABLE 1 (CONTINUED)
**Characteristics of Expedited Permanency Planning (EPP) Sample Cases**

| Variable | % | n | X | Range | SD |
|---|---|---|---|---|---|
| Major illness | 11.2 | 14 | | | |
| Incarceration | | | | | |
| (current or history) | 30.4 | 38 | | | |
| Domestic violence | 54.4 | 68 | | | |
| Homelessness (current | | | | | |
| or history) | 42.4 | 53 | | | |
| Unemployment | 22.4 | 28 | | | |
| Father's problems[a] | | | | | |
| Mental health | 12.0 | 64 | | | |
| Developmental disability | .8 | 1 | | | |
| Major illness | .8 | 1 | | | |
| Incarceration (current | | | | | |
| or history) | 35.2 | 44 | | | |
| Domestic violence | 39.2 | 49 | | | |
| Homelessness (current | | | | | |
| or history) | 12.8 | 16 | | | |
| Unemployment | 9.6 | 12 | | | |
| Substance abuse is a | | | | | |
| current primary problem | 67.2 | 84 | | | |
| Primary substance type ($n = 84$) | | | | | |
| Alcohol | 41.7 | 35 | | | |
| Cocaine | 17.9 | 15 | | | |
| Methamphetamines | 13.1 | 11 | | | |
| Marijuana | 11.9 | 10 | | | |
| Opiates | 4.8 | 4 | | | |
| Heroin | 2.4 | 2 | | | |
| Unknown | 8.3 | 7 | | | |
| Previous child | | | | | |
| maltreatment report | 79.2 | 99 | | | |
| *Service Characteristics* | | | | | |
| Service prior to placement | 30.4 | 38 | | | |
| Number of caseworkers | | | | | |
| during EPP year | | | 2.75 | 1-6 | 1.20 |
| Number of placements | | | | | |
| during EPP year | | | 2.76 | 1-10 | 1.33 |
| First placement type ($n = 125$) | | | | | |
| Receiving home | 32.0 | 40 | | | |
| Family foster care | 54.4 | 68 | | | |
| Relative home | 13.6 | 17 | | | |

## TABLE 1 (CONTINUED)
### Characteristics of Expedited Permanency Planning (EPP) Sample Cases

| Variable | % | n | X | Range | SD |
|---|---|---|---|---|---|
| First service type | | | | | |
| County EPP only | 23.2 | 29 | | | |
| Substance abuse | 23.2 | 29 | | | |
| Mental health | 17.6 | 22 | | | |
| Home-based intervention | 10.4 | 13 | | | |
| Family therapy | 5.4 | 7 | | | |
| Life skills training | 4.8 | 6 | | | |
| Other | 15.2 | 19 | | | |
| Collaborative service planning | | | | | |
| Parents signed the | | | | | |
| family service plan | 57.6 | 72 | | | |
| Concurrent plan in | | | | | |
| family service plan | 80.8 | 101 | | | |
| Family group conference held | 24.0 | 30 | | | |
| Mediation | 25.6 | 32 | | | |
| Possible visiting days per week | | | | | |
| ($n$ = 102) | | | 2.26 | 1-7 | 1.54 |
| *Court Characteristics* | | | | | |
| Days petition to adjudication ($n$ = 119) | | | 49.26 | 7-395 | 63.74 |
| Adjudication to treatment plan ($n$ = 111) | | | 29.69 | 0-393 | 42.11 |
| Days petition to treatment | | | | | |
| plan ordered ($n$ = 110) | | | 77.60 | 7-451 | 67.80 |
| Days petition to permanency hearing | | | | | |
| ($n$ = 100) | | | 194.25 | 29-760 | 116.84 |

a. Multiple responses possible.

sample was selected to maximize the ability to distinguish between successful and unsuccessful cases. This percentage does not reflect the overall 12-month success rate for the program.) Adoption was the most likely outcome (38.4%), but both reunification and permanent relative placement (adoption or guardianship) were well represented, i.e., 29.6% and 22.4%, respectively.

Most of the children in the sample lived in poor families; 59% of families were Title IV-E eligible. The majority of the children were Caucasian (56%), with Latino (24.8%) and African American (14.6%) children being the most prevalent children of color.

Families were most likely to be headed by a single mother (46.4%). Almost 80% of the families had a previous child maltreatment report. More than half of mothers had experienced some mental illness (as noted by a *Diagnostic and Statistical Manual of Mental Disorders* [American Psychiatric Association, 1994] diagnosis or specific mental health needs, assessed by a mental health professional and documented in the file). Of mothers, 30% were incarcerated at some time in their lives. Almost 70% struggled with substance abuse problems, and alcohol was the most prevalent problem substance.

Children had an average of 2.75 caseworkers during the EPP year. Unfortunately, case records were not sufficiently detailed to distinguish between current and consecutive caseworkers. This average reflects both patterns. Children had an average of 2.3 placements during the EPP year, with this number ranging from 1 to 6. Most children were placed directly into family foster care. Only 13% were placed directly with kin. Visiting plans most often called for 1 to 5 hours of contact each week between the birthparents and the child in care. The most prevalent services for parents were counseling for substance abuse and mental health counseling. Patterns of missing data made interpretation of court variables problematic, however, the time between filing of a petition and the order for the treatment plan averaged 77.6 days, with a range from 1 to 451 days.

## Predicting Timely Permanence

The initial step in data analysis involved looking at bivariate relationships between factors and timely permanence, defined as residing in the permanent home after 12 months following the date of initial placement. Table 2 shows chi-square and *t* test results.

### Child Factors

- Children with medical conditions were more likely to achieve timely permanence.

- Children who were younger at the time of placement were more likely to achieve timely permanence.
- Children with emotional or behavioral conditions were less likely to achieve timely permanence.
- Children who were African American were less likely to achieve timely permanence.

## Family Factors

- Children who were Title IV-E eligible were less likely to achieve timely permanence.
- Families with a fewer number of siblings were more likely to achieve timely permanence.
- Children whose mothers have a developmental disability were less likely to achieve timely permanence.
- Children whose mothers have a greater number of problem parental characteristics were more likely to achieve timely permanence.
- Children whose parents have a history of homelessness were less likely to achieve timely permanence.
- Families in which substance abuse is an issue were more likely to achieve timely permanence.

## Caseworker/Agency Actions

- Families who had fewer caseworkers were more likely to achieve timely permanence.
- Children with fewer placements during the EPP service period were more likely to achieve timely permanence.
- Children whose first placement was foster care (compared to receiving home care) were more likely to achieve timely permanence.
- Parents who had signed the family service plan were more likely to achieve timely permanence.
- Families for whom the concurrent plan is clearly identified in the written family service plan were more likely to achieve timely permanence.

# TABLE 2
**Bivariate Relationships**

| Variable | On Time | | | Late | | | $X^2$ | t | p |
|---|---|---|---|---|---|---|---|---|---|
| | % | X | SD | % | X | SD | | | |
| *Permanence* | | | | | | | | | |
| Type of eventual permanent placement | | | | | | | | | |
| Reunification | 81.1 | | | 18.9 | | | 6.598 | | NS |
| Relative placement | 75.0 | | | 25.0 | | | | | |
| Adoption | 68.3 | | | 31.7 | | | | | |
| *Child Characteristics* | | | | | | | | | |
| Age at placement | | 1.88 | 1.79 | | 2.91 | 1.97 | | 3.00 | .003 |
| Ethnicity | | | | | | | 7.82 | | .050 |
| Hispanic | 64.3 | | | 35.7 | | | | | |
| African American | 35.3 | | | 64.7 | | | | | |
| Other ethnicity | 57.1 | | | 42.9 | | | | | |
| White | 69.9 | | | 30.1 | | | | | |
| Title IV-E eligible | 44.6 | | | 55.4 | | | 4.421 | | .035 |
| Emotional or behaviora; problem | 35.6 | | | 71.4 | | | 25.063 | | <.001 |
| Medical condition | 79.4 | | | 20.6 | | | 5.27 | | .022 |
| *Parental Characteristics* | | | | | | | | | |
| Number of siblings | | 1.27 | 1.27 | | 2.24 | 1.69 | | 3.591 | <.001 |
| Number of mother's problems | | 3.23 | 1.25 | | 2.67 | 1.34 | | 2.335 | .021 |

| | | | | | | |
|---|---|---|---|---|---|---|
| Mother's developmental disability | 27.3 | | 72.7 | | 6.694 | .010 |
| Mother's homelessness | 55.7 | | 44.3 | | 3.847 | .047 |
| Father's homelessness | 62.5 | | 37.5 | | 5.211 | .022 |
| Substance abuse | 70.2 | | 29.8 | | 5.174 | .026 |
| *Service Characteristics* | | | | | | |
| Number of caseworkers during EPP year | 2.43 | 0.97 | 3.30 | 1.36 | 4.170 | <.001 |
| Number of placements during EPP year | 2.07 | 1.12 | 2.69 | 1.21 | 3.102 | .002 |
| First placement type | | | | | 6.43 | .041 |
| Receiving home | 42.6 | | 57.4 | | | |
| Family foster care | 62.5 | | 37.5 | | | |
| Relative home | 88.2 | | 11.8 | | | |
| Parents signed the FSP | 70.8 | | 29.2 | | 4.254 | .039 |
| Concurrent plan in the FSP | 58.4 | | 41.6 | | 5.177 | .023 |
| Cross-system staffing | 33.3 | | 66.7 | | 6.53 | .011 |
| Parental options counseling | 36.4 | | 63.6 | | 3.75 | .050 |
| Possible visiting days per week (n = 112) | 2.55 | 1.82 | 1.79 | .70 | -2.459 | .016 |
| *Court Characteristics* | | | | | | |
| Days petition to adjudication (n = 119) | 39.36 | 32.07 | 66.76 | 65.33 | 2.293 | .024 |
| Adjudication to treatment plan (n = 111) | 24.11 | 16.50 | 39.21 | 65.27 | 1.843 | .048 |
| Treatment plan to permanency hearing (n = 100) | 123.33 | 105.99 | 117.48 | 80.93 | -0.279 | NS |

Note: EPP = expedited permanency planning; FSP = family service plan.

- Families who had a cross-system staffing were less likely to achieve timely permanence.
- Parents who had parental options counseling were less likely to achieve timely permanence.
- Families that were offered more possible days of parental visitation per week were more likely to achieve timely permanence.
- Families that received service in some counties were more likely to achieve timely permanence.

### Court/Judicial Actions

- Cases with less time between filing of the petition and adjudication and between adjudication and the order for the treatment plan were more likely to achieve timely permanence.

Although each of these variables is associated with achieving permanency, bivariate relationships can be deceiving because many times variables have an overlapping ability to predict the outcome. For example, among the child factors in this study, children with medical problems were more likely to achieve timely permanence. A closer examination of the overlap between having a medical problem and age revealed that children with medical problems were significantly younger than were healthy children. Indeed, when the two factors were considered together as predictors, only age was significant.

To consider multivariate relationships with timely permanence, a two-stage logistic regression analysis was conducted. Preliminary logistic regression models identified factors within each of the four domains that were most strongly associated with timely permanence (residing in the permanent home by 12 months postplacement). A final model was then constructed using those factors found to be significant in the preliminary analyses.

Logistic regression is used to understand the predictors of a dichotomous outcome and can produce interesting information. Individual significant variables are identified, and their relative strength in predicting the outcome is given in the form of an odds ratio (OR). ORs greater than 1 are interpreted as increasing the likelihood of the outcome. For example, for a dichotomous variable with an OR of 2.3, it might be said that families having this attribute are 2.3 times as likely to experience the outcome than families without this attribute. For ORs less than 1, the interpretation is usually stated as a percentage reduction in likelihood. For example, again for a dichotomous variable, with an OR of 0.2, we could say that families having this attribute are 80% (1 - 0.2) less likely to experience the outcome than those without the attribute. Logistic regression also gives information about the accuracy of a model in predicting the outcome.

For this study, backward logistic regression was used, a type of regression in which all candidate variables are entered into the equation then removed one at a time if they do not significantly contribute to correct prediction of the dependent variable. The final model contains the best predictors. Results of the logistic regression analysis are indicated in Table 3. The following factors are associated with timely permanency:

- Children who were African American (73.9% less likely) or who had an emotional or behavioral problem (88.9% less likely);
- Children who were Title IV-E eligible (90.4% less likely) or situations in which parental substance abuse was an issue (22.77 times more likely);
- Service patterns including fewer caseworkers (each additional worker decreased the odds by 63.2%), fewer placements (each additional placement reduced the odds by 32%), more planned visiting days per week (each day tripled the odds), a first placement into foster care rather than receiving home care (1.72 times more likely), and county of residence; and
- Expedited court time frames (each day less between initial filing and adjudication increased the odds by 1%, and each day less between the adjudication and the order for treatment plan increased the odds by 2.7%).

TABLE 3

**Preliminary Backward Logistic Regression Models**

| Variable | Beta | p | Odds Ratio |
|---|---|---|---|
| *Child Characteristics Model (n = 125)* | | | |
| Ethnicity (White is comparison) | | .049 | |
|    African American | -1.345 | .029 | 0.261 |
|    Latino/Latina | -1.124 | NS | 0.325 |
|    Other | 0.043 | NS | 1.04 |
| Emotional/behavioral problem | -2.199 | <.001 | 0.111 |
| -2 Log Likelihood = 126.89 | | | |
| Cox & Snell $R^2$ = .242 | | | |
| Percentage of cases correctly classified = 76.2 | | | |
| *Family Characteristics Model (n = 125)* | | | |
| Title IV-E eligibility | -2.466 | .002 | 0.096 |
| Substance abuse | 2.466 | .003 | 22.779 |
| -2 Log Likelihood = 63.305 | | | |
| Cox & Snell $R^2$ = .471 | | | |
| Percentage of cases correctly classified = 80.5 | | | |
| *Caseworker/Agency Characteristics Model (n = 112)* | | | |
| County[a] | 0.367 | | |
| Number of caseworkers | -1.000 | .003 | 0.368 |
| Number of expedited permanency | | | |
|    planning placements | -0.386 | .035 | 0.680 |
| Possible visiting days/week | 1.124 | .003 | 3.077 |
| Type of first placement | | | |
|    (Receiving home is comparison) | | .035 | |
|    Family foster care | 0.544 | .037 | 1.724 |
|    Relative home | -1.767 | .368 | 0.171 |
| -2 Log Likelihood = 65.313 | | | |
| Cox & Snell $R^2$ = .494 | | | |
| Percentage of cases correctly classified = 79.4 | | | |
| *Court Actions Model (n = 110)* | | | |
| Days: Petition to adjudication | -0.012 | .028 | 0.990 |
| Days: Adjudication to treatment plan | -0.021 | .050 | 0.973 |
| -2 Log Likelihood = 132.512 | | | |
| Cox & Snell $R^2$ = .101 | | | |
| Percentage of cases correctly classified = 70.9 | | | |

a. Cannot be removed without significantly affecting model fit.

TABLE 4

**Final Backward Logistic Model (*N* = 120)**

| Variable | Beta | p | Odds Ratio |
|---|---|---|---|
| County[a] | | | 0.431 |
| Ethnicity | | | 0.015 |
| African American | -1.162 | .008 | 0.104 |
| Latino/Latina | 0.493 | NS | 1.638 |
| Other | -3.486 | NS | 0.031 |
| Number of caseworkers | 1.742 | .007 | 0.476 |
| Child emotional/behaviora | | | |
|     problem | -0.2594 | <.001 | 0.075 |
| -2 Log Likelihood = 85.754 | | | |
| Cox & Snell $R^2$ = .451 | | | |
| Percentage of cases correctly classified = 85.0 | | | |

a. Cannot be removed without significantly affecting model fit.

The family model performs best in correctly classifying actual outcomes, accurately predicting timeliness for 80.5% of cases.

All of the candidate variables listed above were entered into the final model except visiting frequency and court timelines. Unfortunately, the data related to the frequency of visitation and the court factors were not represented consistently in all case records. Moreover, data were missing for different cases on these variables, leading to an unacceptable reduction to a sample size of less than 100. It is a limitation of the final model that both visiting patterns and court factors were not included. Results from the final model including all other candidate variables can be found in Table 4. This model represents the most parsimonious approach to classifying cases, identifying the following factors as predictors of timely permanence:

- African American (decreased the odds by 89.6%),
- Emotional or behavioral problems (decreased the odds by 92.5%),
- More caseworkers (52.4% less likely for each one), and
- County of residence. (Although this variable was not significant, it cannot be removed from the model without sig-

nificantly decreasing model fit. The large number of counties [9] likely affected significance levels. County success rates ranged from 42% to 100% for this sample.)

The final model successfully predicts timeliness for 85% of sample. It best predicts those cases for which permanency was achieved, successfully predicting 89.5% of cases. The model contains more error in the prediction of failure, correctly classifying 77.3% of cases. For this sample, 63.2% of cases did not achieve timely permanence, therefore a simple model could correctly classify cases 63% of the time by simply predicting that all cases were successful. The model containing these four variables improves on this by correctly classifying an additional 22% of cases.

## Qualitative Method and Results

Interviews were conducted with county and court personnel to gather additional information about experience with the EPP program. A total of 22 county and court personnel were interviewed from four counties. The interviews included the four counties representing the largest number of children in the study and includes two counties with more successful outcomes and two counties with less successful outcomes. The semistructured interview protocol focused discussion in the following three areas: concurrent planning practice and policies, county/court relationships, and child and family characteristics. Key informants were not given the results of the quantitative analysis prior to the interviews.

### Concurrent Planning Practices and Policies

Among the practices associated with concurrent planning models, the counties varied most strongly in practices related to the timing of placement into potentially permanent homes. The decision about the timing of placement into a permanent home was based on a number of factors and perceptions. Although there was uniformity across counties in terms of placing with relatives as soon as possible after an assessment of the relatives was completed, the timing of placements with nonrelatives who may become adoptive parents varied greatly. In some cases, children were placed in foster-adoptive homes within days of the initial placement, and at other times the decision to move a child to a foster-adoptive home was not made until after the permanency planning hearing or when the county filed for TPR. The variance appeared to be related to factors in the child and family (e.g., previous history with the agency), resource availability, and philosophical differences between agencies and individual workers. Key informants in all counties discussed the difficulty in preparing alternative families for the ambiguity inherent in a concurrent planning model.

The language used for alternative permanent families also varied, with counties using the terms *foster-adoptive, legal risk,* or *resource families.* Differences in terms appeared to be related to differences in how families were viewed as a part of the concurrent planning intervention. Counties using the term *legal risk* were more likely to be conservative in the timing of placement with the alternative family. Counties thinking in terms of resource families were more likely to see use of these families as an integral part of concurrent planning.

Although all counties focused on the same goals of timely permanency for children, specific EPP policies vary regarding assignment of workers, preparation of families to care for children, and decisionmaking about when to move a child. Key informant responses revealed significant differences in philosophy and approach across counties. Many respondents also discussed clear philosophical differences within the same county. Many suggested that more consistency and direction are needed.

### County/Court Relationships

Due to the unique relationships within the jurisdictions related to expectations, procedures, and communication, ideas for improving the relationship between the county and the courts were specific to jurisdictions and could not be easily generalized. The reasons for a lack of timely court hearings were perceived to involve multiple variables including the court docket, attorney continuance strategies, respondent attorneys not having opportunities to meet with their clients, and a lack of preparation by workers or attorneys. In some jurisdictions, the court docket was clearly of prime concern. In other jurisdictions, there were concerns about the competency of the players in the system, leading to a serious lack of trust between county workers and court personnel.

### Child and Family Characteristics

Respondents across counties identified similar types of children and families as most at-risk for delayed permanence, including children with severe emotional problems, older children, and children of color. When asked specifically about what makes timely permanence more difficult for children of color, the lack of alternative families was the primary response.

Children with emotional problems and significant behavioral problems were identified by almost every respondent as being the most difficult children for whom timely permanency could be achieved. Respondents saw these children as overrepresented in the child welfare system and the EPP program. Respondents describe the need for lifelong supports, increased recognition by prospective adoptive parents of the possibility of future problems, and difficulties in finding families who can meet children's needs as the greatest barriers to timely permanence.

## Discussion and Implications

### Responding to the Consistent Effect of Race/Ethnicity

Findings of this study are consistent with previous research documenting that African American children are at higher risk for negative placement outcomes. This study focused on the timeliness of permanent placement and found that African American children were less likely to achieve timely permanence. This effect was not explained by family structure or size or by the type of eventual permanent home. As always, this finding raises questions about the nature of child welfare intervention with African American families. At the direct services front-line level, these findings point to a strong need for assertive social work practitioners who are fully aware of the trend and prepared to implement steps to overcome potential time lags for African American children from the onset of a case. At the management level, the findings also underscore the need for honest conversation leading to strategic interventions at many points in the child welfare system.

### Children with Emotional and Behavioral Disturbances

Children with emotional and behavioral disturbances are at higher risk for many negative child welfare events. Moreover, child maltreatment itself has serious emotional consequences for many children, and intervention by child protection agencies, including removal from the family home, may also create emotional trauma and stress (Fahlberg, 1991). The findings of this study point to a need for early identification and early treatment for children with emotional and behavioral problems. These findings also suggest a need for education and support for caseworkers, foster-adoptive families, kinship families, and birthfamilies so that they can effectively address emotional and behavioral disturbances for children. The literature in this area suggests that these children are more likely to reenter care. Careful attention to long-term planning with permanent families is critical.

### Retaining and Supporting Child Welfare Workers

The relationship between the caseworker and the child and family has long been assumed to be important to the outcomes of the case. This study found that the number of caseworkers was associated with timely permanence and may be even more important than the number and types of services provided to a child and family, in that no other service variables remained in the final model. It is logical to assume that if the relationships between workers and clients are important, then a change in workers will affect results for children and families. Both worker turnover and responsibilities diffused across workers may be associated with delays in timely decisions and court processes. Agencies should consider targeted efforts to retain and support competent casework staff. Agencies should also examine internal procedures that require or promote the transfer of cases for specialized or differentiated services.

### Effective Use of Foster-Adoptive Families in Concurrent Planning

Concurrent planning involves developing a primary plan for permanence along with an alternative permanency plan in the event the primary plan is not possible. This study revealed that in almost all cases, concurrent plans were developed for children in placement. However, the manner in which those plans were implemented differed in two key areas: timing of actual placement in an alternative permanent home and preparation and support provided to foster-adoptive families.

Foster-adoptive families are asked to care for children on a temporary basis with the expectation that they will support the plan for reunification. At the same time, foster-adoptive families are asked to agree to adopt the children should the children become legally free for adoption. Committing to divergent plans requires families to love and perhaps lose the children in their homes. Because of this, foster-adoptive families bear additional risks and emotional burdens related to uncertainty. This is the gift that they are asked to give to the children in their care.

All key informants in agencies suggested that the preparation and support of foster-adoptive families is a very difficult and important task. The agency's philosophical perspective and experience with foster-adoptive care, the terminology used to describe the families, and exploration of the emotional issues for both families and staff influence specific practices about the timing of concurrent placement moves and the level and type of preparation and support provided to foster-adoptive families. These practices are likely to directly affect the outcomes for children and should be explored in all agencies implementing concurrent planning.

## Managing the Child Welfare–Court Relationship

Although child welfare practice across the country is based on similar laws and philosophies about the importance of safety, family preservation, permanence, and the well-being of children, practice varies greatly from location to location. It is likely that philosophies, beliefs, and the quality of relationships between child welfare and court personnel influence practice beyond the factors examined here. The level and quality of communication between the agency and the courts, common expectations of role and purpose, and local agency/court procedures were raised as issues in the qualitative portion of this study and are likely to be important factors in successfully achieving desired outcomes.

## Using Research for Program Improvement

Findings from this study raised many questions for county workers and managers. Specifically, the finding that African American children were less likely to "get home on time" challenged EPP counties to examine their agencies and their practices. Similarly, findings regarding county differences in success rates posed difficult questions for counties. How can child welfare professionals best respond to studies such as this one? The responses of some EPP counties are offered as examples.

In response to these findings, one county immediately contacted the researchers and asked for their assistance in facilitating conversations among child welfare and court personnel aimed at fully understanding the findings and examining a wide range of potential intervention points. Following discussion of the study, the group's focus immediately shifted to an examination of county and court processes that might be modified to improve services for families and children most at risk. A second county noted the wide range in timing of court hearings and decided to focus on the relationship between the court and the child welfare agency. The county is arranging for researchers and state child welfare and judicial managers to meet with child welfare managers, county attorneys, and court workers to focus on timely court hearings. Recently, a third county whose EPP project began in fall 2001 met with researchers to discuss these findings in relation to program design and to plans for ongoing program evaluation.

In this study, the following question was asked: What factors predict getting home on time for Colorado's EPP children? The answers reinforce certain trends seen in the broader literature on child welfare placement outcomes. Perhaps more important, they focus local attention on areas in which this successful program can improve its services to those children and families most at risk for delayed permanence.◆

## References

Adoption and Safe Families Act, P.L. 105-89 (1997).

American Psychiatric Association. (1994). *Diagnostic and statistical manual of mental disorders* (4th ed.). Washington, DC: Author.

Barth, R. P. (1997). Effects of age and race on the odds of adoption versus remaining in long-term out-of-home care. *Child Welfare, 76,* 285–308.

Barth, R. P., Berry, M., Yoshiakami, R., Goodfield, R. K., & Carson, M. L. (1988). Predicting adoption disruption. *Social Work, 33*(3), 227–233.

Barth, R. P., Courtney, M., & Berry, M. (1994). Timing is everything: An analysis of the time to adoption and legalization. *Social Work Research, 18*(3), 139–148.

Barth, R. P., Snowden, L. R., Broeck, E. T., Clancy, E., Jordan, C., & Barusch, A. S. (1986). Contributors to reunification or permanent out-of-home care for physically abused children. *Journal of Social Service Research, 9*(2/3), 31–45.

Beeman, S. K., Kim, H., & Bullerdick, S. (2000). Factors affecting placement of children in kinship and nonkinship foster care. *Children and Youth Services Review, 22*(2), 37–54.

Courtney, M. E. (1994). Factors associated with the reunification of foster children with their families. *Social Service Review, 68*(1), 81–108.

Courtney, M. E. (1995). Reentry to foster care of children returned to their families. *Social Service Review, 69*(2), 226–241.

Davis, I., Landsverk, J., & Newton, R. (1997). Duration of foster care for children reunified within the first year of care. In J. Berrick, R. Barth, & N. Gilbert (Eds.), *Child welfare research review* (Vol. 2, pp. 272–293). New York: Columbia University Press.

Fahlberg, V. (1991). *A child's journey through placement.* Indianapolis, IN: Perspectives Press.

Festinger, T. (1996). Going home and returning to foster care. *Children and Youth Services Review, 18*(4/5), 383–402.

Grogan-Kaylor, A. C. (2000a). *The effect of population level characteristics of the foster care caseload on reunification from foster care.* Unpublished dissertation, University of Wisconsin–Madison.

Grogan-Kaylor, A. (2000b). Who goes into kinship care? The relationship of child and family characteristics to placement into kinship foster care. *Social Work Research, 24*(3), 132–141.

Katz, L. (1999). Concurrent planning: Benefits and pitfalls. *Child Welfare, 78*(2), 71–87.

Kelly, C. M., & Taylor, M. (1999). *Fifth annual report to the joint budget committee: Implementation of HB-94-1178: Expedited permanency planning.* Denver: Colorado Department of Human Services.

Lindsey, D. (1991). Factors affecting the foster care placement decision: An analysis of national survey data. *American Journal of Orthopsychiatry, 61,* 272–281.

Lindsey, D. (1992). Adequacy of income and the foster care placement decision: Using an odds ratio approach to examine client variables. *Social Work Research and Abstracts, 28,* 29–36.

McMurtry, S. L., & Lie, G. L. (1992). Differential exit rates of minority children in foster care. *Social Work Research and Abstracts, 28*(1), 42–48.

Nugent, W. R., Carpenter, D., & Parks, J. (1993). A statewide evaluation of family preservation and family reunification services. *Research on Social Work Practice, 3*(1), 40–65.

Rittner, B. (1995). Children on the move: Placement patterns in children's protective services. *Families in Society, 76*(8), 469–477.

Scannapieco, M., Hegar, R. L., & McAlpine, C. (1997). Kinship care and foster care: A comparison of characteristics and outcomes. *Families in Society, 78*(5), 480–488.

Schene, P. (1998). *Expedited permanency planning in Colorado: An evaluation prepared for the Colorado Department of Human Services*. Unpublished manuscript.

Wells, K., & Guo, S. (1999). Reunification and reentry of foster children. *Children and Youth Services Review, 22*(4), 273–294.

Zuravin, S. J., & DePanfilis, D. (1997). Factors affecting foster care placement of children receiving child protective services. *Social Work Research, 21*(1), 34–42.

# Chapter 3

# Psychological Stress in Adoptive Parents of Special-Needs Children

*Katalina McGlone, Linda Santos, Lynne Kazama,*
*Rowena Fong, and Charles Mueller*

This article focuses on the nature and extent of parental stress among adoptive parents of special-needs children. In-depth face-to-face interviews of adoptive parents of 35 children were conducted, on average, four months postplacement (but before adoption). One-year follow-up interviews were conducted with parents of 15 (43%) of these children. Qualitative and quantitative data were collected, including parenting stress scores. Results indicated higher than average levels of stress, particularly on subscales related to parent-child dysfunctional interactions and to raising a difficult child. Increased stress levels were associated with poorer family adjustment and with higher levels of child behavior problems. Stress levels remained mostly unchanged over the year. Responses to open-ended questions identified five stress categories: child characteristics, parent-child interactions, family cohesion, parental adjustment, and adoptions service issues. Practice and research implications are discussed.

*Katalina McGlone, MSEPH, CHES, is Research Associate, Social Welfare Evaluation and Research Unit; Rowena Fong, MSW, PhD, is Associate Professor; and Charles Mueller, PhD, is Professor and Clinical Psychologist, School of Social Work, University of Hawai'i at Manoa. Linda Santos, MSW, LSW, ACSW, is Director—Division Operations and Lynne Kazama, MSW, LSW, ACSW, is Social Work Supervisor, Casey Family Programs, Honolulu Division.*

The Adoption and Safe Families Act of 1997 seeks to promote the speedy adoption of children with special needs who are in the public child welfare system, when reunification with their parents is unlikely. In addition, the Adoption 2002 Initiative set the goal of doubling the number of adoptions or other permanent placements of children in out-of-home care between 1998 and 2002 (Duquette, Hardin, & Dean, 1999; Sullivan & Freundlich, 1999). In fiscal year 1999, 46,000 children were adopted from the public foster care system, and an estimated 134,000 children were waiting to be adopted as of March 31, 2000 (U.S. Department of Health and Human Services, Children's Bureau, 2001). Children in out-of-home care awaiting adoption typically have a range of special needs (Child Welfare League of America, 2000).

Special-needs adoptions generally are regarded as having favorable outcomes, as based on adoptive parent satisfaction and low rates of disruption (Barth, 2000; Gallant, 2000; Rosenthal, 1993). In their review of studies, Kadushin and Martin (1988) found that about 70% of parents regarded their special-needs adoptions as excellent or good, a percentage comparable to adoptions in general. Rosenthal's (1993) review of studies suggested disruption rates for older special-needs children at about 10% to 15%. Although different studies show some contradictory results, disabilities (physical impairments, developmental problems, and serious medical conditions) do not appear to be major risks for disruptions (Rosenthal, 1993). McRoy (1999) found that adoption disruptions and dissolutions were related to various aspects of the adoption service delivery system, adoptive parents, and child characteristics. For example, the child's emotional and behavioral problems and the parent's unrealistic expectations of the child may be linked to disruptions (Barth & Berry, 1988; Rosenthal, 1993).

The small proportion of adoptions that are regarded with some or much dissatisfaction or those that end in disruption or dissolution may indicate stress in these families. Special-needs adoptions are generally believed to be stressful and challenging for adoptive families and parents (Barth & Berry, 1988; Groze, 1996; Groze & Gruenewald, 1991). Hartmann (1984) stated that accompanying the change in view that every child is adoptable, are two assumptions: (1) Families will need help postplacement, and (2) because of the new demands and changes to the parents' lifestyle and to the family system, the family may be in crisis after placement of a child who has special needs.

Parenting stress and parent–child interactions are a function of a complex interplay among variables related to the parent, child, and situation (Abidin, 1990a). Literature about parenting stress in nonadoptive families of children with special needs shows that, despite having an inordinate number of stressors, a significant proportion of parents with children who have disabilities do manage well (Kysela, McDonald, Reddon, & Gobeil-Dwyer, 1988). The severity of disability, the degree of responsiveness of the child to the parent, and the extent of attachment may, however, affect family stress (Kysela et al., 1988). Parents of emotionally impaired and learning disabled children had higher stress scores than parents of children in regular education (Fuller & Rankin, 1994). Mothers of developmentally delayed children had higher stress scores related to child issues but not parent issues (Cameron, Dobson, & Day, 1991). Other studies of nonadoptive families have found correlations between child behavior problems and parenting stress scores related to child characteristics (Cuccaro, Holmes, & Wright, 1993; Eyberg, Boggs, & Rodriguez, 1992).

A theoretical literature is emerging on stress and special-needs adoption (Barth & Berry, 1988; Groze, 1996). Barth and Berry (1988) described a social and cognitive model of adjustment to adoption. The model is based on stress being a function of an individual's (the parent's, the child's, or the family's) resources and appraisal of any situation. Barth and Berry's model identified the following stressors for adoptive parents: misleading expectations, lack of social support, instant parenthood, new roles, financial costs, establishing the parenting role, and nurturance of marital relationships.

Groze (1996) conceptualized the adoptive family system as including stressors from the community, the service system, the family, and the child. In a four-year longitudinal study, Groze identified various stressors in adoptive families of special-needs children. These stressors included significant behavioral difficulties, challenges from placing siblings together or separating them, attachment difficulties, and negative parent/child relations. The lack of background information on the child, regarded as a stressor for parents by Groze, may also be the strongest service-related predictor of disruption (Rosenthal, 1993).

Todis and Singer (1991) interviewed families who had adopted multiple children with severe disabilities and identified four sources of stress: (1) medical emergencies and procedures such as surgeries, (2) crises from adolescents' behavior problems, (3) dealing with service providers to obtain services (special education, physical therapy, and medical), and (4) concern about the future. Families were helped by receiving social support from other parents of children with disabilities, maintaining a positive focus, appreciating the child's progress, learning about the child's condition and what could be controlled, and having no sense of guilt over the child's condition.

In families who adopted children from Romanian orphanages, parenting stress was significantly correlated with the child's behavior problems, whereas the number of developmental delays, number of medical problems, and number of siblings were not correlated with parenting stress (Mainemer, Gilman, & Ames, 1998).

McCarty, Waterman, Burge, and Edelstein (1999) reported that, within three to five months after placement of a prenatally substance-exposed child, adoptive parents scored relatively higher on the amount of stress generated by child issues than by parent issues on the Parenting Stress Inventory (PSI). The majority of these adoptive parents reported parenting to be more difficult than they had imagined, but also more rewarding (McCarty et al., 1999). In the interviews, parents described more difficulty with attachment and development issues of the child than with the child's behavior. Almost one-half of the parents, however, reported clinically significant distress on subscales of the PSI related to the child's mood, demandingness, inability to adapt, distractibility, or acceptability (meeting parents' expectations). At the follow-up interview, within one year, the total stress scores were lower, but the change was not statistically significant.

Casey Family Programs is a national foundation that serves children, youth, and families. Its primary focus is on children who cannot live safely within their own homes. The agency provides direct services to children and families in need, funds national child welfare projects, and collaborates with other organizations in the areas of prevention, permanency, and transition. In 1984, the Honolulu Division of Casey Family Programs began providing long-term foster care for children removed from their homes because of abuse and neglect. In response to an increasing need for permanency options in Hawai'i, the division began working in 1997 with the Hawai'i Department of Human Services to develop an adoption program for these high-risk youth. The goals for the program are to expedite the adoption placement of special-needs children and to support the stability of the placements. The program defines *special needs* as all children from the child protective/foster care system, because they are exposed to losses, issues of neglect and/or abuse, instability, violence, or substance abuse and, therefore, are more at risk than children from intact, safe homes. Children are referred from the child protective services system after the parents' rights have been terminated. Casey licenses the prospective adoptive parents, who are required to participate in intensive preservice training and are expected to participate in ongoing training. Once a child or children are placed, intensive services are provided to assist the family. Services include assisting families to find community resources, providing legal services, and helping the family in dealing with birthfamily issues, cultural identification, and with day-to-day management. Reimbursement for room and board, medical coverage, and limited financial assistance for special situations are provided. Social workers assist families in applying for federal adoption assistance. Adoption usually occurs from 6 to 12 months after placement. Families are invited to participate in postadoption services for one year after the adoption. Longer term follow-up services are being developed. Families are invited to contact the agency as needed, and to attend adoptive parent-support groups, as well as agency-sponsored workshops, training, and social events.

Although models of stress and adoptive parenting have been developed, relatively few empirical studies have addressed the stress of adoptive parents in adoptions of children with histories of abuse and/or neglect. The present study used both quantitative and qualitative methods to explore the nature and extent of parenting stress among a group of new adoptive parents of special-needs children. Data for the present study were derived from an ongoing evaluation of the special-needs adoption program previously described above.

## Method

### Participants

Twenty-five sets of adoptive parents of 35 children who were placed in the adoption program during the evaluation time frame, from the beginning of the program in 1997 through spring 2000, served as the primary participants in the present study. (Two other parents chose not to participate.) Of the adoptive parents, 20 were couples who had been married 2.5 to 42 years at the time of the initial interview. One couple was not married, and four adoptive parents were single. Adoptive parents ranged in age from 27 to 68. Adoptive family household sizes ranged from 2 to 8 persons; 15 of the 25 adoptive homes had other minor children in residence. Of the adoptive parent couples, 15 had birthchildren (one was born subsequent to the adoption of the child in the present program); some of these children had grown and left the household. At least 13 of the 25 parents wanted a child and were either unable or no longer able to have birthchildren. Nine adoptive mothers had never had any birthchildren at the time of the adoption. The adopted child was the first child in eight homes. Twenty of 23 adoptive fathers were employed, and 16 of the 23 adoptive mothers worked outside the home at the time of the initial interview. Seven couples each received two to four siblings placed through the program.

At the time of the initial interview, the children ranged in age from 12 months to 11.5 years (median age 5 years, 5 months). Sixteen were girls and 19 were boys. Reflecting the multiethnic nature of the Hawai'i population, all but 3 of the 35 adopted children were of mixed race/ethnicity. On average, a child was likely to be from three racial groups and to have at least three ethnicities (mean = 3.77). The children's racial background completely matched that of their adoptive parents for 12 of the children, matched 50% or more for 11 children, matched some but less than 50% for 10 children, and did not match at all for 2 children. Of the 35 children in the evaluation, 17 were placed together with siblings. All but one of the children had at least one prior placement; the average was close to three prior placements for each child. Fourteen children were first placed in foster care after birth, often as a result of a positive drug test at time of delivery.

More than one-half of the children at some time had notable health problems or developmental delays. At least 8 children had histories of asthma, 4 children had hearing loss, at least 13 children had language/speech delays, at least 9 children had cognitive delays or impairments, and at least 6 had motor delays. Preplacement Child Behavior Checklist (CBCL) scores were available for 32 of the 35 children in this study. Total behavior problem scores were elevated (above the 85th percentile) for 15 children (47%). Nineteen (59%) demonstrated either an elevated internalizing or externalizing symptom score before placement in the adoptive home. Indeed, nearly one-third (10 of 32) had either internalizing or externalizing symptom scores that exceeded the 98th percentile clinical cut-off score.

## Procedures and Measures

The data collection method had two major components. The first was a formal chart review for each child and preadoptive family enrolled in the adoption program. This review provided demographic and other background information about the children and families, including some baseline data (e.g., standardized scores on a behavioral problem checklist, CBCL, completed before or at the time the child entered the adoption program) and data from follow-up standardized questionnaires routinely collected by the agency across programs (e.g., periodic standardized measures about children in agency programs, such as child behavior problem measures). Second, data were collected directly from adoptive parents via paper-and-pencil surveys (e.g., PSI) and face-to-face interviews. An initial interview was conducted as close as possible to three months after the child was placed in the adoptive home. A second interview was conducted about one year later. Delays occurred in the timing of some interviews for various reasons. For instance, a few adoptive parents had been foster parents first, so their initial interviews were conducted 3 to 27 months after the child's physical placement in the home.

In-depth, face-to-face interviews of adoptive parents, lasting about two hours (longer for parents of sibling adoptions) focused on a variety of topics, including but not limited to: (a) perceptions of the adoption program, (b) satisfaction with being an adoptive parent, (c) parental stress, (d) perceived support, (e) family cohesion and family adjustment to the adoption, (f) near-disruptions of adoption, (g) behavior changes at home and at school, (h) child's attachment, (i) birthfamily issues, and (j) ethnocultural identity issues (McGlone & Mueller, 2001).

The present article focuses on parental stress and primarily relies on data collected on this topic. During or shortly before each of the interviews, adoptive parents were asked to complete the PSI-Short Form (Abidin, 1995). The PSI provides a total stress score and four subscale scores (Defensive Responding, Parental Distress, Parent-Child Interaction, and Difficult Child). The parents with multiple sibling placements were asked to complete the first two sections of the PSI only once (providing scores on Defensive Responding and Parental Distress). They completed the remaining two sections (Parental-Child Dysfunctional Interaction and Difficult Child), however, for each adopted child. A total stress score was then calculated for each child, by taking the parent's score on the Parental Distress subscale and adding the unique scores from the latter two subscales.*

The PSI–Short Form is a 36-item, 5-point, disagree–agree self-report scale designed to identify the level and sources of parent–child stress (Abidin, 1990b, 1995). The measure produces a total parenting stress score, one validity subscale, and three substantive subscales (Parental Distress, Parent–Child Dysfunctional Interactions, and Difficult Child). The total stress scale assesses the overall level of parenting stress, but it does not include stresses associated with other life roles or events (Abidin, 1995). The Parental Distress subscale indicates the level of distress a person is experiencing in his or her role as parent. The Parent–Child Dysfunctional Interactions subscale focuses on the parent's perception that the child does not meet expectations and that parent–child interactions are not reinforcing to the parent. The Difficult Child subscale focuses on some behavioral characteristics of children that make them easier or more difficult to raise. Both total scores and subscale scores can be compared to the responses from the normative sample used to develop the index. The PSI and the

---

* Given the combined use of two subscales and the absence of independence of observation, care needs to be exercised in interpreting findings based on the total stress scores.

PSI–Short Form have been used in a wide variety of studies and have demonstrated solid psychometric properties (Abidin, 1995).

Using a Likert-type, five-point disagree–agree format, participants were asked to respond to a series of statements related to family functioning. The first nine statements were taken directly from the Family Cohesion Subscale of the Family Environment Scale (Moos & Moos, 1986). The remaining nine items, specifically developed for this study, focused on how well the family was adjusting to the adoption (e.g., "The addition of [child's name] is causing problems that seem to be hurting our family," and "Our family's adjustment to having [child's name] still is a struggle").

During the initial interview, parents were asked to identify the most stressful aspects related to having the adopted child and to·identify other causes of stress related to the adoption. In the second interview, participants were asked to reflect on the kinds of problems, challenges, or stresses they or their family were having postadoption. Responses to these open-ended questions and any other spontaneous descriptions related to stress were recorded and collected. Each interview was sorted by themes. Files were created that combined all participants' stress-related responses. All of this information was sorted and organized by using WordPerfect. Two of the authors reviewed, discussed, and analyzed these data, then they developed the thematic organization.

Finally, data from the PSI were compared to scores from available CBCL scores ($n = 14$) provided by the adoptive parents approximately one year after placement (between the first and second interview).

*Parenting Stress Levels*

Table 1 depicts the parenting stress scores (total and the three substantive subscales) reported around the time of the initial interviews. Prior normative data indicate a median raw score of 69 for the total stress scores. As shown in Table 1, mean scores for total parenting stress indicate a significant elevation, $t(34) = 2.36$,

## TABLE 1

**Parenting Stress Scores: Normative Sample Median Raw Score, Participants' Mean (Standard Deviation), and Percentage Above 85th Percentile Clinical Cut-Off**

| Scale | Normative Sample Median Raw Score | M(SD) | Percentage Above 85th Percentile Cut-Off |
|---|---|---|---|
| Total Parenting Stress | 69 | 76.89*(19.80) | 34.3 |
| Parental Distress | 25 | 21.88*(5.26) | 00.0 |
| Parent-Child Dysfunctional Interactions | 19 | 24.06*(7.75) | 40.0 |
| Difficult Child | 25 | 30.06*(9.93) | 42.9 |

*$p < .05$, one-sample $t$ tests, compared to test value equal to sample median raw score.

$p < .05$. In addition, raw scores at or above 86 are thought to be clinically significant, as they place the parent above the 85th percentile of the normative sample. That is to say, about 15% of parents in the normative sample scored at this elevated level. In comparison, 12 of 35 (34.3%) of the total parental stress scores in the present study were at or above this cut-off. As such, more than twice as many adoptive parents in the present study reported clinically significant levels of stress relative to the normative sample.

PSI subscale scores provide an opportunity to examine factors that contribute to elevated stress levels. Table 1 displays stress level scores across the three substantive subscales. One-sample $t$ tests, using each subscale's normative median raw score as the test value, indicated that parents in the present study scored lower on parental distress, $t(24) = -2.96$, $p < .01$, but higher on Parent-Child Dysfunctional Interactions, $t(34) = 3.86$, $p < .01$, and Difficult Child subscales, $t(34) = 3.01$, $p < .01$, than seen in the normative sample. As can be seen in the right column of Table 1, the percentage of participants who reported stress levels above the 85th percentile cut-off followed the same pattern. Specifically, no adoptive parents reported clinical elevations on the Parental Distress subscale, but about 40% (14/35) indicated elevated scores on the Parent-Child Dysfunctional Interaction and the Difficult Child subscales (15/35).

The PSI has a Defensive Responding subscale. On 6 of the 25 (24%) administrations at Time 1, scores exceeded this cut-off, indicating a tendency for the adoptive parents (as a group) to respond in a more defensive manner than seen in the normative sample. These somewhat elevated defensive responding scores, consistent with prior literature about scores on other measures (Dalton, 1994), might indicate that parental stress levels were somewhat higher than reported here, adding further support to the finding of elevated stress in this sample of parents.

Although follow-up data were limited to 15 of the 35 children, no significant change occurred in mean stress scores (total or subscale) over time. Total stress scores, Parent-Child Dysfunctional Interactions and Difficult Child scores rose slightly, but not significantly, $t(14) = 0.51$, 1.41, and 0.44, respectively. Parental Distress scores showed a nonsignificant trend toward lower scores, $t(14) = -2.04, p < .10$. In addition, PSI scores at Times 1 and 2 were fairly highly correlated ($r = .63$ for total stress), indicating that parents who reported higher levels of stress at Time 1 were likely to do so again at Time 2.

To examine more closely factors that may have contributed to parenting stress, Time 1 PSI scores were correlated with the Family Cohesion and Family Adjustment to Adoption scores collected during the same interview and with CBCL scores (Achenbach & Edelbrock, 1983) completed by adoptive parents approximately one year postplacement. As shown in Table 2, Family Adjustment and, to a lesser extent, Family Cohesion were inversely related to parenting stress scores. Similarly, CBCL total and Internalizing scores were significantly correlated with the Parent–Child Dysfunctional Interactions subscale and the Difficult Child subscale. CBCL scores were not significantly correlated with Family Cohesion or Family Adjustment scores (all $r$s < .23).

TABLE 2

**Pearson Correlations Between Measures of Parental Stress and Family and Child Functioning**

|  | CBCL Total | CBCL Internalizing | CBCL Externalizing | Family Cohesion | Family Adjustment |
|---|---|---|---|---|---|
| PSI Total | .52* | .53* | .45 | -.49* | -.81* |
| Parental Distress | -.42 | -.15 | -.31 | -.65* | -.51* |
| Parent-Child Dysfunctional Interactions | .56* | .57* | .45* | -.38 | -.80* |
| Difficult Child | .60* | .59* | .53* | -.36 | -.73* |

Note: PSI = Parenting Stress Inventory; CBCL = Child Behavior Checklist.
*$p < .05$.

## Responses to Open-Ended Interview Questions

Responses to open-ended questions about stress and adjustment both support and expand on the quantitative findings. When asked, nearly all parents identified stressors, and the majority of these responses were organized into five major categories.

**Child Characteristics.** Particular characteristics of the child were said to be stressful for parents. Many parents reported stressful externalizing behavior problems, including lying, stealing, physical and verbal aggression, tantrums, hyperactivity, and inattention. Naturally, parents found their child's threat of violence to others quite stressful. Parents also were stressed by the child's threats of violence to self, sleeping problems, lack of self-confidence, fears and insecurities, retreat into fantasy, and other internalizing problems.

Other emotional and behavioral problems exhibited by the child were stressful. In the first few months of placement, some children's poor hygiene and self-care abilities were reported as stressful. Several children were reported to "still need help wiping." Enuresis and encopresis, especially among older children, were stressful.

Other sources of stress for some parents were children's chronic medical problems, such as asthma and chronic bladder infections, and the routines, treatments, and appointments needed to manage them. Insurance and medical coverage issues were also mentioned.

**Parent-Child Interactions.** Responses reflected stressors related to the parent-child relationship. Parents expressed that the children's lying to them was especially stressful. Other stressful forms of inadequate communication were lack of disclosure and withdrawal (e.g., "You ask him what he's thinking, but he doesn't speak, he doesn't really talk"). One parent was upset by the child's lack of remorse about his misbehavior. Another parent was challenged by her child's anger: "I hate you. You're not my real mom. I wish you were dead." A few children at times said they wanted to be with their prior foster parents or to go home with their teacher. Also stressful was when the child tried to "play the adoptive mother and father against each other."

Other perceived stressors that were related to the parent–child relationship included the child's disobedience, not listening, stubbornness, and pushing limits. Some parents seemed to have a low tolerance for their child's expression of emotional needs, especially crying. A child's clinginess and strong need for attention were stressful for a few parents.

**Family Cohesion.** Challenges to family adjustment and maintaining family cohesion were identified as parental stressors. Some parents with birthchildren noted difficulties with sibling adjustment and sibling rivalry, for example, teasing, fighting, and a sense of having been displaced. "Most parents can put up with just about anything without having to choose between one child and another, if you're being pulled both ways. That's what makes or breaks an adoption." For example, one family described a birthchild's anger with the adopted child's behavior problems, as well as the birthchild's feelings about receiving less attention and even worry about the parent's stress level. This family was describing an older child who avoided being home and, when home, tried to ignore the new child. Parents also reported that attempting to meet different family members' needs was stressful when cohesion was low.

**Adjustment Issues for Parents.** Parents expressed stress from the extra workload, new routines, child's food preferences, becoming a new parent of an older child, and the restructuring of home life brought on by the placement. Some parents mentioned challenges to finding time for themselves as a couple. Parents reported as stressful a lack of needed support because respite care was unavailable or because of changes resulting from moving or from a spouse's absence for an extended period. Several parents also mentioned issues related to the birthfamily, finances, or other sources of stress unrelated to adoption.

**Adoption Service Issues.** Three themes emerged concerning stressors related to the service system, primarily preplacement practice. First, some parents thought they did not have adequate information about the child, although most parents had access to the child's record at the agency before placement. Some parents suggested that a more thorough evaluation of the child before placement, including the effects of prenatal substance exposure and/or the severity of medical or behavioral problems, would have avoided the situation of having a child who did not fit their preferences. Second, parents described as "rushed" about 40% of the children's placements. These placements caused additional stress and may have contributed to ongoing problems for some families. Placements were rushed for a variety of reasons, most commonly service system concerns about abuse and/or neglect by the foster family before the child entered the preadoptive home. Third, several parents reported being stressed about a perceived lack of partnership, mostly about decisions contrary to their wishes that were made by service professionals. These service system-related stressors are congruent with those described in the literature, and, in this study, were found in the context of a program regarded with high overall satisfaction by the adoptive parents.

## Discussion

Data presented here, derived from an ongoing evaluation of a new special-needs adoption program, indicate elevated stress levels among new adoptive parents. In parallel with prior literature on adoption disruptions and parenting stress, the present findings demonstrate the important role of stress related to parent–child interactions, child behavior, family cohesion, and adjustment to the adoption, and adoption service issues (Barth & Berry, 1988; Groze, 1996; Mainemer et al., 1998; McCarty, Waterman, et al., 1999; McRoy, 1999; Rosenthal, 1993; Rosenthal, Groze, & Aguilar, 1991). As seen in other studies, parental distress, as a source of stress alone, was relatively low (McCarty et al., 1999). The low Parental Distress score may be a result of effective program support of parents (reported in the interviews, but not included in the present study), parental defensive responses, or effective recruitment and screening of prospective parents. Also congruent with the results of McCarty et al. (1999), little evidence was found of significant change in stress levels over the first year of placement.

Given the comparability of findings across the literature on parenting stress and on adoption disruption, high levels of parenting stress may be a risk for potential disruption. If so, ongoing assessment of and interventions for parenting stress might be productive.

The present results need to be viewed with some caution. Other factors that can influence parenting stress in relation to adopted children who have special needs were not examined. For instance, little emphasis was placed on the child's type and degree of disability or on other theoretically important variables, such as community attitudes (Groze, 1996). In addition, the present sample was small, and participants were adoptive parents from a new adoption program for children with special needs. Whether parents from similar adoption programs or systems would respond in the same way is not known. Thus, further research might focus on operationalizing the various factors believed to influence parenting stress in the special-needs adoption context and on examining these variables in a larger sample of participants.

Given persistently elevated parental stress levels found in this and other studies, adoption program planners should consider how parental stress levels might be formally addressed in various aspects of special-needs adoption programs. In the areas of parental selection and preparation, the program should attempt to identify and to anticipate parental stress. Assessing parental readiness to adopt special-needs children—including clearly identifying expectations of prospective parents while also reviewing the reality of parenting special-needs children—is particularly important. In addition, specific screening and interviewing questions should be included that focus on parental stress management, sources of satisfaction, and beliefs about raising children with significant emotional and behavioral needs. Providing stress management training to parents during preplacement services may also be useful.

Adoption changes family dynamics and affects birthchildren of adoptive families, as suggested in this study and other literature (Babb & Laws, 1997; Keck & Kupecky, 1995). Therefore, it is important to assess likely adjustment issues for birthchildren of prospective adoptive parents. As suggested by Mullin and Johnson (1999), services for birthchildren and previously adopted children are recommended as part of the preparation and postplacement support of families who adopt children with special needs.

The results of this research support suggestions made elsewhere about family–child matching (Barth & Berry, 1988; McRoy, 1999). Adoptive parents should be given all available information about the child and should have time to digest this information (Babb, 1999; Freundlich & Peterson, 1998). Program staff should do everything in their power to ensure adequate time for visitation before placement. Programs can also use a matching checklist so that anticipated challenges with the child (e.g., internalizing or externalizing behavior problems) can be compared with parenting expectations, styles, and tolerance levels.

Programs should provide frequent, intensive, and ongoing worker and agency support to the parents and family in the preadoptive period, especially the first three to six months. The program might monitor parenting stress levels or teach parents how to monitor stress themselves. When parenting stress is high, or when factors that contribute to high levels of stress are present (poor sibling adjustment, low family cohesion, persistent emotional or behavioral problem manifestations by the adopted child), the program should link the family to individual and family therapy with a therapist who is knowledgeable about adoption issues and who has experience in working successfully with adoptive families. In addition, parents may benefit from respite care as a stress management strategy. Programs can help by providing or facilitating the availability of respite care both pre- and postadoption. Programs can also provide ongoing training and support pre- and postadoption to increase parental skills, manage parenting stress, promote family cohesion and adjustment, advocate for effective services, and deal with the day-to-day challenges of parenting a child with special needs. Much of this work can be done in groups in which parents and other family members of adopted children who have special needs can provide support and mentoring to each other. Programs should maintain long-term connections with families as they deal with ongoing issues and work toward ensuring that families have access to strong formal and informal support systems. When indicated, programs might offer training and information to these support systems to strengthen their understanding of special-needs adoption issues. Finally, throughout the whole adoption process, programs should maintain a partnership practice model (Kramer & Houston, 1999; Smith & Howard, 1999). In this model, adoptive parents and adoption services work together for the betterment of the child and the family.◆

## References

Abidin, R. (1990a). Introduction to the special issue: The stresses of parenting. *Journal of Clinical Child Psychology, 19*(4), 298–301.

Abidin, R. (1990b). *Parenting Stress Index* (3rd ed.). Charlottesville, VA: Pediatric Psychology Press.

Abidin, R. (1995). *Parenting Stress Index: Professional manual* (3rd ed.). Odessa, FL: Psychological Assessment Resources.

Achenbach, T. M., & Edelbrock, C. S. (1983). *Manual for the Child Behavior Checklist and Revised Child Behavior Profile.* Burlington: University of Vermont.

Babb, L. (1999). *Ethics in American adoption.* Westport, CT: Bergin & Garvey.

Babb, L. A., & Laws, R. (1997). *Adopting and advocating for the special needs child: A guide for parents and professionals.* Westport, CT: Bergin & Garvey.

Barth, R. (2000). What works in permanency planning: Adoption. In M. Kluger, G. Alexander, & P. Curtis (Eds.), *What works in child welfare* (pp. 217–226). Washington, DC: Child Welfare League of America.

Barth, R., & Berry, M. (1988). *Adoption and disruption: Rates, risks, and responses.* New York: Aldine de Gruyter.

Cameron, S., Dobson, L., & Day, D. (1991). Stress in parents of developmentally delayed and nondelayed preschool children. *Canada's Mental Health, 39*(1), 13–17.

Child Welfare League of America. (2000). *CWLA standards of excellence for adoption services* (Rev. ed.). Washington, DC: Author.

Cuccaro, M., Holmes, G., & Wright, H. (1993). Behavior problems in preschool children: A pilot study. *Psychological Reports, 72*, 121-122.

Dalton, J. (1994). MMPI-168 and Marlowe-Crowne profiles of adoption applicants. *Journal of Clinical Psychology, 50*(6), 863-865.

Duquette, D., Hardin, M., & Dean, C. (1999). *Adoption 2002: The President's initiative on adoption and foster care: Guidelines for public policy and state legislation governing permanence for children.* Washington, DC: U.S. Department of Health and Human Services; Administration for Children and Families; Administration on Children, Youth, and Families; Children's Bureau.

Eyberg, S., Boggs, S., & Rodriguez, C. (1992). Relationships between maternal parenting stress and child disruptive behavior. *Child and Family Behavior Therapy, 14*(4), 1-9.

Freundlich, M., & Peterson, L. (1998). *Wrongful adoption: Law, policy, and practice.* Washington, DC: Child Welfare League of America; New York: Evan B. Donaldson Adoption Institute.

Fuller, G., & Rankin, R. (1994). Differences in levels of parental stress among mothers of learning disabled, emotionally impaired, and regular school children. *Perceptual and Motor Skills, 78*(2), 583-592.

Gallant, N. (2000). What works in special needs adoption. In M. Kluger, G. Alexander, & P. Curtis (Eds.), *What works in child welfare* (pp. 227-234). Washington, DC: Child Welfare League of America.

Groze, V. (1996). *Successful adoptive families: A longitudinal study of special needs adoption.* Westport, CT: Praeger.

Groze, V., & Gruenewald, A. (1991). PARTNERS: A model program for special-needs adoptive families in stress. *Child Welfare, 70*(5), 581-589.

Hartmann, A. (1984). *Working with adoptive families beyond placement.* New York: Child Welfare League of America.

Kadushin, A., & Martin, J. (1988). *Child welfare services* (4th ed.). New York: Macmillan.

Keck, G., & Kupecky, R. (1995). *Adopting the hurt child: Hope for families with special needs kids: A guide for parents and professionals.* Colorado Springs, CO: Pinon.

Kramer, L., & Houston, D. (1999). Hope for the children: A community-based approach in supporting families who adopt children with special needs. *Child Welfare, 78*(5), 611–636.

Kysela, G., McDonald, L., Reddon, J., & Gobeil-Dwyer, F. (1988). Stress and supports to families with a handicapped child. In K. Marfo (Ed.), *Parent–child interaction and de-*

*velopmental disabilities: Theory, research, and intervention* (pp. 273–289). New York: Praeger.

Mainemer, H., Gilman, L., & Ames, E. (1998). Parenting stress in families adopting children from Romanian orphanages. *Journal of Family Issues, 19*(2), 164–180.

McCarty, C., Waterman, J., Burge, D., & Edelstein, S. (1999). Experiences, concerns, and service needs of families adopting children with prenatal substance exposure: Summary and recommendations. *Child Welfare, 78*(5), 561–577.

McGlone, K., & Mueller, C. (2001). *Evaluation of the Casey Family Program Honolulu Division's Permanency Options Initiative: Year three report.* Honolulu: University of Hawaii, Social Welfare Evaluation and Research Unit, School of Social Work.

McRoy, R. (1999). *Special needs adoptions: Practice issues.* New York: Garland.

Moos, R. H., & Moos, B. S. (1986). *Family Environment Scale manual* (2nd ed.). Palo Alto, CA: Consulting Psychologists Press.

Mullin, E., & Johnson, L. (1999). The role of birth/previously adopted children in families choosing to adopt children with special needs. *Child Welfare, 78*(5), 579–591.

Rosenthal, J. (1993). Outcomes of adoption of children with special needs. *The Future of Children, 3*(1), 77–88.

Rosenthal, J., Groze, V., & Aguilar, G. (1991). Adoption outcomes for children with handicaps. *Child Welfare, 70*(6), 623–636.

Smith, S., & Howard, J. (1999). *Promoting successful adoptions: Practice with troubled families.* Thousand Oaks, CA: Sage.

Sullivan, A., & Freundlich, M. (1999). Achieving excellence in special needs adoption. *Child Welfare, 78*(5), 507-517.

Todis, B., & Singer, G. (1991). Stress and stress management in families with adopted children who have severe disabilities. *Journal of the Association for Persons with Severe Handicaps, 16*(1), 3-13.

U.S. Department of Health and Human Services, Children's Bureau. (2001). *The AFCARS (Adoption and Foster Care Analysis and Reporting System) report: Preliminary estimates as of April 2001.* Available online at www.acf.dhhs.gov/program/cb

Chapter 4

# Making Visits Better: The Perspectives of Parents, Foster Parents, and Child Welfare Workers

*Wendy L. Haight, James E. Black, Sarah Mangelsdorf, Grace Giorgio, Lakshmi Tata, Sarah J. Schoppe, and Margaret Szewczyk*

Mothers of children recently placed in foster care, foster mothers, and child welfare workers participated in semistructured, clinical interviews focusing on the challenges of parent visitation with young children. Mothers described their feelings of grief, trauma, and rage about the forced separation from their children and stressed the importance of emotional expression and communication during visits. Child welfare workers described the complexities of supporting emotionally close parent-child interactions while monitoring and assessing parental behavior during visits. Foster mothers described the importance of preparing children for visits and the difficulties of supporting the children afterward. Implications of understanding mothers', foster mothers', and child welfare workers' perspectives on enhancing the quality of visits with young children are discussed.

*Wendy L. Haight is Associate Professor and Lakshmi Tata is Doctoral Student, School of Social Work; Sarah Mangelsdorf is Professor of Psychology; Grace Giorgio is Lecturer in Speech Communication; and Sarah J. Schoppe and Margaret Szewczyk are*

Parent visitation, the scheduled face-to-face contact between parents and their children in foster care, is considered the primary child welfare intervention for maintaining parent–child relationships necessary for successful family reunification (Downs, Costin, & McFadden, 1996; Hess & Proch, 1993), a permanency goal for the majority of children in foster care. Visitation also is viewed as providing an opportunity for professionals to better understand the parent–child relationship (Kessler & Greene, 1999). Organized visits are considered so critical to the effort to reunite families that P. L. 96-272 (Adoption Assistance and Child Welfare Act of 1980) explicitly requires their inclusion in family preservation efforts. In Illinois, visits take on even greater significance, given state statutes enacted in 1998 requiring that permanency plans, for children ages 8 or younger, be in place within six months after the child's placement in care.

Yet existing research and clinical reports (e.g., Haight, Kagle, & Black, in press) suggest that, too often, visits fall short of meeting their goals. Indeed, social workers' reports (Fanshel, 1982), and direct observations (Haight, Black, Workman, & Tata, 2001) indicate considerable variation in the extent to which mothers and young children sustain mutually engaging and developmentally appropriate interactions during visits. Furthermore, adult participants vary widely in their understanding of appropriate and supportive social work practice during visits. In the following unpublished excerpts, a child welfare worker and her client discussed during separate interviews how to make visits better:

> I think praising the parents helps when they have done a good visit, recognizing "that was good." [Praise] is not some-

*Doctoral Students in Psychology, University of Illinois at Urbana-Champaign. This study was funded by a grant from the Children and Family Research Center, a collaboration between the University of Illinois School of Social Work and the Illinois Department of Children and Family Services. We thank Karen Burkhart for her help in developing the coding system, and Ian Kodis and Richard Kim for their help in conducting the interviews.*

thing you hear enough. I mean we all like praise. It was something from my boss—and, basically, we're their [the parents'] bosses at this point in time. (Child welfare worker)

I'm serious! The [child welfare workers] sit there and look at you like you are stupid! Or they're patronizing. "You did really good!" What do you mean, "Really good?" I have had day care in my home for eight years! I raised my children! I've got an 11-year-old. I raised him for 10 1/2 years before you took him. I don't need you to tell me I did "really good." (Mother)

These excerpts illustrate the emotional and interpersonal complexities of visits. The clinical literature increasingly recognizes the effect of children's grief and emotional pain on visits (Beyer, 1999; Department of Children and Family Services [DCFS] clinical materials; Haight et al., in press). Remarkably few systematic efforts have been made, however, to understand the subjective experiences of parents, foster parents, and child welfare workers surrounding visits. In general, parents involved with public child welfare systems have reported emotional suffering (Jenkins & Norman, 1975), anger, fear, powerlessness (Diorio, 1992), and dissatisfaction with services (Poertner, Harris, & Joe, 1997). Low income, minority parents with children in Head Start agreed that most parents need help, but child protective services were viewed with distrust, anger, and fear (Keller & McDade, 2000). Clinical discussions suggest that foster parents (Edelstein, Burge, & Waterman, 2001) and child welfare workers also may experience grief, anger, and powerlessness (DCFS clinical materials), as well as burnout and secondary trauma (Dane, 2000). Some child welfare workers even express condemnation of parents (Ong, 1985; Smith & Smith, 1990).

This article examines the perspectives of mothers, foster mothers, and child welfare workers for clues as to how to improve parent visits with very young children. Understanding the subjective experiences and perceptions of parents, foster parents, and caseworkers can be critical to making visits better for several related reasons. First, the voices of individuals actually involved in visits may illuminate neglected psychological and interpersonal issues that affect visits. For example, participants' subjective experiences of grief, rage, and powerlessness can affect their energy level, emotional availability to the child, and ability to collaborate with other adults during visits. (See Edelstein, et al., 2001, for a discussion of "disenfranchised grief.") Once these issues have been identified, interventions to better support parents, foster parents, and child welfare workers may be developed.

Second, mothers, foster mothers, and child welfare workers have a wealth of experience with visits, but gained from very different vantage points. For example, mothers can describe what visits mean to them personally and can suggest how their children, and their relationships with their children, may be affected over time. Child welfare workers schedule, organize, supervise, and evaluate the responses of many children and parents during visits. Foster mothers observe, prepare, and support children before and subsequent to the visits; sometimes they even supervise visits. By including the perspectives of all three groups of adults, a more complete picture may be obtained of the issues involved in visiting. Attempts to enhance practice can then be informed by a systematic exploration of the diverse "practice wisdom" of those individuals directly involved in all phases of the routine conduct of visits.

Third, given their differing roles during visits, mothers, foster mothers, and child welfare workers sometimes have divergent perspectives. For example, mothers may prioritize intimacy with their children during visits, whereas child welfare workers may prioritize supervision and assessment. These differing perspectives may result in mismatched agendas and conflicts that are disruptive to the visits. Attempts to improve the quality of parent visitation can anticipate key adults' divergent perspectives that may affect their participation in visits.

# Method

## Participants

Participants were 28 mothers, 13 foster mothers, and 24 child welfare workers associated with a public child welfare office (DCFS) in a medium-sized, midwestern city. Mothers were participants in an observational study of parent-child interaction during visits (Haight et al., 2001; Mangelsdorf, Haight, Black, Schoppe, Szewczyk, & Tata, n.d.)

This study focused on mothers because they comprise the majority of visitors of preschool- and toddler-aged children in the state in which this study was conducted. Mothers of preschool- and toddler-aged children were the focus because very young children are entering the foster care system at increasing rates and are staying for longer periods of time (Berrick, Needell, Barth, & Jonson-Reid, 1998; Downs et al., 1996). Furthermore, because early parent–child relationships undergo considerable development during the first few years of life (e g., Thompson, 1998), these relationships are especially vulnerable to disruption through foster care placement. The study also focused on mothers with children in care for 12 months or less, because child welfare workers increasingly recognize the significance to later reunification of the establishment of regular visits early in placement. Only mothers whose children had been in care for a minimum of one month were included so that initial visiting patterns were established.

In summary, mothers of all children between 24 and 60 months of age who had been in foster care from 1 to 12 months were identified through DCFS records. Children's caseworkers were contacted and asked to screen out any children who were not receiving visits or for whom a permanency plan was not to "return home." Caseworkers then contacted mothers and obtained permission for the researchers to contact them regarding participation in the study.

It was explained to each mother that, to develop better social work practices, the researchers at the university were interested in learning more about visits. Although DCFS had granted permission for this study and even designated the researchers as "visit supervisors" for the purposes of this study, the researchers were not employed by DCFS and did not report to DCFS employees regarding any individual mother's or child's participation (or lack thereof) in the study.

Approximately 38% of the eligible mothers referred by caseworkers agreed to participate. Mothers were paid $30.00 for their time. They also were given an additional supervised visit with their children, which the researchers supervised.

Of the 28 mothers, 15 were Caucasian, 12 were African American, and 1 was Hispanic. The mean age of mothers was 27 years (range, 16–42 years). Of the mothers, 15 had less than a high school education, 9 had completed high school, 3 had earned GEDs, and 1 had an associate's degree from a community college. Ten mothers were employed at service or factory jobs; the others did not have steady employment. Nine mothers had a history of or ongoing problems with substance abuse, nine were struggling with mental heath issues, with clinical diagnoses of depression ($n = 6$), manic depression ($n = 1$), anxiety disorder ($n = 1$), and posttraumatic stress disorder/anxiety disorder ($n = 1$); one had brittle diabetes. Although the issue was not probed systematically, domestic violence incidents occurring around the time of their children's placement in foster care were mentioned spontaneously by 25% of the mothers. Mothers had a mean of 2.4 children (range, 1–5) with a mean age of 6 years (range, less than 1 year to 22 years). Twenty-seven mothers had become involved with the child welfare system involuntarily. One mother, overwhelmed by substance abuse and domestic violence, voluntarily placed her children in care.

Children in the group were in care primarily because of neglect ($n = 19$). Six children were in care because of physical abuse, one because of sexual abuse, and two because of domestic violence. Twenty-five mothers reported participating in at least one visit per week with the their children; 18 reported that their visits currently were supervised.

## Foster Mothers and Child Welfare Workers

Foster mothers were included in the study because they were the primary caregivers of the children involved with DCFS. Foster mothers in the study were randomly selected from all foster mothers involved with DCFS. All child welfare workers at the local level DCFS office were invited to participate. A letter of introduction from DCFS announced the study to foster mothers and child welfare workers. The letter stated that DCFS was participating with researchers from the University of Illinois in a project to improve the quality of visiting. Unless they contacted DCFS to express their disinterest in participating, they should expect a call from the researchers.

Of the foster mothers contacted, approximately 35% ($n = 13$) agreed to participate. They received $20 for their participation. Seven foster mothers were African American, and six were Caucasian. Two had completed junior high school, six had completed high school or earned a GED, and five were college graduates. The mean number of years these mothers had provided foster care through DCFS was 7 years (range, 2.5–14 years).

Approximately 50% of the child welfare workers contacted agreed to participate ($n = 24$). Eighteen child welfare workers were female. Six workers were African American, and 18 were Caucasian. Twenty-three child welfare workers were college graduates, and 9 had graduate degrees (7 of these were master's of social work degrees). The mean number of years participants had worked in child welfare was eight years (range, 3–17 years). All had experience with parent visits. Four participants currently were employed as supervisors. The other 20 were involved in direct services, typically described as child welfare specialists or caseworkers.

## Procedure

Each participant responded to an individual, semistructured, in-depth, tape-recorded interview lasting approximately one to two hours. Interviews were conducted at a location of the participant's choosing, typically a private office at the university (mothers), the local DCFS office (child welfare workers), or at home (foster mothers). Each interview was conducted by a graduate research assistant or by a psychiatrist from the local community mental health center. Participants were aware that the interviewer was not affiliated with DCFS and that their conversations would remain confidential. They were invited to narrate their experiences with visits, to articulate their own beliefs regarding the role of visits in child welfare services, to describe factors which facilitate or impede visits, and to provide advice to DCFS professionals. (Protocol is available on request.) Child welfare workers and foster mothers were asked to focus on visits with young children, ages 2 to 5. Mothers were asked to focus on their experiences with their own 2- to 5-year-old children. Audiotapes were transcribed, verbatim, in their entirety.

## Analysis

A subset of 12 randomly chosen interviews (4 each for mothers, foster mothers, and child welfare workers) was read by two individuals who independently, and then through discussion, generated a list of factors identified by participants as affecting the quality of visits. Two other independent raters then used this list to code the interviews. They overlapped on approximately 10% of the interviews for mothers ($n = 3$), foster mothers ($n = 2$), and child welfare workers ($n = 2$). The mean agreement was 86% (range, 83%–100%). Disagreements were resolved through discussion. (Details are available on request.) The factors coded are described in the relevant portions of the Results and Discussion section below. This article is restricted to those factors described as affecting visits by at least 50% of mothers, foster mothers, or caseworkers.

## TABLE 1

**Percentage of Mothers, Foster Mothers, and Child Welfare Workers Identifying Historical/Contextual Factors as Affecting the Quality of Visits**

| Factors Identified by at Least 50% of Mothers, Foster Mothers, or Child Welfare Workers | Mothers (n = 28) | Foster Mothers (n = 13) | Child Welfare Workers (n = 24) |
| --- | --- | --- | --- |
| Historical/Contextual Factors | 100 | 100 | 100 |
| Services | 100 | 100 | 100 |
| Frequency and Consistency of Visit Schedule | 93 | 62 | 71 |
| Quality of Services | 82 | 85 | 83 |
| Parents' Compliance with Mandated Services | 79 | 77 | 67 |
| Quality of Child's Foster Care | 86 | 69 | 63 |
| Feelings About the Separation | 100 | 31 | 58 |
| Parents' Feelings About the Separation | 100 | 8 | 33 |
| Child's Feelings About the Separation | 75 | 23 | 50 |

## Results and Discussion

### Historical/Contextual Factors

As shown in Table 1, participants agreed that the history and context of the case, that is, conditions occurring outside of a specific visit in time and space, can affect the quality of that visit. In particular, participants discussed the quality of services provided to the family, as well as parents' and children's feelings about separation.

**Services to Families.** All participants discussed the quality of services provided to families by DCFS or by agencies contracted by DCFS. Participants emphasized that the frequency and consistency of visits can affect the quality of future visits. For example, some participants felt that frequent and consistent visits help young children to anticipate and eventually adjust to visiting their parents. The majority of participants also agreed that visits may be affected by the adequacy of other services (e.g., parenting classes, and mental health and substance abuse treatment) to meet the real needs of families. Most participants also viewed parents' compliance with mandated services as affecting visits. Some child welfare workers used mothers' compliance with services as an index of their motivation to reunite with their children. Unfortunately, some mothers characterized their participation in mandated services as "jumping through the hoops," which is necessary to maintain adequate relations with DCFS workers, but not effective in addressing the real needs of their families.

Participants also identified quality foster care and support provided by foster mothers as key facilitators of visits. Some participants argued that when children are emotionally supported and well cared for in their foster homes, parents and children are better able to relate during visits. Conversely, some mothers described their distress when young children arrived at visits appearing uncared for or unhappy. In the following excerpt, a young mother contrasts the effect of two foster mothers on the quality of her visits with her two young children.

> [The current foster mom is] pointing out a lot, telling [them] to call me "Mom."...They used to be with a different foster mom, and when they came to visit me they were—I don't know how to put it—very shy. They didn't want to show their enjoyment or whatever. I had to go to them. They wouldn't come to me. It was like they were little statues, and they were ordered to do whatever. Now they're with [the current foster mother], and it's totally different. They're like what they were with me. Like they have their own personalities back again. I like that.

**Feelings About the Separation.** The discussions of mothers, foster mothers, and child welfare workers diverged primarily around the issue of parents' and children's feelings about the separation—for example, the extent to which any trauma associated with the involuntary placement had been resolved. All the parents spoke of their feelings about the separation, and most spoke of their children's feelings. More specifically, nearly all mothers expressed, both verbally and nonverbally, feelings of grief, depression, and trauma over the loss of their children. Many mothers also spoke of hopelessness and a lasting rage toward the child welfare system. As one young mother stated:

I just feel like I've lost everything [crying]. I'm scared if I don't get my kids back and I fight 'em [DCFS] as much as I can, but what else do they want me to do? I hate DCFS, and I've never told them that, but I want to....You can't tell them that, because then they write a bad report about you.

Other mothers spoke quite specifically about how their and their children's feelings about the separation affected visits per se. For example, one mother in treatment for substance abuse described her visits with her three young children:

Every time I see him, it's like, "You better yet? You better yet?" I'm like, "Not yet. Almost." She's like, "I want to come home!" It's hard, too, because the little one is so attached to her foster parents. She's so young [voice breaking] and it's hard. Very hard [sobbing]....They [foster parents] are all right, and we're working on getting them back, so you've gotta, you know, take time. It's hard when they're so young. The two-year-old doesn't play much [during visits]. It's very hard on her. She hugs and kisses me, you know. The most important thing in my life is Thursdays. Being with my kids [crying] makes me feel better. Very much better [laughs, sadly].

Another mother of a 4-year-old girl described her own complex feelings during visits:

I felt guilt because I made the mistake, and she shouldn't have to be going through all this. She is so little, and she shouldn't have to be taken out of her home. I just felt bad and angry at myself for doing what I did. I mean, it was stupid of me. Oh, I was excited to go see her [for visits]. And then I would see her and act like nothin' really changed when we're together. But I knew the time had to come when I had to leave, and I was trying to make up ways to try to tell her what was going to happen, why I had to leave.

Another mother, who visited at her children's foster home, described the grief she felt when watching another care for her baby:

I give my kid a lot of love. I rock him and all that, and [the foster parents] don't have time to do that, you know? He was crying, and they said, "Just let him cry, he'll fall asleep." I don't like to let my kids cry, that's just the way I am. So, I told my mom to just take me home because I started crying, you know. It's hard for me. I know they do well taking care of him. It's hard for me to see him and to know that we're not together and to see him crying. Because I should be the one to be there with him.

In the following example, a mother relates a discussion with her 4-year-old daughter, during a visit, about the child's placement in foster care after her mother left her alone in their apartment.

She did ask me the other day, "Why didn't you come back? They knew you were off, and you didn't come back." And she's says, "You didn't bring me any gummy bears." You know, I really didn't think she remembered that. And she's says, "Why didn't you come back?" I said, "I came back, but when I came back, they were already gone." And she's like, "The cops took me!" That made me feel real bad.

Foster mothers and child welfare workers typically did not spontaneously identify mothers' feelings about the separation as affecting the quality of visits. Only one-half of child welfare workers and approximately one-fourth of foster mothers spoke of children's feelings about the separation. Even when child welfare workers did discuss parents' feelings about the separation, they showed little recognition of or concern for parents' complex grief reactions. Rather, the focus was on difficulties caused by parents' anger. For example, one worker noted,

> I think that if parents are still really angry and blameful, that can be really tense during a visit. Their body language tends to demonstrate that, and I get concerned because I think the kids pick up on that.

### Implications for Practice

Participants' responses suggest the importance of considering how the history and context of each case may affect mothers' and children's abilities to maintain and strengthen their relationships through visiting. Consistent with the clinical literature (e.g., DCFS training materials), participants' responses underscore the importance of providing frequent, regular visits and high quality foster care and services to families. Most striking, however, was mothers' articulation of their own feelings of grief, trauma, hopelessness, and rage about the forced separation from their children. These intense responses raise several issues.

First, how might a mother's unresolved feelings related to the child welfare intervention affect her short- and long-term ability to parent? For example, unresolved grief and trauma surrounding a mother's forced separation from her child may leave her with little energy to engage actively in services that could strengthen her abilities to parent now and in the future. Such responses also could affect a mother's abilities to focus on and interact with her young child during visits. Clearly, for reunification to succeed, child welfare interventions must go beyond what many mothers described as punishment or even trauma to themselves and their families. Interventions must actually strengthen women to become more effective people, i.e., women who, when their children do return home, are less likely to succumb to depression and substance abuse, less likely to become involved with violent men, and more likely to protect their children from abusive family members.

Second, how might a mother's unresolved feelings affect child welfare workers and foster parents? For example, a mother's unresolved grief and trauma may manifest itself as intense anger and hostility toward the child welfare system, making it very difficult, uncomfortable, and ineffective for workers to provide essential reunification services to families. Given the low percentage of child welfare workers and foster mothers who identify mothers' feelings about the separation as affecting the quality of visits, education regarding mothers' mourning may be warranted so that their grief and despair are not misattributed by child welfare workers and foster mothers as a lack of concern for their children, lack of motivation, or lack of fundamental ability to benefit from necessary services.

Finally, how might professionals support mothers in resolving complex issues of grief surrounding the forced separation from their children? The majority of the mothers in this study experienced their grief in isolation. Most lived complex and difficult lives. Few had relationships with reliable, nurturing adults who could provide support to them in times of crisis. Many also described feelings of stigmatization because of their involvement in the child welfare system. Remarkably, many mothers expressed gratitude simply for having someone listen to their stories and hear their sadness. At a minimum, child welfare agencies could create opportunities for allowing mothers, particularly those new to the system, to share their feelings of grief and to gain perspective with a supportive, empathic person who is knowledgeable about the child welfare system, e.g., a mental health professional, parent advocate, or member of the clergy. Such opportunities could be in place from the very initiation of services and, for some mothers, remain in place throughout their contact with the child welfare system.

## TABLE 2

**Percentage of Mothers, Foster Mothers, and Child Welfare Workers Who Identify Visit Preparation As Affecting the Quality of Visits**

| Factors Identified by at Least 50% of Mothers, Foster Mothers, or Caseworkers | Mothers (n = 28) | Foster Mothers (n = 13) | Child Welfare Workers (n = 24) |
|---|---|---|---|
| Visit Preparation | 32 | 100 | 96 |
| Quality of Preparation of the Parent | 7 | 0 | 54 |
| Quality of Preparation of the Child | 4 | 77 | 13 |
| Quality of Support for the Child in the Transition to and from Visits | 36 | 100 | 58 |

## *Visit Preparation*

As shown in Table 2, the importance of preparing for the visit emerged as a theme for all foster mothers and most child welfare workers, but for fewer than one-half the mothers. For the child welfare workers, visit preparation may include coordinating the schedules of foster parents, parents, and children; planning and preparing a location; ensuring supervision and transportation; and supporting all participants in anticipation of a possibly stressful event. Visit preparation for a foster mother may include adjusting her family's schedule to accommodate the visit, informing the child of the visit, making any special preparations with the child for the visit, and helping the child make the transition to and from the visit.

Approximately one-half the child welfare workers discussed the importance of preparing the parent for the visit. These discussions focused almost solely on issues of planning activities and rules.

> If they [the mothers] can do some planning before they have the visits and say, "What would the child really like to do? Would the child like to go to the park? Would the child like to go out and get ice cream?"...Something that would be positive, and channel that so they are not coming to the DCFS office, landing in a chair, watching the

child sit there putting blocks together. Not that there's anything wrong with that...but a little interaction that is positive—more than just getting together.

Another child welfare worker elaborated:

In improving visits, we really need to be working hard to talk to...parents ahead of time about the purpose of visits. Things like how the visit should go and what kind of things would cause the visit to end prematurely, or what kinds of things we need to see you doing so we can look at extending visits.

Foster mothers emphasized the importance of preparing the child for the visit. For example, they discussed comforting rituals such as fixing the child's hair or dressing the child in good clothes to make the visit feel special to the child. Both child welfare workers and foster parents also emphasized the importance of providing emotional support to the child during the often stressful transition to and from the visits. As one foster mother elaborated:

You know, you get a different transporter constantly. And these kids have problems enough, and they bond with a person on transport and then get pulled. And the bonds that they have are so important. When it's somebody who just takes them to a visit to see a parent, they bond with that person. And then when that person is constantly changing, it's very frustrating. Especially if that child is kind of shy in the first place. When you're dealing with little, little kids, it's hard to hand your little child over to someone new....It's like, all of a sudden someone new is at your door...I've talked to them on the phone, because I've made the arrangements for transporting, but the kid doesn't know this person, and all of a sudden it's someone new to take them. And you can set them up and say,

"Listen, someone else is gonna come, and so-and-so is not going to be here anymore," but that's someone new that they are getting in the car with and driving away.

In contrast, a child welfare worker describes the emotional support that she is able to give a 4-year-old girl whom she has consistently escorted to and from visits.

She has made up a game called "caseworker." She plays the caseworker, and I'm the child. Her name is Lynn, and I'm Kerry. She'll ask me questions about my visit with my parents, and I'll talk to her and I'll say, "When am I going to see my mom and dad again?" And she says, "Next week." Then I say, "How many more days is that?" because that is what she does, and she says, "You go to bed at night, and you go to sleep, and it's going to be five more nights." We go back and forth, and she loves the game. She loves it.

## Implications for Practice

Consistent with the clinical literature (e.g., DCFS training materials), participants' responses highlight the importance and complexity of preparing for the visit, including communicating with mothers and children about the visit and ensuring that children receive adequate support in the sometimes difficult transition to and from foster mothers and mothers. Most striking, however, was mothers' apparently minimal involvement in visit preparation. Less than 50% of the mothers even discussed preparing for the visit. Furthermore, almost no mothers or foster mothers, and only about one-half of child welfare workers, discussed preparing *the mother* for the visit. Furthermore, these discussions focused on planning activities and rules, not on the complex psychological and interpersonal issues confronting mothers during visits. Child welfare workers could create a context, e.g., a period of 10 or 15 minutes before the visit, in which mothers would have an opportunity to meet with a supportive, empathic person to discuss and plan for these complex issues in relation to the upcoming visit.

*Visit*

As shown in Table 3, all participants discussed characteristics of the actual visit, focusing on the physical and social context as well as on the parent-child relationship and interaction.

**Context.** Nearly all participants agreed that contextual factors affect visits. Mothers, foster mothers, and child welfare workers alike emphasized the importance of an adequate physical context. In particular, many participants described the need for a comfortable, child-proofed environment with adequate privacy and opportunities to engage children in age-appropriate activities. A homelike room might have comfortable furniture and clean, unbroken, interesting toys. Mothers and child welfare workers also elaborated on the importance of scheduling visits of adequate duration. Many mothers, in particular, felt that one-hour visits simply did not allow them enough time to comfort, reassure, and discipline their children; engage in familiar, routine activities; and learn about their child's activities during the week.

Participants also agreed that a positive parent–supervisor relationship is essential. When mothers feel that their interactions with their children are being scrutinized and judged, spontaneous, self-assured interaction becomes difficult. As one mother explained:

> The worst [visit] was when he came home and had to be supervised. That was the worst visit because I felt like I was under a microscope and I had to be on my best behavior. I couldn't really be "Mama." I was just there with him, because he didn't really get a chance to know that I was Mom, because someone else was there. He was just as used to her as he was to me. That was the worst visit.

## TABLE 3
**Percentage of Mothers, Foster Mothers, and Child Welfare Workers Describing Characteristics of the Visit**

| *Factors Identified by at Least 50% of Mothers, Foster Mothers, or Caseworkers* | *Mothers (n = 28)* | *Foster Mothers (n = 13)* | *Child Welfare Workers (n = 24)* |
|---|---|---|---|
| Visit | 100 | 100 | 100 |
| Context | 100 | 100 | 100 |
| Physical Context | 100 | 92 | 92 |
| Quality of Parent-Supervisor Relationship/Interaction | 93 | 69 | 92 |
| Duration | 93 | 38 | 71 |
| Parent-Child Relationship/Interaction | 100 | 100 | 92 |
| Emotion Expression/Communication | 89 | 8 | 58 |
| Play | 64 | 23 | 29 |
| Caretaking | 61 | 0 | 25 |
| Practice/Assess Competence | 0 | 0 | 46 |
| Monitor for Inappropriate Behavior | 7 | 85 | 83 |

Another mother described a conflict between her need to be physically close to her toddler and the visit supervisors' perceptions of age-appropriate behavior:

> When I—when my daughter wants me to hold her, and the [supervisor] said "She needs to walk." You only have an hour with your child, and she loves to be held by her mommy, and you have someone tell you, "No." So you do "no," because that's what they told you—and you [need] to make *them* happy.

In contrast, some mothers described feelings of support from and even friendship with their visit supervisors. These mothers described visits as not only comfortable but allowing the exchange of meaningful information, e.g., learning strategies for disciplining and comforting the child. In addition, one foster mother who hostesses visits in her own home viewed her support of parents during visits as helpful to children's adjustment to foster care:

Let them [parents] think they have the freedom of the home. That way, the foster child sees that you and their parents are friends. That makes the children feel safer with you, because they see that you like their mom or dad, and that makes them more comfortable.

**Parent-Child Relationship/Interaction.** Mothers, foster mothers, and child welfare workers alike emphasized the importance of the parent–child relationship/interaction during visits. Aspects of the parent–child interaction/relationship that were emphasized diverged, however. Mothers emphasized visits as an opportunity to care for their children, e.g., to feed them, do their hair, and simply "be Mama." Parents also emphasized emotional expression and communication, especially simple physical contact and affection, "spoiling," laughing, and playing with their children.

Mothers also described the emotional challenge of managing their own and their children's grief and anger, especially during leave taking. In the words of one mother:

Oh, God. It's like tearing my heart out. It's the most hurtful thing to be on a schedule to see your own child. It's just something that is inconceivable. The pain is just so deep. To tell your own child, "good-bye," as bad as you want to be with him. That's one of the hardest things I've ever had to experience, next to giving him up. And it's terrible for him, too, because I know he loves me

Child welfare workers' discussions of the parent–child interaction/relationship during visits reflected the multiple roles that they are expected to fulfill during visits: supporting parent–child closeness to facilitate reunification, protecting children from parents' possibly inappropriate behavior, and assessing parents' progress and the parent–child relationship. Like mothers, child welfare workers elaborated on the importance, for supporting parent–child closeness, of expressing emotion and communicating during visits. The monitoring function of visit supervision was reflected in a large percentage of child welfare workers and foster mothers who elaborated on inappropriate behavior they had observed during the visits. They described in detail the insensitive, cruel, and abusive behavior that they had witnessed during parent–child visits. Their narratives included accounts of a sexually abusive father who discreetly fondled his toddler during visits, a mother who pressured her young son to recant his account of physical abuse by her boyfriend, and a mother who continued to scapegoat her young son and pointedly left him out as she provided gifts for his sisters and asked them about their week.

Child welfare workers also emphasized visits as one of the very few (if not only) contexts in which parents can practice skills learned through other services and the worker can assess their progress. In the words of one worker:

> The visits are essential. [They are] the only way. Parents [can] go through services, and they can go through them with flying colors, complete them, and do all that stuff. But if they cannot interact with the kid appropriately, if they cannot demonstrate what they've learned, then we cannot send the kids back home. The place to see that is the visits.

More specifically, many child welfare workers indicated the importance of using visits to assess mothers' abilities to discipline their children appropriately. Many mothers, however, described a reluctance to discipline during visits. For example,

> Sometimes they get a little edgy because I'm not...around them all of the time. When you don't see them that much, it's hard. They say something about me not chastising the kids enough, sometimes, but I don't think I'm with them enough to chastise them. I mean, once a week for two hours! That's not enough time to be putting no pressure on a child I don't see that much.

Some child welfare workers articulated the complexities of negotiating the various roles required of the visit supervisor. One experienced caseworker described how she took the perspective of a mother to respond to the challenges inherent in monitoring and supporting:

> I think it important for the caseworker to step back and let the parent be the parent. [But] we have to be there, and we have to make sure we're in the room, or in earshot of what's going on, and see what's happening. Mom was very nervous at first, and I didn't focus on that because I didn't think that was going to help her. She knew why she was there, and she knew I was watching her and monitoring it, but I didn't sit there and say, "You don't have to be nervous." Of course she's going to be nervous. I would be nervous. You have somebody watching you and your kid—I'd be nervous! So, don't disregard those feelings and emotions parents are having.

This worker and a number of others described specific strategies for balancing the roles of supporting, monitoring, and supervising mothers, such as sharing their notes with mothers, allowing them to write in any comments, and explaining the child welfare system to mothers, including persons to whom they can appeal to if visits are not satisfactory. Some less-experienced workers described strategies that were punitive to parents when dealing with the complexities of visits. For example, some assumed that all parents had made "bad choices" and, therefore, warranted close scrutiny.

### Implications for Practice

Consistent with the practice literature (e.g., DCFS training materials), participants stressed the need for an adequate physical context for the visit. Most striking, however, were participants' discussions of complex psychological and interpersonal issues.

For example, mothers discussed their difficulties in saying good-bye to their children at the end of visits. All participants discussed the complexities of the parent–supervisor relationship and how that relationship may affect the quality of visits. Supervisors have multiple, sometimes conflicting roles: supporting children's close-ness to their parents to facilitate reunification, protecting children from possible harm from their parents, and assessing parents' progress and the parent-child relationship.

This discussion raises two issues. First, are parents provided with adequate support and coaching for dealing with the psy-chological and interpersonal complexities of visits? We recom-mend that parents be provided with support and coaching be-fore the visit. Second, is it realistic to expect visit supervisors to adequately support parents, monitor their behavior, and assess their progress? Child welfare workers may need to prioritize and simplify goals for visits. The primary goal for visits is to support the parent–child relationship. Goals related to assessment can undermine this primary function by making parents uncomfort-able and/or reluctant to act, for example, in setting limits or dis-ciplining their children. Workers do need time to observe and assess parenting, but opportunities should be made for them to do so separately from the weekly visit. For example, parenting classes could include practicing and assessing parenting skills during actual parent–child interaction. In addition, monitoring children's safety is necessary during visits, but if done insensi-tively, monitoring also can undermine the primary goal of visits. Several experienced child welfare workers shared excellent strat-egies that they use to help put parents at ease about necessary monitoring, and these strategies could be shared with less expe-rienced workers.

*Postvisit*

As shown in Table 4, relatively few participants discussed the significance of the postvisit period, but the voices of foster moth-

**TABLE 4**

Percentage of Mothers, Foster Mothers, and Child Welfare Workers Describing Characteristics of the Postvisit Period

| Factors Identified by at Least 50% of Mothers, Foster Mothers, or Child Welfare Workers | Mothers (n = 28) | Foster Mothers (n = 13) | Child Welfare Workers (n = 24) |
|---|---|---|---|
| Postvisit | 46 | 100 | 71 |
| Quality of Child's Reactions to Visits | 11 | 100 | 8 |
| Quality of Support for Child | 0 | 77 | 17 |
| Match Between Child's Expectations and Visits | 0 | 69 | 8 |
| Cancellations of Visits | 39 | 69 | 17 |

ers are most distinctly heard through these comments. Foster mothers emphasized the significance of the child's reactions to visiting and the importance of providing appropriate and sensitive support after the visit has ended:

> When the kids come back, I have to deal with whether it was a good visit or not. If it wasn't, then I have to spend maybe three hours nurturing, showing all of the affection, and promising that, hopefully, this won't happen again. The foster parent is the one there to nurture and give the affection and stuff if [it has] been a bad visit.

Children's negative reactions after visits, however, were not restricted to visits that went poorly. As one foster mother described,

> sometimes [the children] come back, and they are kind of sad. I think it is because they want to be with their parents. Children have a lot of different reactions when they go on visits. Some kids will have nightmares the night before or have trouble sleeping. Some of them have nightmares they get back home. Wake up in the middle of the night crying.

Another foster mother described the reaction of her young foster son:

He would cry. He would actually cry. I mean literally cry and cry. I would go in and try to comfort him. Sometimes he would come in [from the visit] and not say anything. He'd just rush by, stompin' like he couldn't get away from people fast enough.

Foster mothers also strongly emphasized the emotional harm to young children when visits are canceled or parents fail to appear for a scheduled visit. For example, one foster mother explained:

When the parents don't show up, the [children] come in stompin'. I don't have to ask them, but I ask, "What's wrong?" "Oh, she didn't show up." Makes me sick! I said, "Wait a minute, if she didn't show up, there must be a good reason." But I stop making excuses, because the parents show up and say, "I just didn't want to." Here I am, trying to make excuses, and the parents will tell the children they don't want to [visit]. I said, "I be shuttin' my mouth."

Mothers also described the emotional harm to themselves and their children when visits are canceled by child welfare workers or others.

Foster parents also emphasized the importance of meeting the child's expectations for the visits, that is, keeping promises to the child regarding who will be at the visit or having favorite activities or toys.

### Implications for Practice

Foster parents elaborated on the intensity and complexity of children's responses to visits, cancellations of visits, and unfulfilled expectations for visits. Many foster parents also expressed uncertainty about how to respond to children's sad and angry responses. These discussions raise the issue of whether or not foster parents and children are given adequate support subsequent to the visit. Absent from discussions of the postvisit period is any mention of support for parents.

## Conclusion

The goal of this research was to examine the perspectives of mothers, foster mothers, and child welfare workers for clues as to how parental visits with very young children may be improved. The adults who were actually involved in visits shared a wealth of practice wisdom, converging on the importance of attending to the historical/contextual factors of each case and to the physical and social contexts of visits. These adults also drew attention to complex, but neglected, psychological and interpersonal issues that may affect visits. These issues include mothers' feelings of grief, trauma, and rage; the complexities of leave taking; mothers' uncertainty and discomfort with limit setting and discipline during visits; child welfare workers' dilemmas surrounding their multiple—and sometimes conflicting—roles of supporting, monitoring, and assessing parents; and foster mothers' difficulties in responding to some children's intense and problematic responses to visits.

The mothers, foster mothers, and child welfare workers also revealed some divergence in perspectives. In some instances, these differences simply seemed to reflect the various roles played by the participants. For example, many foster mothers emphasized the importance of preparing children before visits and supporting them afterwards, whereas many mothers focused on historical/contextual factors and the actual visit. In other instances, differences in perspective, particularly when unarticulated, may be problematic for the visit. For example, many mothers prioritized emotional expression and communication with their children, but many child welfare workers prioritized supervision and assessment of parenting skills. It is easy to imagine how such mismatched agendas, particularly if unarticulated, may result in confusion, frustration, and dissatisfaction with visits.

The voices of these mothers, foster mothers, and child welfare workers raise many issues for practice and policy. First, many mothers may require support in resolving feelings of trauma, grief, and anger over their children's placement before they benefit fully from necessary services. In addition, they may need coaching and support in dealing with the psychological and interpersonal complexities of visiting, such as saying good-bye and setting limits. Second, many foster mothers may require education and training to support adequately children whose responses to visits are intense and problematic. Third, child welfare workers may require education to be able to juggle successfully the multiple, and sometimes conflicting, roles they play during visit supervision, such as encouraging parent–child closeness and monitoring for possible inappropriate parent behaviors. Next, contexts may need to be created for all the adults involved in visiting to share their convergent and divergent perspectives, thereby achieving better collaboration in parent–child visits. Finally, goals for visits need to be reevaluated and simplified. If the primary goal of visits is to strengthen the development of the parent-child relationship, then other contexts may be required to achieve secondary goals that might otherwise undermine natural and spontaneous parent–child interaction during visits. For example, parenting skills might be assessed in special sessions of parenting classes that include children.

In interpreting the discussions with mothers, foster mothers, and child welfare workers, it is important to remember that the focus was on visits with mothers and young children who were relatively new to foster care. Other issues may come to the fore in discussions centered on visits involving infants, older children, and adolescents; visits with other family members (fathers and grandparents); and visits with children in care for longer periods of time. It also is important to keep in mind that the mothers who participated in this study may be high-functioning and highly motivated compared with other mothers involved with DCFS. Although these mothers clearly led difficult and complex lives, they were organized enough to participate in the study, and they were in contact with DCFS and their children. A sizable number of mothers whose children are in foster care do not visit their children and are not even in contact with DCFS.

It also is important to remember that these were relatively open-ended discussions. The intent was to encourage the participants to define the issues most relevant to them, not to conduct a systematic assessment of all factors with each participant. For example, feelings about the separation from their children emerged as very salient to mothers. The fact that this issue was mentioned by relatively few foster parents and child welfare workers does not, however, mean that these individuals necessarily are insensitive to parents' feelings.

In conclusion, the results of this study highlight the need to examine more fully the complex psychological and interpersonal processes involved in parent visitation of young children in foster care. Although visitation is mandated by law, and is essential for reunification, little previous research has examined the perspectives of individuals actually involved in visits. The present study revealed how difficult visits can be, both psychologically and interpersonally, for mothers, foster mothers, and child welfare workers. Future researchers and policymakers must focus on ways to make visits better for all involved, so that we can best serve the needs of vulnerable children.◆

# References

Berrick, J. D., Needell, B., Barth, R. P., & Jonson-Reid, M. (1998). *The tender years: Toward developmentally sensitive child welfare services for very young children.* New York: Oxford University Press.

Beyer, M. (1999). Parent–child visits as an opportunity for change. National Resource Center for Family Centered Practice. *Prevention Practice, 1,* 2-12.

Dane, B. (2000). Child welfare workers: An innovative approach for interacting with secondary trauma. *Journal of Social Work Education, 36,* 27–38.

Diorio, W. (1992, April). Parental perceptions of the authority of public child welfare caseworkers. *Families in Society: Journal of Contemporary Human Services*, pp. 222–235.

Downs, S., Costin, L., & McFadden, E. (1996). *Child welfare and family services: Policies and practice* (5th ed.). White Plains, NY: Longman.

Edelstein, S., Burge, D., & Waterman, J. (2001). Helping foster parents cope with separation, loss, and grief. *Child Welfare, 80,* 5–25.

Fanshel, D. (1982). *On the road to permanency: An expanded database for children in foster care.* New York: Child Welfare League of America.

Haight, W., Black, J., Workman, C., & Tata, L. (2001). Parent–child interaction during foster care visits: Implications for practice. *Social Work, 46,* 325-338.

Haight, W., Kagle, J., & Black, J. (in press). Understanding and supporting parent-child interactions during foster care visits: Clues from universal, developmental, and culturally variable dimensions of attachment relationships. *Social Work.*

Hess, P., & Proch, K. (1993). Visiting: The heart of reunification. In B. Pine, R. Warsh, & A. Maluccio (Eds.), *Together again: Family reunification in foster care* (pp. 119-140). Washington, DC: Child Welfare League of America.

Jenkins, S., & Norman, E. (1975). *Beyond placement: Mothers view foster care.* New York: Columbia University Press.

Keller, I., & McDade, K. (2000). Attitudes of low-income parents toward seeking help with parenting: Implications for practice. *Child Welfare, 74,* 285–312.

Kessler, M., & Greene, B. (1999). Behavior analysis in child welfare: Competency training caseworkers to manage visits between parents and their children in foster care. *Research on Social Work Practice, 9,* 148–170.

Mangelsdorf, S., Haight, W., Black, J., Schoppe, S., Szewczyk, M., & Tata, L. (n.d.). Maternal beliefs and parent-child interaction in families with young children in foster care.

Ong, B. N. (1985). Understanding child abuse: Ideologies of motherhood. *Women's Studies Forum, 8,* 411-419.

Poertner, J., Harris, G., & Joe, S. (1997). *Parent with children in care: Assessment of service satisfaction.* Unpublished manuscript of the University of Illinois, Urbana-Champaign, School of Social Work, Children and Family Research Center.

Smith, B., & Smith, T. (1990). For love and money: Women as foster mothers. *Affilia, 5,* 66–80.

Thompson, R. (1998). Early sociopersonality development. In W. Damon (Ed.), *Handbook of child psychology* (5th ed., Vol. 3, pp. 25–104). New York: John Wiley & Sons.

# Chapter 5

# Expedited Permanency Planning: Evaluation of the Kentucky Adoptions Opportunities Project

*Mavin H. Martin, Anita P. Barbee, Becky F. Antle, and Bibhuti Sar*

This article presents the evaluation findings of a Kentucky Adoptions Opportunities Project (KAOP), a three-year project funded by the U.S. Department of Health and Human Services, Administration on Children, Youth and Families, Children's Bureau. The primary goal of the KAOP was implementation of three permanency planning activities: (1) risk assessment/concurrent planning, (2) one child/one legal voice, and (3) early placement in kinship or foster/adoptive homes. These activities were designed to expedite a permanency placement decision within 12 months for high-risk children. The evaluation of 124 high-risk children in the KAOP revealed that the majority of children had one or both parents coping with multiple risk factors, including mental illness, substance abuse, mental retardation, or family violence. The major barriers to permanency are discussed, as well as the policy and practice implications in the context of Adoption and Safe Families Act of 1997.

*Mavin H. Martin, PhD, is Assistant Research Professor; Anita P. Barbee, PhD, is Associate Research Professor; Becky F. Antle, MSSW, ABD, is Doctoral Student; and Bibhuti Sar, PhD, is Associate Professor, University of Louisville, Louisville, KY.*

Millions of children are maltreated each year. A child's increased vulnerability to an array of psychological and health disorders as a consequence of maltreatment and out-of-home placement is well documented (Briere, Berliner, Bulkley, Jenny, & Reid, 1996). Similarly, it is well documented that children who are removed from their homes are better served when the out-of-home placement is brief and without disruptions (Barth & Price, 1999). Despite this evidence, effective and enduring interventions by child protective service (CPS) agencies remain elusive. Although many low-risk families are successfully helped, an increasing number of children from high-risk families are lingering in foster care. The literature (Katz, 1999; Katz & Robinson, 1991; Katz, Spoonemore, & Robinson, 1994) has identified very young children from problem-saturated families as most at risk of lingering in care. In the late 1990s, federal and state funding supported implementation and evaluation of innovative approaches to combating foster care drift (Katz, 1999), facilitating termination of parental rights (TPR) and adoption for children in the child welfare system.

This article summarizes evaluation findings of the multisystem permanency planning approach of the Kentucky Adoptions Opportunities Project (KAOP), a pilot project funded in 1997 by the U.S. Department of Health and Human Services, Administration on Children, Youth and Families, Children's Bureau. The primary goal of the KAOP was implementation of three permanency planning activities. The KAOP was a collaborative initiative of child welfare, the courts, and the county attorney's office. Specifically, the stakeholders were an urban family court, a rural circuit/district court, the Administrative Office of the Courts (AOC), the Cabinet for Families and Children (CFC), and the county attorney in the urban region and the commonwealth attorney in the rural county region. This article summarizes the multisystem permanency planning activities of the KAOP, as well as its preliminary outcomes.

## Goal and Principal Activities of the KAOP

The goal of the KAOP was expedited permanency planning for high-risk children who were deemed most at risk of lingering in the child welfare system. Specifically, the KAOP attempted to achieve a permanency placement decision within 12 months of the petition for these high-risk children. Since its inception, the KAOP had three primary program activities: risk assessment and concurrent planning; one child/one legal voice; and early placement in foster/adoptive and kinship homes.

### Risk Assessment and Concurrent Planning

*Risk assessment* refers to identification of high-risk cases using the court's Risk Assessment Matrix (see Table 1). Concurrent planning was defined as early placement of a child in a kin or foster/ adoptive family that was willing to accept permanent custody of a child should family reunification efforts fail. The entire KAOP rested heavily on the pioneering work of Linda Katz, who developed one of the most well-known models of concurrent planning (Katz, 1990, 1999; Katz & Robinson, 1991; Katz et al., 1994). The court's risk assessment was a modified version of the risk assessment matrix developed by Katz and her colleagues (1994).

### One Child/One Legal Voice

*One child/one legal voice* was defined as a dedicated project attorney. In the urban county, one assistant county attorney was dedicated, and in the rural county region, one assistant commonwealth attorney was dedicated to the project. These dedicated attorneys prosecuted a KAOP case from filing of the dependency action to permanency, which in some cases included TPR. Prior to the collaborative activities of the KAOP, the county attorney in the urban area prosecuted a case from adjudication to disposition. In the rural region, the dependency action was prosecuted in district court and TPR was continued in circuit court. The stakehold-

## TABLE 1
### Court Risk Assessment Matrix

Child must be 8 and younger (child should be excluded if child has any older siblings in the home).

AND

Parent (must be parent, and not merely a primary caregiver) has killed or seriously harmed *another* child through abuse or neglect, and no significant change has occurred since.

OR

Child has documentation (i.e., medical records, physical examination, reliable interview) of extreme physical or sexual abuse by a parent and must be removed from the home.

OR

Parental rights to another child have been terminated following a six-month period of service delivery to the parents, and no significant change has occurred since.

OR

Child has been in out-of-home care on at least one other occasion for a period of six months or more or has had at least two prior placements with Cabinet for Families and Children (CFC) interaction.

OR

Parent has a documented history of a chronic mental disorder (i.e., schizophrenia, bipolar disorder) and has not responded to previously delivered mental health services. Symptoms continue that prevent parent from being able to protect and nurture the child.

OR

There have been three or more CFC interventions for separate incidents, and there is a chronic pattern of abuse or severe neglect.

OR

Parent has a documented history of substance dependence and has a history of treatment failures.

OR

Child has been abandoned with friends, relatives, foster caregivers, or hospital workers, or, after being placed in care, parents do not visit of their own accord. Parents disappear or appear rarely.

OR

Parent has a documented history of mental retardation or other persisting and pervasive developmental disorder (i.e., autism), has shown significant impairment in caring for the child, and has no support system of kin to share in parenting.

Source: Modified indicators found in Katz, Spoonemore, and Robinson's (1994), *Concurrent planning: From permanency planning to permanency action* (Lutheran Social Services of Washington).

ers anticipated that in the event of TPR, permanency would be expedited when one attorney with historical memory of the case prosecuted throughout the court process.

The concept of one child/one legal voice also refers to one guardian ad litem (GAL) throughout the court process. The project intended to assign one GAL to each KAOP child to provide both legal advocacy and continuity for each child. It was hypothesized that one GAL throughout the court process would contribute to better representation and expedited permanency decisions.

### Early Placement in Foster/Adoptive and Kinship Homes

The third and final activity of this project was early placement of KAOP children in foster/adoptive or kinship homes. It was anticipated that early placement in a potentially permanent placement would reduce placement disruptions and emotional distress related to disruptions. The aforementioned program activities were designed to support accelerated hearings, including adjudication, disposition, permanency planning, TPR, and adoptions for high-risk children. In addition, KAOP activities emphasized early service provision, discouragement of judicial delays, and waivers of reasonable efforts when parents failed to avail themselves of services or indicated lack of motivation to address the issue that led to their child's coming into care.

Throughout the project, cross-training was conducted with all KAOP stakeholders including site coordinators, judges, attorneys, CFC staff, community agency representatives, foster parents, foster care review board members, and other interested parties. This training included GAL education about the Adoption and Safe Families Act (ASFA), concurrent planning principles, community resources, and methods to increase interagency collaboration, coordination, and communication.

### Evaluation Questions

The evaluation was driven by three broad questions:
- Can stakeholders implement the program activities designed to expedite permanency planning?

- What is the affect of KAOP activities on permanency outcomes?
- What are the barriers to achieving a permanency decision
  within 12 months?

To evaluate the activities of the KAOP and answer the evaluation questions, case review, key informant interviews, and CFC
and court observations were conducted. Selection of the KAOP
cases commenced after cross-training and the three program activities had been implemented.

## Method

When review of the petition that led to the child coming into state
custody indicated a possible KAOP case, the court risk assessment matrix was completed by the county attorney in the urban
county and the commonwealth attorney in the rural county in
consultation with supervisors from CFC at the two KAOP urban
and rural sites. The court risk assessment was implemented at
the time of the petition to screen cases appropriate for the project,
i.e., appropriate for concurrent planning, dedicated attorneys, and
kin or foster/adoptive placement. The following criteria were
used to select KAOP cases:

1. Case must be screened according to court risk assessment
   matrix.
2. Child must be removed from the home.
3. Child must not be of Native American heritage due to special
   legislation that covers Native American children.
4. Child must remain in an out-of-home placement beyond the
   temporary custody hearing.

During the first two years of the KAOP, there were 84 cases
selected in the urban county and 30 cases in the rural region for
the KAOP. The principal source of data was CFC case files and
court records. These records were reviewed using a protocol developed by the evaluation team. In addition to case review, inter-

views were conducted with caseworkers, supervisors, service providers, attorneys, and judges when additional information was warranted.

## Variables

### Case Demographics

Demographic variables were gathered for age, race/ethnicity, and gender of all key individuals including children, mother, father (or the primary caregiver), and perpetrator (or the person responsible for incident). Initial reporting source, type of maltreatment, and history of previous allegations were also recorded.

### Case Severity

To validate data collected at the time of the petition that led to the child coming into state custody from the court risk assessment matrix, data on comorbid factors were also collected for mothers, fathers, and other caregivers involved at the time of the petition. Documented history of mental illness, substance abuse, mental retardation/developmental disorders, domestic violence, and history of child abuse were of particular interest in understanding factors contributing to repeated involvement with child welfare.

### Casework Process

To capture casework practice, including concurrent planning principles, a detailed analysis was conducted of case plans based on principles of solution-based casework (SBC) (Christensen, Todahl, & Barrett, 1999), Kentucky's statewide casework intervention model. Although a simple concept in theory, concurrent planning requires sophisticated casework practice when planning permanency alternatives from the inception of a case (D'Andrade, Choice, Martin, & Berrick, 2000). Concurrent planning (Katz, 1999) and SBC integrate the principles of family-based assessment, full disclosure, collaboration with family and outside agencies to address the issue that led to the petition, adherence to timelines, and documentation of behavior. Case plans were scored according to their compliance with principles of concurrent planning and SBC, such as presence of a prevention plan, use of family and individual objectives, and use of the family's language in a written agreement. Scoring of case plans also took into account documentation of service referrals, appointments missed and attended, and adherence to visitation schedules. Types of contact were operationalized by evaluating phone calls, visits, letters, court reports, reports from service providers, and changes in persons involved with the family (caseworker, supervisor, attorney, GAL, etc.). Court process variables were also measured by reviewing custody orders, hearing dates, court orders, citizen review board recommendations, permanency goal changes, and TPR petitions.

*Case Outcomes*

Placement outcomes focused on number of placements, placement disruptions, and type of placement at the time of removal. Permanency outcomes compared length of time to achieve permanency relative to the general foster care population in that region, in addition to final permanency arrangements.

## Results

Table 2 summarizes demographics for children and parents in the KAOP. The gender and race of the KAOP children were consistent with the distribution in the general foster care population of these geographic areas. Consistent with the objectives of the KAOP and the assumptions of concurrent planning, both sites identified young children. Both the urban and the rural sample differed significantly from the general foster care population in

## TABLE 2
**Child Demographics (in percentages)**

|  | KAOP Sample | | Foster Care Population | |
|  | Urban (n = 84) | Rural (n = 30) | Urban (n = 1,239) | Rural (n = 89) |
|---|---|---|---|---|
| Male | 53.6 | 43.3 | 54.7 | 49.4 |
| Female | 46.4 | 56.7 | 45.3 | 55.1 |
| Caucasian | 35.7 | 100.0 | 34.2 | 100.0 |
| African American | 58.7 | 0.0 | 60.2 | 0.0 |
| Biracial | 6.0 | 0.0 | 5.6 | 0.0 |
| Younger than 3 Years | 73.5 | 30.0 | 17 | 24.1 |
| Average Age (in years) | 2.25 | 5.67 | 11.1 | 10.4 |

Note: KAOP = Kentucky Adoptions Opportunities Project.

these areas, $t(82) = -34.52$, $p < .0001$, and $t(10) = -4.53$, $p < .001$, respectively. The number of children younger than the age of 3 in the sample was significantly different than expected from the population, $X^2(3) = 53.34$, $p < .0001$. There were significantly fewer children than expected in both the urban and rural counties.

Data for mothers of the KAOP cases were easy to access, however, approximately half of the cases at both sites did not have information on fathers. Approximately 53.1% of KAOP cases in the urban sample and 83% of cases in the rural sample had siblings in the home. Table 3 summarizes the average age and range of mothers and fathers in the KAOP when data were available.

### Case Severity

The majority of the KAOP cases at both sites met multiple criteria of the court risk assessment matrix. Chronic CPS involvement, substance abuse, and abandonment were the most frequently recorded issues at the time of the petition. Table 4 summarizes data collected from the matrix. A significant number of children were considered neglected when they were born exposed to substances, usually cocaine, which is consistent with data collected for pa-

TABLE 3

**Parent Demographics (in percentages)**

|  | Mother | | Father | |
|  | Urban (n = 84) | Rural (n = 30) | Urban (n = 42) | Rural (n = 15) |
|---|---|---|---|---|
| Average Age | 26.8 | 30.2 | 32.4 | 37.4 |
| Age Range | 17-38 | 20-38 | 18-63 | 23-60 |
| Percentage Living with Child | 66.6 | 90 | 20.6 | 24.1 |

rental comorbid factors. The mother was most often held responsible for the incident.

### Risk Factors Contributing to Abuse and Neglect

Table 5 summarizes the comorbid risk factors of the mothers of the KAOP children. Data were collected on these risk factors to check the reliability of data collected for the court risk assessment matrix, which was completed at the time of the petition. A mother was considered to have a documented history of one of the comorbid factors if the case record included a psychological, medical, forensic, or other independent assessment or evaluation to this effect. In other words, a report of mental illness or a caseworker assessment of substance abuse without collateral documentation was not sufficient to be recorded for the evaluation. Data on maternal comorbid factors of mental illness, chronic CFC history, substance abuse, and developmental disorders differ from data collected on the court risk assessment. These differences were attributed to a lack of historical data available to the dedicated project attorneys at the time of petition. Of the 67 mothers (79.8%) in the urban county who had documented histories of mental health concerns, 48 of these (71.6%) had documented histories of multiple mental disorders. The most frequently occurring disorders were mood disorders, anxiety disorders, and chronic psychotic disorders. Only eight mothers had sufficient documenta-

TABLE 4

**Percentage of Kentucky Adoptions Opportunities Project Cases by Court Risk Assessment Matrix Indicator**

|  | *Urban* | *Rural* |
|---|---|---|
| Child is Age 8 or Younger | 92.9 | 70.0 |
| Previously Killed | 16.6 | 10.0 |
| Extreme Abuse | 9.5 | 23.3 |
| Previous Terminations of Parental Rights | 34.5 | 6.7 |
| History of Out-of-Home Placement | 21.4 | 33.3 |
| Chronic Mental Illness | 20.2 | 3.3 |
| Chronic Child Protective Service | 80.9 | 83.3 |
| Substance Abuse | 75.0 | 53.3 |
| Abandonment | 39.3 | 40.0 |
| Mental Retardation/Developmental Disability | 5.9 | 0.0 |

tion of a personality disorder; often, this was in addition to another Axis I mental disorder, substance abuse problem, or mood disorder. In the rural area, unipolar mood disorders and anxiety disorders were the most frequently documented mental health concerns. As mentioned earlier, mental health issues were coupled with other risk factors in both areas.

*Casework Process*

There was a significant difference in implementation of concurrent planning between the urban and rural areas, $t(75) = 4.83, p < .0001$. The mean case plan score was 10.35 in the urban county and 5.42 in the rural area. This finding suggests that concurrent planning and SBC had different levels of implementation at the two sites. There were no differences in implementation of concurrent planning and SBC as a function of race. The mean case plan score was 9.71 for African Americans and 8.05 for Caucasians.

Case plan scores by type of maltreatment indicated that implementation was more difficult for physical abuse and sexual abuse cases. There was a significant difference in the case plan score with and without physical abuse, $t(61) = -2.88, p < .01$. The mean

**TABLE 5**

**Percentage of Mothers with Documented Risk Factors**

|                                  | Urban | Rural |
|----------------------------------|-------|-------|
| Mental Illness                   | 79.8  | 30.0  |
| Chronic CFC Case                 | 80.9  | 56.7  |
| Substance Abuse                  | 85.7  | 83.3  |
| Mental Retardation               | 8.3   | 0.0   |
| Other Developmental Disorders    | 11.9  | 0.0   |
| Adult Child of Child Abuse       | 60.7  | 6.7   |
| Adult Child of Foster Care       | 16.7  | 6.0   |
| Domestic Violence                | 40.5  | 73.3  |

Note: CFC = Cabinet for Families and Children.

case plan score when physical abuse was present was 8.03, and the mean score in the case when physical abuse was not present was 11.85. Similarly, there were significant differences in case plan development with and without sexual abuse, $t(47) = -3.56$, $p < .001$. The mean case plan scores with or without sexual abuse were 7.27 and 11.52, respectively, suggesting that workers were able to use SBC to a higher degree with sexual abuse cases. The application of the model to cases of sexual abuse may be due to the use of relapse prevention concepts through SBC. High implementation scores were achieved in all cases involving neglect and emotional abuse, again supporting the usefulness of relapse prevention and cycle work for these forms of child maltreatment.

In cases with historical involvement with child welfare, case plan scores were high and significantly different from cases with no historical involvement, $t(39) = 8.50$, $p < .0001$. The mean score for chronic families was 8.83, whereas the mean for nonchronic families was 2.40. As would be expected, this effect was also evident in case plans of families with previous TPR, $t(54) = 2.63$, $p < .05$. The mean for families with previous TPRs was 9.63, whereas the mean for families without previous TPR was 5.93. These data suggest that concurrent planning and SBC were appropriately implemented with families with repeated involvement with CPS.

Case plan scores were significantly higher when comorbid factors such as mental illness, substance abuse, and developmental disorders were present. The mean for cases with mental illness was 11.00, versus a mean of 5.05 when mental illness was not present, representing a significant difference, $t(24) = -3.67$, $p < .001$. Case plan scores for cases involving substance abuse were significantly different, $t(79) = 2.05$, $p < .05$. The mean for case plans involving substance abuse was 9.35, whereas the mean score for cases without substance abuse was 6.00.

This trend continued when parental mental retardation and developmental disorders were issues. The mean case plan scores involving mental retardation was 16.33, versus a mean case plan score of 5.97 when mental retardation was not evident, a significant difference, $t(33) = 3.55$, $p < .001$. These results suggest that workers are able to implement SBC to an even greater degree when there are complex comorbid factors.

*Compliance*

Cases that achieved a high implementation score demonstrated higher client compliance, as evidenced by fewer missed appointments with workers, $X^2(3) = 14.81$, $p < .01$. Approximately 73% of families that kept all appointments had case plans with high implementation scores. Similarly, high implementation scores were related to client follow-through with collaterals, $X^2(3) = 15.58$, $p < .001$. Approximately 87.5% of clients who followed through with referrals were in the high implementation group. These clients were more likely to complete tasks assigned by the case worker, $X^2(3) = 19.07$, $p < .0001$, and adhere to visitation schedules, $X^2(4) = 20.87$, $p < .0001$. Whereas 31.4% of clients in the high implementation group always completed tasks, only 2% in the low implementation group completed tasks. In the high implementation group, 33.3% of the families followed visitation guidelines, whereas only 2% in the low implementation group followed guidelines. Finally, workers were more likely to attend collateral meetings with clients when there was high implementation of SBC, $X^2(3) = 26.23$, $p < .0001$. All workers who were implementing SBC attended collateral meetings, whereas all workers who did not attend collateral meetings were not implementing SBC.

### Court Process

In an attempt to measure the expeditiousness, stability, and continuity of representation in the KAOP cases, data were collected on length of time between hearings and on the number of changes in key persons involved during the court process. Although expedited timelines were a goal of this project, data collected suggested that cases progressed well initially but stalled later in the court process. Timely permanency planning hearings and periodic reviews were the hearings most likely to be delayed.

The majority of cases at both sites experienced stability and continuity of representation across systems. In terms of CFC supervisors, 91% of cases in the urban and 100% of cases in the rural county had no changes. In 57% of cases in the urban county and 63% in the rural county there was no change in worker. Attorney representation of child and parents was extremely stable; 82% of children in the urban county and 77% of children in the rural county had no change in GAL.

### Case Outcomes

**Placement History.** In the urban county, 63% of the children had two or fewer placements, with a comparable achievement in the rural county, in which 50% of the children had one or two placements. In the urban county, 60% of the KAOP children were placed with kin, 24% were placed with foster/adoptive homes, and the balance were placed in foster homes. In the rural counties, 23% were placed with kin, 20% were placed in foster/adoptive homes, and 57% were placed with traditional foster families. In the urban county, the most frequently occurring kinship placement was with maternal grandmother

($n$ = 14, 30.4%), maternal aunt ($n$ = 7, 15.2%), and other distant kin ($n$ = 9, 19.6%). All cases of kinship placements in the rural area were with the birthfather.

**Permanency Outcomes.** In the urban county, 33% of the cases achieved a permanency placement within 12 months. Ten children were reunified with parents, nine were permanently placed with kin, and nine were adopted by foster/adoptive families. In the rural counties, 27% of children were in the process of adoption by foster/adoptive homes, although no adoptions had been completed at the time of the evaluation. There were no reunifications and no permanent placements with kin in the rural county.

**Length of Stay in Care.** The children in the KAOP had significantly shorter lengths of stay relative to the general foster care population in their region. In the urban county, the length of stay was 11.6 versus 31.8 months for children in the general population, $t(80)$ = -24.87, $p < .0001$. In the rural region, children in the KAOP had a length of stay of 16.9 months versus 24.7 months for the general population in this region, $t(10)$ = -3.98, $p < .001$, in this region. These results are promising given the new 12-month time frame under ASFA.

## Discussion

The primary goal of the KAOP was implementation of cross-system permanency planning activities. It was anticipated that these activities would result in a permanency placement decision within 12 months of the petition. Reviews of case plans revealed that the court risk assessment matrix was implemented, and the majority of children in the KAOP were young children who were most likely to benefit from expedited timelines. Based on the results of the court risk assessment matrix, these children were from families with multiple risk factors. As both KAOP sites, substance abuse issues coupled with chronic involvement with the CFC were the most predominant risk factors. These data also suggest that the KAOP cases in the urban county represented a significantly more chronic CFC sample relative to the sample in the rural region, which had significantly fewer previous substantiated allegations, fewer previous removals, and significantly fewer previous TPRs. The relatively few previous TPRs in the rural area relative to the urban county reflect the Appalachian setting in which many families here have lived for generations. Key informant interviews revealed that the court risk assessment and other activities of KAOP were more difficult to implement in a close-knit rural context in which most people knew each other.

However, qualitative interviews with stakeholders revealed that there was evidence of misconceptions across systems and across pilot sites about the goals and activities of the KAOP. Structured interviews with AOC coordinators, CFC caseworkers, KAOP attorneys, GALs, and judges indicated disparate approaches to the KAOP. To address the misconceptions about the goal and intent of the KAOP, the first several months of the evaluation were spent defining, in operational terms, the objectives and principal activities of the KAOP. These misconceptions led to some problems with the sample choice.

In the evaluation, an attempt was made to apply a very high standard of caseworker understanding with reference to the implementation of risk assessment and concurrent planning. As mentioned, concurrent planning is a well-recognized model that appears simple in theory but requires advanced casework practice skills (D'Andrade et al., 2000). For this evaluation, rather than surveying caseworkers about their level of knowledge of concurrent planning, a more complex level of assessment was conducted by evaluating the implementation of understanding, as all caseworkers had purportedly been trained. Caseworker understanding of concurrent planning and other advanced casework skills were not consistently thorough within sites or across sites. These casework skill inconsistencies impeded outcomes, such as expedited permanency planning or expedited TPR, whichever was most appropriate. Thus, although the court risk assessment matrix was used and training in advanced casework skills was conducted, a greater focus on concurrent planning and SBC principles might have improved permanency outcomes, particularly in the rural area.

*One child/one legal voice* was defined as a dedicated project attorney and one GAL throughout the court process. When TPR was the likely permanency outcome, the dedicated project attorney prosecuted a case from filing of the dependency action through TPR. Continuity of legal representation was established in the KAOP. These dedicated project attorneys improved the court process, particularly in cases involving TPRs. Given the high-risk nature of the KAOP, the stability and continuity of representation can be attributed to the coordination of these cases by stakeholders.

Despite the continuity of GAL representation, the effect of the one GAL model was less clear relative to the significant effect of the dedicated project attorneys. Interviews with attorneys and observations during court activities indicated that there were GAL misconceptions about concurrent planning, ASFA, and their roles relative to those of the child welfare workers. Future attempts should involve GALs more aggressively in training and collaboration so as to achieve permanency for high-risk children.

The early placement of KAOP children in foster/adoptive and kinship homes was another promising success of the project, in that this practice contributed to a stable placement history for these children. When comparing the KAOP children to the general foster care population in Kentucky, most of these children experienced fewer placement changes, thereby increasing the likelihood that first placements would be permanent placements. The increased availability of kinship and foster/adoptive homes contributed to this stability and permanency.

The second question of the evaluation addressed the effect of the aforementioned activities on permanency outcomes. This

question was more difficult to address, as there were several activities and multiple stakeholders. The KAOP heightened awareness of early assessment, adherence to timelines, reasonable efforts, and coordination, communication, and collaboration across
systems. It was, however, difficult to isolate the effect of activities on outcomes. As mentioned, these children experienced stability of placement, continuity of advocacy representation, and
shorter lengths of stay relative to the foster care population in
their counties. One-third of the cases achieved permanency within
the 12-month period. The mean length of stay was 12 months in
the urban county and 16 months in the rural county, both shorter
than the length of stay in the general foster care population. It
can be concluded that these outcomes were the result of the combined efforts of all involved in the project. However, the fact that
all children did not reach permanency suggests that some barriers were present and need to be explored.

### Barriers

The final evaluation question was designed to identify barriers
to expedited permanency for high-risk children. The KAOP attempted to achieve the goal of a permanency decision within 12
months while reducing the number of placement disruptions and
improving placements with families committed to the children
in their care. Although some cases have achieved these goals, high-
risk cases continue to linger due to systemic barriers related to
assessment, case plans, service coordination, court process, and
role confusion.

The lack of early, accurate assessments of parental and child
risk factors contributed to inappropriate referrals in some cases.
Referrals that were perfunctory, rather than individualized, delayed permanency, as the central issue that led to the petition
was not addressed (Katz, 1999). The court risk assessment matrix
at both KAOP sites demonstrated that substance abuse issues
coupled with chronic involvement with the CFC were the most

predominant risk factors. Other data collected for this evaluation suggested that the incidence of mental illness, multigenerational abuse, and domestic violence were often underestimated. These are important risk factors to consider in permanency planning of these high-risk children.

In some instances, the parent's, usually the mother's, main issue that led to the petition was not assessed or not recognized, leading to inappropriate referrals that in turn contributed to delays in permanency planning. A frequent occurrence in the KAOP cases was a mother diagnosed with a primary substance abuse issue, which was actually secondary to a chronic mental disorder such as schizophrenia or bipolar disorder. Another scenario was the custodial parent with a substance abuse issue and mental retardation. A referral only to a substance abuse treatment facility for a mother coping with mental retardation will lead to greater confusion on the part of the mother, which may be interpreted as lack of motivation, when the lack of requisite cognitive abilities is the actual issue.

It was also evident from the case review that service providers were not clear about their role or expected work product in the court process. Best practice protocols for treatment providers and psychological evaluations should be developed to improve the written reports to the court. In addition, it was challenging to determine when and how long a particular treatment provider was involved in a case. In KAOP cases with significant CFC histories, treatment providers were many and varied with little coordination or communication, which contributed to competing treatment plans and less success for clients.

Kentucky implemented two excellent case management models, SBC (Christensen et al., 1999) and concurrent planning. Although these two models appeared to have different conceptual frameworks, both concurrent planning and SBC have integrated similar principles. These principles include thorough family and individual assessment, collaboration with family and outside agencies, timelines, and documentation of behavior. SBC is a sophisticated model in terms of behavioral family case plans that are designed to work in conjunction with family and individual prevention plans. These results suggest that concurrent planning and solution-focused models such as SBC interface well but require thorough training.

Despite laudatory efforts on the part of judges and court administrators to streamline the process, the court system remains complicated and daunting to many families. Court delays continue to be the norm, particularly in rural settings where lack of transportation, childcare, and other services contributed to delays. There were identified delays from TPR to adoptions, particularly to foster/adoptive and concurrent planning homes. The process typically takes three months from TPR to adoption largely as a result of completing the adoption subsidies. The final barrier is related to role confusion across child welfare, the courts, and service providers. There is evidence from this evaluation that the roles of child welfare workers, their supervisors, GALs, other attorneys, and volunteers need role and task clarification to ensure quality advocacy and representation for high-risk children.

## Conclusion

Overall, the evaluation of the KAOP revealed the challenge of multiple systems working toward a common goal. Despite galvanizing stakeholders from the courts, child welfare, and the service community, the KAOP could not prevent some of the children from remaining in care for lengthy periods of time. The barriers to success included poor communication, lack of collaboration, and lack of role clarity across systems. The lack of involvement of service providers for mental health, substance abuse, and domestic violence issues was a glaring hole in the collaboration process. If it was difficult for these motivated stakeholders to communicate, coordinate, and collaborate, then the difficulty of day-to-day work of child welfare has been underestimated. Glisson and his colleagues found that the biggest predictor of children lingering in care was the failure to adequately assess and respond to the complex needs of high-risk families (Glisson, 1994, 1996; Glisson, Bailey, & Post, 2000; Martin, Peters, & Glisson, 1998; Nugent & Glisson, 1999). Although the KAOP made a gallant effort in this regard, system responsiveness to the needs of these children and their families remains a daunting challenge.◆

## References

Adoption and Safe Families Act, P.L. No. 105-89 (1997).

Barth, R. P., & Price, A. (1999). Shared family care: Providing services to parents and children placed together in out-of-home care. *Child Welfare, 78,* 99–107.

Briere, J., Berliner, L., Bulkley, J. A., Jenny, C., & Reid, T. (1996). *The APSAC handbook on child maltreatment.* Thousand Oaks, CA: Sage.

Christensen, D. N., Todahl, J., & Barrett, W. C. (1999). *Solution-based casework: An intro-duction to clinical and case management skills in casework practice.* New York: Aldine de Gruyter.

D'Andrade, A., Choice, P., Martin, M., & Berrick, J. D. (2000, January). *Concurrent plan-ning: The influence of new practices on child welfare permanency outcomes.* Paper pre-sented at the Fifth Annual Conference of the Society for Social Work and Research, Atlanta, GA.

Glisson, C. (1994). The effects of service coordination teams on outcomes for children in state custody. *Administration in Social Work, 18,* 1-23.

Glisson, C. (1996). Judicial and service decisions for children entering state custody: The limited role of mental health. *Social Service Review, 70,* 257–281.

Glisson, C., Bailey, J. W., & Post, J. A. (2000). Predicting the time children spend in state custody. *Social Service Review, 74,* 253–280.

Katz, L. (1990). Effective permanency planning for children in foster care. *Social Work, 35,* 220–226.

Katz, L. (1999). Concurrent planning: Benefits and pitfalls. *Child Welfare, 78*(1), 71–87.

Katz, L., & Robinson, C. (1991). Foster-care drift: A risk assessment matrix. *Child Welfare, 70*, 347–358.

Katz, L., Spoonemore, N., & Robinson, C. (1994). *Concurrent planning: From permanency planning to permanency action*. Seattle: Lutheran Social Services of Washington.

Martin, L. M., Peters, C. L., & Glisson, C. (1998). Factors affecting case management recommendations for children entering state custody. *Social Service Review, 72*, 521–544.

Nugent, W. R., & Glisson, C. (1999). Reactivity and responsiveness in children's services systems. *Journal of Social Service Research, 25*, 41–60.

Chapter 6

# Overcoming Hopelessness and Social Isolation: The ENGAGE Model for Working with Neglecting Families Toward Permanence

*Donna D. Petras, Carol Rippey Massat, and Elizabeth Lehr Essex*

The Adoption and Safe Families Act of 1997 (ASFA) mandates policies designed to increase the frequency and speed with which permanency is achieved for children in the child welfare system. ASFA's focus is on child safety, permanency, and well-being. The expectation that parents correct neglectful conditions within specified time frames places an increased ethical responsibility on child welfare staff. Carrying out this responsibility requires vigorous and innovative approaches to engaging and working with neglectful families. Drawing on a well-established conceptual framework for understanding the determinants of effective parenting, the authors derive the ENGAGE (Engagement, Needs assessment, Goal setting, Assessment of progress, Goal achievement, Ending work) model for achieving permanency within the policy structure. The model incorporates creative client engagement, assessment of family needs, mutual goal setting, the goal achievement process, termination, and aftercare.

*Donna D. Petras is Assistant Professor, Carol Rippey Massat is Associate Professor, and Elizabeth Lehr Essex is Assistant Professor, Jane Addams College of Social Work, University of Illinois at Chicago.*

Child neglect is the most prevalent form of child maltreatment in the United States today. In 1999, 826,000 children nationwide were abused or neglected. Of these, 58.4% were cases of child neglect (U.S. Department of Health and Human Services [DHHS], 1999). The consequences of neglect for children are severe and include physical, emotional, and developmental impairment. In its most severe forms, child neglect results in death. Nationally, an estimated 1,100 children died as a result of child abuse and neglect in 1999; 38% of these child deaths were associated with neglect, more than with any other form of maltreatment.

Because of the incidence and prevalence of child neglect as a reason for family involvement with child welfare services, permanency planning for such families affects the majority of families involved with the child welfare system. Little attention has been given to this area, however, when compared to child abuse (Garbarino & Collin, 1999). As a result, practice models for work with families affected by child neglect are lacking.

## Framework for Service Provision Mandated by the Adoption and Safe Families Act

The 1980 Adoption Assistance and Child Welfare Act was an attempt to stop the drift of children in foster care. The act required guarantees that "reasonable efforts" be made to prevent family breakup, establish permanency goals, create service plans, regularly review progress toward permanency goals, and plan for alternative permanent placements for children if reunification is not feasible. The number of children in foster care dropped initially, but soon the number increased (Lindsey, 1994).

Enacted in November 1997, the Adoption and Safe Families Act (ASFA), P.L. 105-89, amended the 1980 Adoption Assistance and Child Welfare Act. ASFA includes provisions that affect permanency planning for families in which neglect has occurred. Key elements emphasized child safety, permanence, and child well-being, as well as timelines and conditions for filing of termination of parental rights. Reunification may be eliminated as an initial goal for neglectful families if a child has been abandoned or parental rights to another child have previously been terminated. The abbreviated timelines for initial reviews for permanence and for initiation of proceedings to terminate parental rights also provide for less time to prepare children and families for safe reunification. The strengthened focus on the safety of the child in permanency planning places additional pressure on states to ensure the physical well-being of children, which could result in a "raising of the bar" for reunification.

These changes mean that workers and families must start rapidly if reunification is the goal, and workers must work quickly with families to reach resolution of ambivalence (Hess & Folaron, 1991) and to establish evidence that the home is a safe, permanent place for the child. The literature on child neglect, however, suggests that neglect tends to be a long-term and intractable problem for families, thus implementation of these guidelines becomes a challenge (Polansky, Chalmers, Buttenwieser, & Williams, 1981).

ASFA also brought about another trend in permanency planning, termed *concurrent planning*. Concurrent planning was originally defined as the development of two different service plans for the same case. One plan would be to reunify the family, and the second would be pursuit of an alternative permanent plan for a child, such as adoption. This planning would occur simultaneously (Tracy & Pine, 2000). As it exists today, concurrent planning has been interpreted in many different ways. In Illinois, for example, concurrent planning is often interpreted as the development but not implementation of plans for an alternative placement should reunification not occur.

## Conceptual Model for the Predictors of Child Neglect

Studies have identified a wide variety of factors that influence child neglect, including individual pathology of parents, such as substance abuse (Harrington, Dubowitz, Black, & Binder, 1995); family dynamic issues, such as family dysfunction (Polansky, Gaudin, & Kilpatrick, 1992); parent-child interaction (Fagan & Dore, 1993); and interactions between the parent and the environment, such as social isolation (Gaudin, Polansky, Kilpatrick, & Shilton, 1993). Current theorists posit that child neglect emerges through the interactions of multiple factors at the individual, family, community, and societal levels (Dubowitz, Black, Starr, & Zuravin, 1993).

The conceptual framework that has been selected to guide the ENGAGE model (Engagement, Needs assessment, Goal setting, Assessment of progress, Goal achievement, Ending work) for intervention with neglectful families has been widely cited within the literature on child neglect. It is a process model of the determinants of parenting developed by Belsky and Vondra (1989). Characteristics that make it especially appropriate as the guiding conceptual framework for this practice model include the ability to examine multiple interrelated factors identified in the literature as influencing child neglect; the systems perspective of the model, which incorporates both stressors on and support for parenting; and the capacity to identify sources of both vulnerability and resilience in parents (Belsky & Vondra, 1989). This model identifies three domains that influence parental functioning: the parent's own developmental history and personal characteristics, the child's individual characteristics, and parental social connectedness to the environment. Three assumptions underlie the model: (1) Parenting is multiply determined, (2) the variable domains are not equally influential in supporting or undermining growth-promoting parenting, and (3) the parent's developmental history and personal characteristics influence parenting both directly and indirectly through the broader social context in which parenting occurs (Belsky & Vondra, 1989). The literature on child neglect has identified key factors related to each domain, which are briefly reviewed below.

## Parental Developmental History and Personal Characteristics

The importance of the quality of parenting one receives in promoting healthy development of the individual and the capacity to provide positive parenting for one's own children has long been recognized. Bowlby (1969) theorized that children grow into healthy adults in the context of a secure attachment to their parents. Secure attachments are developed through a warm, nurturing relationship provided by the parent, in which the needs of the child are met. According to Bowlby, failure to experience such a nurturing relationship—and instead, experiencing maltreatment in childhood—can have severe consequences for development, leaving individuals without the internal resources to parent their own children adequately. Indeed, the intergenerational cycle of child maltreatment has long been recognized in the child abuse and neglect literature (Zuravin, McMillen, DePanfilis, & Risley-Curtiss, 1996). Early experiences of maltreatment are thought to have an adverse effect on personality development, especially the child's view of self and relationship to others, and to predispose one to select situations that reinforce negative experiences (Zuravin et al., 1996). Childhood experience of maltreatment is hypothesized to be an important predictor of child neglect in the next generation.

Personal characteristics of the parents have also been found to predict neglect. Polansky et al. (1981) coined the term "apathy-futility syndrome" to describe the sense of hopelessness that they observed in neglecting parents. The syndrome they described included a "pervasive conviction that nothing is worth doing...emotional numbness...desperate clinging...intense loneliness" (p. 39). Other researchers have consistently found an association between child maltreatment and maternal depression (Belsky & Vondra, 1989). Researchers have repeatedly documented that depressed mothers are likely to be withdrawn, to provide a rejecting and hostile home environment, and to be neglectful of their children, especially in the area of physical neglect (Ethier, Lacharite, & Couture, 1995; Rosenzweig & Kaplan, 1996).

According to the literature, one of the most firmly established predictors of child maltreatment is parental substance abuse. Studies have found that the rate of child abuse and neglect among substance-addicted parents is significantly higher than in the general population. Likewise, studies examining the family circumstances of children who are involved with child protective services have found that a significant proportion, ranging from 13% to more than 70%, come from families in which at least one parent is involved in substance abuse (Magura & Laudet, 1996). Parental substance abuse has been associated not just with maltreatment in general but specifically with greater incidence of child neglect. The existing literature strongly supports an association between substance abuse and child neglect (Chaffin, Kelleher, & Hollenberg, 1996; Harrington et al., 1995; Magura & Laudet, 1996; Peterson, Gable, & Saldana, 1996).

### Child Characteristics

A considerable body of evidence has been developed that supports the perspective that the parent-child relationship is not unidirectional from parent to child, but rather it is bidirectional, involving influences of the child on the parent as well (Belsky & Vondra, 1989). A number of characteristics of children have been found to be associated with child maltreatment including age, maladaptive behavior, presence of a disability, and limitations in adaptive functioning (Browne, 1988). Child neglect primarily affects young children; for example, more than 86.1% of the children who died from child neglect in 1999 were younger than age six (U.S. DHHS, 1999).

### Social Connectedness

Parenting occurs in a social context replete with potential sources of support and stress. Growth-promoting parenting has been positively associated with social support (Lee & Coletta, 1983). One of the most important sources of both support and stress in the parenting environment is the relationship between the parental partners (Belsky & Vondra, 1989; Coohey, 1996). High levels of positive spousal support are positively associated with increased maternal responsiveness and competence. On the other hand, children whose parents have a troubled relationship show increased behavior problems and poorer adaptive functioning than children whose parents have harmonious marital relationships (Belsky & Vondra, 1989). A growing body of evidence confirms a strong link between domestic violence and child maltreatment (Doyle, 1996; McKay, 1994). Partner abuse significantly increases the risk of child neglect (Lecklitner, Malik, Aaron, & Lederman, 1999). These findings suggest that the relationship between intimate partners can be a strong influence on parenting behaviors.

Although social support can come from an intimate partner, parenting is also influenced by the degree of connection to multiple sources of support. Unfortunately, neglectful parents have fewer connections to others and, therefore, fewer potential sources of support than their non-neglecting counterparts (Coohey, 1996). Numerous studies have found that social isolation is associated with child neglect (Gaudin et al., 1993; Polansky, 1985). Social connectedness is a significant factor both in research on child neglect and conceptually in the Belsky and Vondra (1989) model of the determinants of parenting behavior.

Formal social services are potential resources for parents who have weak social networks. DePanfilis (1996) found that social service interventions can provide parents with support that may be missing from their natural social networks. In turn, improvements in parenting behavior of neglectful parents can be achieved. DePanfilis's review of intervention models suggests that the mechanism by which neglectful behavior is reduced is through connection to others in a variety of ways.

## Practice Applications

ASFA has created a new urgency and time pressures in work with families affected by neglect, but the obstacles for these families cannot be legislated away and constitute challenges to workers who must work quickly and effectively with families. The EN-GAGE model has been developed by the authors based on the Belsky and Vondra theoretical model of determinants of parenting and the research literature on child neglect. The ENGAGE model spells out the steps in working with neglecting parents toward permanency planning.

These steps are important no matter what the permanency goals are for a family. To paraphrase an aphorism, "You can take a child out of a family, but you can't take the family out of the child." Adoptive or guardianship arrangements may be with relatives or others willing to sustain some level of contact with birthparents, and this may well be beneficial to the child. Reaching such goals cooperatively with families can be considered similar to an amicable divorce, in that it is likely that less harm will result to children who are separated from birthparents in a nonadversarial fashion.

### Engagement

Client engagement has been defined as "the therapist's continuous modification of his/her own behavior and responses to ensure that family members feel sufficiently acknowledged and involved to continue to attend" (Jackson & Chable, 1985, p. 65). Successful engagement with the family is a necessary first step to movement toward either reunification or a decision to relinquish parental rights.

Among the immediate obstacles to engagement is the adversarial nature of the child welfare system. The relationship begins with an accusation of child maltreatment, placing the parent in a defensive posture. The worker has a dual responsibility to engage the family while ensuring the safety and well-being of the child. The worker has to build a relationship but is also required to report child maltreatment or give negative testimony about a family in court. The worker's level of accountability regarding child safety also makes workers cautious about reaching out. The isolation and pervasive sense of hopelessness that characterize neglecting parents are both obstacles to engagement and conditions that make engagement a critical precondition to successful intervention (Winefield & Barlow, 1995). In light of all of these factors, initial reactions of families—which may be expressed as anger or "no-shows"—must not be overinterpreted or misinterpreted to represent the full capacity of families.

Some literature suggests that client engagement is enhanced by longer contacts with clients, more instruction, and a perception of feeling understood by the worker (Tryon, 1989). Empathy is related to more positive relationships between clients and workers (Florentine & Hillhouse, 1999). Thus, the ENGAGE model attempts to build on these elements in the initial and ongoing engagement of families. Workers and families can move from coercion to cooperation through education about the culture of the child welfare system, instillation of hope, and development of partnerships.

## Education of Families About the Culture of the Child Welfare System

The authors have found it helpful to provide direct instruction to families regarding the language and culture of the child welfare system. This perspective is supported by research showing that teaching is an important component in client engagement (Tryon, 1989). Families who are new to the child welfare system may need to learn the meaning of new phrases and acronyms, as well as to learn the unwritten rules. This direct instruction can help families negotiate the system and assist them in achieving success in their goals. Parents need to understand that the decisions of child welfare agencies and the courts are based to a large extent on parental behavior, not parental feelings or intentions, and that those behaviors are judged through punctuality, use of language, attire, communication with the worker, and follow-through with tasks outlined in the service plan.

Punctuality may or may not be an important value to a family, but it is a paramount indicator for many members of the child welfare system and the courts. Achievement of goals in a set time period and timely appearances at visits and appointments are interpreted by decision-makers as critical indicators of a parent's ability and desire to parent. ASFA sets forth specific time limitations as key components in the drive toward permanency. Parents need to understand the implications of these time limits for their efforts to parent their children. Workers need to directly address these issues by using clear, jargon-free language to explain to families what is expected of them and the criteria on which they will be judged. This discussion needs to continue until it is clear that understanding has been reached.

### Instillation of Hope

What Polansky et al. (1981) termed the "apathy-futility syndrome" common to neglectful parents creates a necessity for instilling hope. This may be a daunting task for a worker who may be drawn into the despair of the family. Hope can be instilled through the recognition of the parent's feelings, development of focus, partialization of goals, and vigorous efforts to communicate the worker's own hopefulness, which implies respect and empathy on the part of the worker.

Recognition of the legitimacy of parental feelings is critical, especially because parents enter the relationship in a defensive posture. Whether the allegation of neglect is true is a separate issue from acknowledging the legitimacy of the emotions a parent may experience as a result of the exposure of their failings.

Anger should be seen as part of the common human experience and may also serve to motivate and mobilize clients who may otherwise be stuck in the apathy-futility syndrome. Acknowledgment of expected parental reactions does not imply the condoning of child maltreatment. The worker must understand the experience and emotions of parents while helping them move to new levels of functioning. Understanding does not mean acceptance of the status quo. It is a recognition of the starting place for working together.

The initial experience of many families that come to the attention of the child welfare system is one of great chaos. Multiple demands, lack of clarity about goals and process, and lack of familiarity with the many individuals involved with their family often make the initial intervention seem fragmented and confusing. Helping the family develop a focus for the achievement of progress is an essential step for instilling hope. Dividing the ultimate goal into small steps and having families develop and complete the steps toward that goal can create forward movement. Each small success of the family needs to be acknowledged and credited to them, not the worker, so that the family can build its own sense of efficacy.

*Partnership Development*

Despite the inherent power imbalance between the worker and the client, a partnership can be developed with families. Helping parents to correct the conditions that led to their involvement with the child welfare system is not something that can be done for families or to families. To paraphrase Carl Rogers (1961), the child welfare worker must create an environment that is conducive to growth and change, but the parent must do their own growing and changing. Factors that compose such a relationship include shared decisionmaking and goal setting, respectful behavior and demeanor toward the parent, and continual crediting of success to the efforts of the client rather than the expertise of the worker. Genuineness and authenticity on the part of the worker are also critical elements in the development of such a partnership.

Correcting the imbalance of power involves the sharing of information, including educating parents about the child welfare system and fully disclosing information about their case so that they can make informed decisions. Informing parents about and inviting their participation in decisions and actions regarding their family are fundamental aspects of successful partnerships.

Rapid and vigorous efforts on the part of agencies and workers are demonstrations of good faith in working to achieve partnerships with families. Such efforts include: (a) availability of workers to meet with families at hours and locations that are feasible for families, (b) frequent reaching out to families through letters and telephone calls, (c) provision of needed information and linkage to services, and (d) provision of concrete resources to families who identify such needs as food, clothing, and housing. As Winefield and Barlow (1995) pointed out, the relationship with the caseworker in which "trust was established and simple acts of kindness performed, which seemed like going the extra mile" (p. 898) was key to successful outcomes for maltreating parents who had often experienced severe emotional deprivation themselves.

## Needs Assessment of Families Affected by Neglect

Work toward permanence cannot be effective without an understanding of the specific strengths and obstacles faced by families affected by neglect. Based on the theoretical understanding that multiple factors influence parenting, the ENGAGE model proposes that assessment of family needs has multiple foci. The worker evaluates strengths and needs in the three major domains of the conceptual model—parental developmental history and personal characteristics, child characteristics, and sources of stress and support. It is important to note that the assessment process is not a faultfinding session. Rather, it is a means of determining ways to help families and ways in which their strengths can be used to move toward permanence. Within the domains of the Belsky and Vondra (1989) model, the focus is on factors that have been found to be significantly associated with child neglect. Assessment of those factors identified earlier and a description of the standardized measures that may assist workers in understanding their significance for individual families will be addressed. A common failing of assessment in child welfare settings is the gathering of a great deal of information without an objective means of analyzing it to develop an understanding of the strengths and needs of families. Therefore, the use of standardized instruments for assessment is recommended.

One factor found to have an effect on parenting, which is therefore important to assess, is the parent's own developmental history. Often, much can be learned from the social history process of asking open-ended questions of parents about their own childhood and development. Key areas include history of abuse or neglect, family history of substance abuse, possible separation from parents during childhood, level of conflict in the home, and methods of managing conflict. In addition, learning about current relationships with extended family can assist the worker in understanding the family network and possibly who should be involved in the permanency planning process. Family meetings with kin and fictive kin who are closely involved with the parents may tap into significant resources, either for support of the family or for placement of the child. Use of genograms and ecomaps can help to map out the family history and current relationships. Another potentially useful tool is the Family of Origin Scale (Hovestadt, Anderson, Piercy, Cochran, & Fine, 1985), a 40-item, Likert-type scale designed to assess the emotional health of one's family of origin. The scale has satisfactory internal consistency, stability, and validity. Hudson's (1992) Index of Family Relations may be used to get a sense of the current level of relationships with extended family members. The Childhood Trauma

Questionnaire (Bernstein et al., 1994) can also be used to assess the level of neglect or emotional, physical, or sexual abuse the parents experienced in childhood. The scale is a 70-item measure and thus is somewhat long, but it has good reliability and validity.

The parental level of hope is another dimension that has been found to be an obstacle for neglectful families, whereas depression, closely negatively related to a sense of hope, has been found to be common among maltreating parents. Thus, measurement of parental depression is another important focus of assessment. A number of assessment instruments have satisfactory reliability and validity in screening for depression in adults. Suggested measures include Hudson's (1992) Generalized Contentment Scale, the Beck Depression Inventory (Beck & Beck, 1972), the Cognitive-Triad Inventory (Beckham, Leber, Watkins, Byer, & Cook, 1986), the Costello-Comrey Depression Scale (Costello & Comrey, 1967), and the Center for Epidemiologic Studies Depression Scale (Radloff, 1977). These measures are brief and easy to score and use in assessing the level of hope or depression of parents.

Parental substance use is another critical area of assessment. "Being clean" may be a source of pride for a family member, and the recovery community may be a source of support. Problems with alcohol or other substances, however, will contribute significantly to difficulties in parenting and must be addressed. Even if substance abuse has not been identified as an issue, all cases should be screened. One useful tool is the Addiction Severity Index (Urschel, Blair, & McLellan, 1991), which is administered in an interview format. This instrument has been found to be reliable and valid and has been translated into nine languages.

There are realistic issues that may inhibit candid responses from family members to questions regarding drug and alcohol use. For this reason, random urine tests are frequently used when substance abuse has been identified as a factor in a case. If a family meeting is held to discuss permanency planning with extended family, the need for substance abuse services may be discussed as well.

Another area of assessment is the health and development of children. Different child temperaments and the presence of chronic illness or disability of a child affect parenting behaviors and thus must be considered when assessing possible needs of families in which neglect has occurred. If a child has a learning disability, developmental disability, or chronic health condition, demands on the parent are increased. Children with medical conditions require assessment by a physician or other health care provider with expertise in the child's area of need. Children suspected of having learning or behavioral disorders that could affect their school performance should be evaluated for special education services by the educational system, including infancy and early childhood programs. Perhaps the most widely used instrument for assessing child behavior problems is the Child Behavior Checklist (CBCL) developed by Achenbach (1991). The CBCL is used to assess behavior problems and social competence of children ages 4 to 18. A separate instrument has been developed to assess children ages 2 to 3. The CBCL has high reliability and validity; different versions have been designed for reports by a parent, teacher, or child.

Partner relations also affect parenting. Not all parents in contact with the child welfare system will have a current intimate partner, but many do. Such a relationship can be a tremendous resource, but if problems such as violence are occurring, these are detrimental to parenting. Often, the intimate partner is not a marital partner and may either be a heterosexual or same sex partner. Therefore, the assessment process should include a diverse range of potential relationships. One brief, seven-item screening instrument is the Relationship Assessment Scale (Hendrick, 1988), which is used as a measure of satisfaction in intimate relationships. Another instrument is the Marital Comparison Level Index (Sabatelli, 1984). Although *marital* is in the title, the actual wording used for the scale is *partner*, so the measure can be used to assess nonmarital relationships.

All cases should be screened for domestic violence, because of the frequent co-occurrence of child maltreatment and domestic violence. The Conflict Tactics Scale (Straus, Hamby, Boney-McCoy, & Sugarman, 1996) is probably the best-known scale, but the Hudson (1992) Non-Physical Abuse of Partner Scale, Partner Abuse Scale: Non-Physical, and Partner Abuse Scale: Physical are also options.

In the literature on both maltreatment in general and child neglect, social connectedness of parents is a key factor. It is critical to determine the amount of social support available to parents, particularly in relation to the parenting role. An eco-map and genogram, as mentioned earlier, can be helpful in determining support for parents. The Maternal Sense of Social Support Index (Pascoe, Loda, Jeffries, & Earp, 1981) includes questions regarding the amount of support available in general and specific to parenting. The University of California, Los Angeles, Loneliness Scale (Russell, Peplau, & Cutrona, 1980) can help to assess the level of isolation experienced by a parent.

## Goal Setting

Permanency goals and objectives to meet them must be set with the family and must be related to the specific needs identified in the assessment process. This apparently simple action is rarely carried out in practice. Plans may be developed in the absence of the family and may be virtually identical for all cases, despite wide variations in family needs and circumstances. The inclusion of a visitation objective, parenting classes, and individual counseling in most case plans suggests that goals are rarely individualized to meet the specific needs of families. Given the urgency of the timelines set by ASFA, specific, focused, and achievable goals and objectives developed to meet the individual needs of the family are necessary to meet permanency goals.

A valid service plan, if met by the parent, will result in the parental provision of a safe, permanent environment that ensures the well-being of the child. The service plan must be based on the assessment findings and must identify measurable indicators of problem resolution. Failure to do this may result in a situation in which the parent has fulfilled the service plan but is unable to provide a safe, nurturing environment for the child.

It is important to differentiate between formal service plans and intermediate goals that may be set from week to week with the worker. To instill hope and empowerment, families need to develop small, achievable steps toward the larger goal. Achievement of each step can then be celebrated.

The results of the assessment of family needs and the maltreatment investigation are the bases for the family service plan. The conditions that brought the family to the system must be corrected, and family service needs identified in the assessment must be addressed. For each condition identified, services must be developed and utilized. Parental developmental history and characteristics (e.g., substance use and mental health), social connectedness (e.g., partner relations and social isolation), and child characteristics are assessed and goals are developed for domains identified as areas of need.

## Assessment of Reasonable Progress Toward Permanence

Although the law requires the assessment of reasonable progress toward permanence, this assessment is rarely performed in a systematic fashion. Therefore, the results of the assessment of reasonable progress are sometimes disputed and may be difficult to defend. The ENGAGE model proposes that the single system design method be used to assess progress toward permanency goals. Single system design is a widely recognized method of evaluating the change in clients and involves regular measurement of specific behaviors (Bloom, Fischer, & Orme, 1999). If assessment reveals a specific area that needs to be addressed, baseline measurement of the problem is taken, followed by interventions to address the problem and daily or weekly measurements of progress.

The use of the single system design approach with families has several potential benefits. Data are available to demonstrate to workers, families, and others how much progress has been made. These data can be used to adjust intervention strategies or to develop and adjust case goals if it appears that goals are not likely to be achieved. If progress is made, regular measurement of that progress provides the opportunity to reinforce and strengthen changes in behavior. If progress is not being made, then it may be necessary to change strategies, motivate families, or revise goals.

Measurement of progress can be achieved by using some of the same instruments discussed in the assessment section of this article. In addition, self-anchored measures or measures of specific behaviors can be used. For example, if a significant contributing problem is poor housekeeping, daily goals can be set and measured for specific behaviors such as washing dishes, sweeping the floor, or making beds.

### Goal Attainment: Maintaining Engagement with Families

The regular contact necessitated by the use of single system design to assess progress has the potential benefit of supporting the relationship between the worker and the family. In addition, the regular recognition and reinforcement of new behaviors is likely to make the relationship more positive for families and workers.

The engagement strategies spelled out earlier must be continued throughout contacts with the families. These families are likely to have been wounded by many previous disappointing relationships, so it is critical that workers make every effort to provide the consistent, caring contacts that can move families toward a permanent plan for children. If this is done, visitation is more likely and reunification becomes more possible. In addition, the continued acceptance of families who are unable to parent their children may assist them in helping to make another permanent plan for their children.

Before moving on to the final stage, the key decision is determining if goals have been attained and, if they have, whether these circumstances constitute a safe, permanent setting in which the child's well-being is provided for. If goals set with the family are objective and measurable, it will be possible to determine when they have been met. Difficulty arises when there is continuing uncertainty regarding child safety. This can occur if the initial or revised service plan failed to address important aspects of parental need.

### Ending Work: Service Termination and Care After Permanence

Aftercare following achievement of a permanent plan may depend greatly on the specifics of that plan. Adoptive placement, guardianship, or reunification should never be treated as the happy ending of a fairy tale. If anything, service needs may initially intensify. These needs are the reason there is generally some waiting period before adoptions are finalized and guardianship is not relinquished on the day children are returned home. Indeed, the return of children to their families after placement has been found to be a process with predictable crisis points that need to be planned for and addressed to effect successful and permanent reunification of families.

Although intrusion is undesirable, support is essential through the adjustment periods when changes in placement and legal status occur. If engagement with an agency and worker has occurred, supportive relationships should be continued through periodic contacts and referrals for ongoing services so that resources are available to meet new family needs. If hopelessness and isolation were long-term family patterns, then resources for ongoing support need to be in place prior to termination of agency involvement, as old patterns may recur.

As with all clinical interventions, a primary objective of child welfare intervention is to foster independence and empowerment of families so that they can provide for the long-term safety, permanency, and well-being of their children. Children who enter foster and kinship care have been found to have greater medical, emotional, and behavioral needs than children in the general population. Therefore, these children frequently require formal and informal supports throughout childhood and adolescence. True permanency planning requires that the child welfare system help families develop the ability to meet these needs after the case is closed.

Several major issues need to be addressed when ending work with families (Petras, Terry, Schiff, & Gleeson, 2000). The adequacy of the permanency plan should be assessed. Does the parent have an adequate support system to keep the child safe without the monitoring and assistance of the child welfare system? Has the parent and support system considered the changing needs for care as the child grows older? The family needs to be helped to identify and to access both informal community supports and formal social services in their community. The family should be assisted in anticipating potential risks to the child and developing plans to minimize those risks. Ongoing communication with extended family members should be encouraged to strengthen their involvement and commitment to the child and the parents. The feelings of the child, parents, and members of the support network about termination of services by the child welfare system should be explored. Progress should be reviewed with the family to help them appreciate and gain a sense of accomplishment from their steps forward in correcting conditions and meeting the child's needs for safety, permanence, and well-being. Finally, the family must be assisted in establishing next steps in meeting the child's needs following disengagement by the child welfare system.

## Summary

The ENGAGE model is a systematic approach to permanency planning with neglecting parents, the largest group of parents involved with the child welfare system. Through careful and compassionate engagement of the parents in services, followed by careful assessment and mutual and individualized goal setting, it may be possible to meet the demands of ASFA legislation for faster timelines in permanency planning. Workers must continue to maintain engagement with families throughout the process of goal attainment. If careful service plans have been developed, it is likely to be clear whether or not goals have been met, so that decisions can be made and ending work can begin. This final stage of the ENGAGE model may be the most critical in the long-term success of the permanent plan. Careful disengagement of the agency from the family involves considerable assurance that current and future needs have been anticipated and that the barriers the family has faced, such as hopelessness and isolation, have been addressed.◆

## References

Achenbach, T. M. (1991). *Manual for the Child Behavior Checklist/4-18 and 1991 profile.* Burlington: University of Vermont Department of Psychiatry.

Beck, A. T., & Beck, R. W. (1972). Beck Depression Inventory—Short Form. Screening depressed patients in family practice: A rapid technique. *Postgraduate Medicine, 52,* 81-85.

Beckham, E. E., Leber, W. R., Watkins, J. T., Byer, J. L., & Cook, B. (1986). Development of an instrument to measure Beck's cognitive triad: The Cognitive Triad Inventory. *Journal of Consulting and Clinical Psychology, 54,* 566-567.

Belsky, J., & Vondra, J. (1989). Lessons from child abuse: The determinants of parenting. In D. Cicchetti & V. Carlson (Eds.), *Child maltreatment: Theory and research on the causes and consequences of child abuse and neglect* (pp. 153-202). Cambridge, UK: Cambridge University Press.

Bernstein, D. P., Fink, L., Handelsman, L., Foote, J., Lovejoy, M., Wenzel, K., et al. (1994). Initial reliability and validity of a new retrospective measure of child abuse and neglect. *American Journal of Psychiatry, 151,* 1132-1136.

Bloom, M., Fischer, J., & Orme, J. G. (1999). *Evaluating practice: Guidelines for the accountable professional.* Boston: Allyn & Bacon.

Bowlby, J. (1969). *Attachment and loss: Volume I: Attachment.* New York: Basic Books.

Browne, D. (1988). High risk infants and child maltreatment: Conceptual and research model for determining factors predictive of child maltreatment. *Early Child Development and Care, 31*(1-4), 43-53.

Chaffin, M., Kelleher, K., & Hollenberg, J. (1996). Onset of physical abuse and neglect: Psychiatric, substance abuse, and social risk factors from prospective community data. *Child Abuse and Neglect, 20*(3), 191-203.

Coohey, C. (1996). Child maltreatment: Testing the social isolation hypothesis. *Child Abuse and Neglect, 20*(3), 241-254.

Costello, C. G., & Comrey, A. L. (1967). Scales for measuring depression and anxiety. *Journal of Psychology, 66,* 303-313.

DePanfilis, D. (1996, February). Social isolation of neglectful families: A review of social support assessment and intervention models. *Child Maltreatment, 1*(1), 37-52.

Doyle, C. (1996). Current issues in child protection: An overview of the debates in contemporary journals. *British Journal of Social Work, 26,* 565-576.

Dubowitz, H., Black, M., Starr, R. H., & Zuravin, S. (1993). A conceptual definition of child neglect. *Criminal Justice and Behavior, 20*(1), 8-26.

Ethier, L. S., Lacharite, C., & Couture, G. (1995). Childhood adversity, parental stress, and depression of negligent mothers. *Child Abuse and Neglect, 19*(5), 619-632.

Fagan, J., & Dore, M. M. (1993). Mother-child play interaction in neglecting and non-neglecting mothers. *Early Child Development and Care, 87,* 59-68.

Florentine, R., & Hillhouse, M. P. (1999). Drug-treatment effectiveness and client-counselor empathy: Exploring the effects of gender and ethnic congruence. *Journal of Drug Issues, 29*(1), 59-74.

Garbarino, J., & Collin, C. (1999). Child neglect: The family with a hole in the middle. In H. Dubowitz (Ed.), *Neglected children: Research, practice, and policy* (pp. 1-23). Thousand Oaks, CA: Sage.

Gaudin, J. A., Polansky, N. A., Kilpatrick, A. C., & Shilton, P. (1993). Loneliness, depression, stress, and social supports in neglectful families. *American Journal of Orthopsychiatry, 63*(4), 597-605.

Harrington, D., Dubowitz, H., Black, M. M., & Binder, A. (1995). Maternal substance use and neglectful parenting: Relations with children's development. *Journal of Clinical Child Psychology, 24*(3), 258-263.

Hendrick, S. S. (1988). A generic measure of relationship satisfaction. *Journal of Marriage and the Family, 50*, 93-98.

Hess, P. M., & Folaron, G. (1991, July-August). Ambivalences: A challenge to permanency for children. *Child Welfare, 70*(4), 403-424.

Hovestadt, A. J., Anderson, W. T., Piercy, F. A., Cochran, S. W., & Fine, M. (1985). A Family-of-origin scale. *Journal of Marital and Family Therapy, 11*(3), 287-297.

Hudson, W. W. (1992). *The WALMYR Assessment Scales scoring manual.* Tempe, AZ: WALMYR.

Jackson, S., & Chable, D. G. (1985). Engagement: A critical aspect of family therapy practice. *Australian and New Zealand Journal of Family Therapy, 6*(2), 65-69.

Lecklitner, G. L., Malik, N. M., Aaron, S. M., & Lederman, C. S. (1999). Promoting safety for abused children and battered mothers: Miami-Dade County's Model Dependency Court Intervention Program. *Child Maltreatment, 4*, 175-182.

Lee, D. M., & Coletta, N. D. (1983, April). *Family support for adolescent mothers: The positive and negative impact.* Paper presented at the biennial meeting of the Society for Research in Child Development, Detroit, MI.

Lindsey, D. (1994). *The welfare of children.* New York: Oxford University Press.

Magura, S., & Laudet, A. B. (1996). Parental substance abuse and child maltreatment: Review and implications for intervention. *Children and Youth Services Review, 18*(3), 193-220.

McKay, M. M. (1994). The link between domestic violence and child abuse: Assessment and treatment considerations. *Child Welfare, 73*, 29-39.

Pascoe, J. M., Loda, F. A., Jeffries, V., & Earp, J. A. (1981). The association between mothers' social support and provision of stimulation to their children. *Behavioral Pediatrics, 2*, 15-19.

Peterson, L., Gable, S., & Saldana, L. (1996). Treatment of maternal addiction to prevent child abuse and neglect. *Addictive Behaviors, 21*(6), 789-801.

Petras, D. D., Terry, T., Schiff, A., & Gleeson, J. P. (2000). *Kinship care practice project: Casework implications of research findings.* Chicago: University of Illinois at Chicago, Jane Addams College of Social Work, Jane Addams Center for Social Policy and Research.

Polansky, N. A. (1985). Determinants of loneliness among neglectful and other low-income mothers. *Journal of Social Service Research, 8*(3), 1-15.

Polansky, N. A., Chalmers, M. A., Buttenwieser, E. W., & Williams, D. P. (1981). *Damaged parents: An anatomy of child neglect*. Chicago: University of Chicago Press.

Polansky, N. A., Gaudin, J. M., & Kilpatrick, A. C. (1992). Family radicals. *Children and Youth Services Review, 14*, 19-26.

Radloff, L. S. (1977). The CES-D Scale: A self-report depression scale for research in the general population. *Applied Psychological Measurement, 1*, 385-401.

Rogers, C. R. (1961). *On becoming a person*. Boston: Houghton Mifflin.

Rosenzweig, H. D., & Kaplan, S. J. (1996). Child and adolescent neglect and emotional maltreatment. In S. J. Kaplan (Ed.), *Family violence: A clinical and legal guide* (pp. 37-72). Washington, DC: American Psychiatric Press.

Russell, D., Peplau, L. A., & Cutrona, C. E. (1980). The Revised UCLA Loneliness Scale: Concurrent and discriminant validity evidence. *Journal of Personality and Social Psychology, 39*, 472-480.

Sabatelli, R. M. (1984). The Marital Comparison Level Index: A measure for assessing outcomes relative to expectations. *Journal of Marriage and the Family, 46*, 651-662.

Straus, M. A., Hamby, S. L., Boney-McCoy, S., & Sugarman, D. B. (1996). The Revised Conflict Tactics Scale (CTS2): Development and preliminary psychometric data. *Journal of Family Issues, 17*, 283-316.

Tracy, E. M., & Pine, B. A. (2000). Child welfare education and training: Future trends and influences. *Child Welfare, 79*(1), 93-114.

Tryon, G. S. (1989). Study of variables related to client engagement using practicum trainees and experienced clinicians. *Psychotherapy, 26*, 54-60.

Urschel, H. C., Blair, J., & McLellan, A. T. (1991). *Addiction Severity Index* (5th ed.). Philadelphia: Treatment Research Institute.

U.S. Department of Health and Human Services, Children's Bureau. (1999). *Highlights of findings*. Retrieved from http://www.acf.dhhs.gov/programs/cb/publications/cm99/high.htr

Winefield, H., & Barlow, J. (1995). Client and worker satisfaction in a child protection agency. *Child Abuse and Neglect, 19*(8), 897-905.

Zuravin, S., McMillen, C., DePanfilis, D., & Risley-Curtiss, C. (1996). The intergenerational cycle of child maltreatment: Continuity versus discontinuity. *Journal of Interpersonal Violence, 11*, 315-334.

# Chapter 7

# Judges', Caseworkers', and Substance Abuse Counselors' Indicators of Family Reunification with Substance-Affected Parents

*Brad R. Karoll and John Poertner*

The decision to reunify children with their substance-affected parent is highly complex and requires a tremendous amount of work and change on the part of the affected parent. This exploratory study identified indicators for safe reunification of children placed in foster care due to parental substance abuse. Judges who hear juvenile cases, private agency child welfare caseworkers, and substance abuse counselors from a large midwestern state were surveyed using an instrument composed of a preliminary list of indicators identified through focus groups with these professional groups. Responses from 196 professionals who rated the importance of each item and subsequent factor analysis resulted in identification of 97 indicators. These indicators were grouped into the categories of motivation, recovery, competency, and reliability; social support; parenting skills; and legal issues. Implications of the findings for practice are discussed.

*Brad R. Karoll, MSW, LCSW, is Research Assistant, and John Poertner, DSW, is Professor and Interim Dean, University of Illinois at Urbana-Champaign, School of Social Work,Urbana, IL. This project was funded in part by the Illinois Department of Children and Family Services.*

Reunification of children in foster care with their birthfamilies has been a long-standing goal of child welfare (Maluccio, Fein, & Davis, 1994). Federal legislation strengthened this function by passing the Adoption Assistance and Child Welfare Act of 1980 (P.L. 96-272). This legislation was intended to remedy the problem of the growing number of children placed in foster care who remained there for extended periods of time. The Adoption and Safe Families Act of 1997 (ASFA) (P.L. 105-89) amended P.L. 96-272. Although it re-emphasized reasonable efforts, its greatest concern was the safety and health of the child (Hollingsworth, 2000; Larsen, 2000).

ASFA reduces the maximum allowable time for making permanency decisions to 12 months (Poertner & Garnier, 1998). ASFA also mandates states to automatically initiate proceedings to terminate parental rights for children who were in foster care for at least 15 of the most recent 22 months. Although there are exceptions included in the law, the degree to which these might be applied to substance-abusing parents is unknown.

Judges who hear juvenile cases, substance abuse counselors, and child welfare professionals suggest this renewed emphasis on moving children to a safe and permanent home in a short period of time causes difficulties for parents with substance use disorders (Semidei, Radel, & Nolan, 2001). It is often argued that the time required for a substance-affected parent to achieve stable recovery is longer than that allowed by this legislation.

To assist decisionmaking in this important area, the Miami Substance-Exposed Newborn Project sought to create standards for judicial decisionmaking involving parents with substance use disorders (Larsen, 2000). Input was solicited from lawyers, social workers, neonatologists, psychologists, drug and alcohol assessment specialists, and treatment providers, as well as available literature. Criteria identified as necessary for returning the child home included:

Parent has made striking progress toward recovery from drug-alcohol involvement and has verifiable plans to continue treatment; if co-morbidity was indicated, parent's psychiatric/psychological reports state that there are no serious mental impediments to parenting and parent has accepted recommended treatment; parent has consistently visited with child as permitted by the agency and treatment provider; parent has successfully completed appropriate parent skills training; a report on family strengths and/or mother-child bonding indicates that parent can offer adequate nurture for the child; and a recent home assessment indicates that unhealthy factors have been sufficiently reduced to render the home safe; and child's developmental status is not so vulnerable as to make a return home perilous. (Larsen, 2000, p. 3)

The study reported here sought to identify indicators that are more specific, which judges who hear juvenile cases, child welfare workers, and substance abuse treatment staff can use to determine when it is safe to reunify children with their recovering parents.

## Substance-Affected Families and Reunification

Child welfare caseworkers are often involved with parents with substance use disorders (U.S. General Accounting Office [GAO], 1994, 1998). An estimated 15% of women of childbearing age currently abuse substances (National Institute of Drug Abuse, 1995), and approximately 11% of children (8.3 million) are under the care of at least one drug- or alcohol-abusing parent (Wingfield, Klempner, & Pizzigati, 2000). Evidence from various national studies suggests 40% to 80% of all confirmed neglect and maltreatment cases involve substance abuse (Wingfield et al., 2000).

Working with substance-affected individuals can be difficult and frustrating. Recovery from addiction is an ongoing process with multiple pitfalls, setbacks, and formidable tasks (Brown & Lewis, 1999; M. Miller, Gorski, & Miller, 1992; GAO, 1998). The process of family reunification only adds to these tasks. Given the conflicting time clocks between child welfare policy and recovery, decisionmakers are confronted with the challenging task of identifying indicators for safe reunification or termination of parental rights.

The combination of overcoming addiction along with acquiring learning skills needed for effective parenting is difficult. The literature suggests that parents, predominantly women, face systemic problems, social attitudes, relapse, and their own individual histories as multiple challenges to their recovery and reunification.

## Systemic Problems

One systemic problem for recovery and successful reunification is the potential conflict arising from the focusing on the child or the parent as the client. From the child welfare caseworker's perspective, the child is the client. Substance abuse counselors treat the substance-affected individual as the client. These opposing viewpoints often conflict with respect to suggested interventions and perceptions of success.

Additional systemic barriers include the particular obstacles faced by African American parents. One study found that pregnant African American women and those of lower socioeconomic status were found to be more likely to be reported to authorities for substance abuse than were Euro-American women (Chasnoff, Landress, & Barrett, 1990). In addition, the addiction treatment system is not responsive to the needs of African American families (Child Welfare League of America, 1992; Rebach, 1992).

Poverty is another barrier to recovery and reunification (Dore & Doris, 1997; Freundlich, 1997). Women with substance use disorders tend to be financially or psychologically dependent on drug-using or abusive partners (W. Miller & Cervantes, 1997). Their inability to move to a safer environment is a threat to prolonged abstinence. Related barriers are insufficient medical insurance, support from family or friends, and openings available at treatment centers for financially destitute people. Inadequate or nonexistent transportation and childcare characterize additional obstacles to both treatment and long-term recovery.

## Social Attitudes

Numerous social attitudes inhibit women's recoveries and reunifications. Stigma prevents many women with substance use disorders from seeking treatment (Copeland, 1997; Royce & Scratchley, 1996). Ironically, professionals wishing to protect the image of female clients often make ineffective referrals, resulting in women's being denied access to appropriate care (Loneck, Garrett, & Banks, 1997). Society does not, however, release substance-affected mothers from the obligations of child-rearing or management of family affairs (Hanke & Faupel, 1993). Mothers with substance use disorders are considered unfit and, therefore, are subjected to societal disapproval for failing to meet the cultural standards of motherhood (Baker & Carson, 1999).

Social attitudes also suggest that substance abuse is a male disorder (Wilke, 1994). Most screening instruments were developed and validated with male samples (Karoll, 2000). In-depth assessment protocols also fail to investigate gender-specific issues relevant to women's life experiences and chemical use (Wilke, 1994). Finally, most treatment modalities focus on the needs of men (Goldberg, 1995), evidenced by the many treatment programs that are unwilling or unable to serve women who are pregnant (Blume, 1997).

## Relapse

Policymakers, judges, and child welfare caseworkers often do not understand the meaning and nature of relapse (Azzi-Lessing & Olsen, 1996). Women experience high recidivism rates, estimated to exceed 70% within the first year after treatment (Pagliaro & Pagliaro, 2000). Prochaska, DiClemente, and Norcross (1992) described relapse as a recycling process moving toward final, total behavioral change. Professionals in the field of substance abuse treatment recommend using relapse as a tool to help the substance abuser identify what triggers their substance use and from this develop new coping strategies (Katz & Ney, 1995).

Parenting requires a woman to take on additional demands that may force her to place greater focus on her children than on her own recovery, thus potentially contributing to relapse. Relapse challenges caseworkers to re-evaluate the case, and many may believe that the relapsing mother is hopeless and the child's safety is threatened. However, many women are capable of caring for their children during recovery despite an occasional relapse.

### Individual and Family Histories

Individual characteristics and personal histories present still other obstacles to recovery and reunification. A history of childhood sexual and physical abuse has been identified as a major cause of relapse (Kang, Magura, Laudet, & Whitney, 1999). Frequently, recovery involves the return of traumatic memories, and these feelings often lead to relapse.

Women with histories of childhood abuse often lack effective parenting and other life skills (Kang et al., 1999). They have learned parenting through their parents' models, who may not have had good parenting skills (Young, 1990). In addition, women from substance-affected families tend to develop caregiving behaviors in lieu of self-care. Family roles are overtly and covertly imposed and enforced (Black, 1981; Wegscheider-Cruse, 1989). The rules of "don't talk," "don't trust," and "don't feel" are the norm. Women experiencing this parental modeling often repeat these same behaviors.

## Method

Given the multiple challenges faced by mothers who have substance abuse problems and the added difficulties of trying to regain custody of their children, the recovery and reunification process is clearly complex. This study sought to identify specific indicators of safe reunification for children placed because of parental substance abuse. Five focus groups were conducted with judges who hear juvenile cases, child welfare caseworkers, and substance abuse counselors from a large midwestern state. Indicators of safe reunification were derived from a theme analysis of the groups' responses. The identified indicators were the basis of a questionnaire. Because there were such a large number of items (181), the items were categorized into 26 areas of functioning. The respondents were asked to rate the importance of each item from 0 (low) to 100 (high). The survey was mailed following the procedures suggested by Salant and Dillman (1994).

*Sample*

The population of interest was judges who hear juvenile cases, private agency child welfare caseworkers, and substance abuse counselors who work with child welfare clients in a large midwestern state. The administrative office of the state's courts provided a list of 78 judges throughout the state who hear juvenile cases. Because of the small number of judges, all were included in the study sample. Administrators from private child welfare agencies were asked to participate in the study and to provide lists of their current caseworkers. This resulted in identification of 420 caseworkers. Of the caseworkers, one-third ($n = 140$) were randomly selected for the study. Finally, the state's substance abuse certifications board provided a list of 3,500 currently certified counselors. Because this list did not include identification of those who worked with child welfare clients, it was anticipated that many would not respond or would return the questionnaire unanswered, so a larger random sample of 311 counselors was selected. Response rates ranged from 62% ($n = 48$) of the judges to 55% ($n = 74$) of caseworkers to 49% ($n = 113$) of the counselors.

# Results

The majority of judges who responded were male (68%), whereas the majority of caseworker and counselor respondents were female (73% and 71%, respectively). Overall, the ages of the judges (mean = 49, $SD$ = 5.02) and counselors were similar (mean = 46, $SD$ = 9.71). Caseworkers tended to be younger, with an average age of 33 years ($SD$ = 8.95).

The majority of judges identified themselves as Euro-American ($n$ = 32, 91.4%). Two (5.7%) were African American, and one (2.9%) was Hispanic. The ethnic distribution of caseworkers was 47% ($n$ = 27) Euro-American, 40% ($n$ = 23) African American, 5% ($n$ = 3) Asian American, 5% ($n$ = 3) Hispanic, and 2% ($n$ = 1) Native American. Of the counselors, 48% ($n$ = 45) were African American, 39%($n$ = 35) were Euro-American, 9% ($n$ = 8) were Hispanic, and 2% ($n$ = 2) were Native American.

Most judges (92%) reported having a doctoral degree. The majority of caseworkers possessed a baccalaureate degree (62%, $n$ = 38), whereas 34% ($n$ = 21) had a master's degree and 3% ($n$ = 2) had a doctorate. Most counselors reported having a master's degree (62%, $n$ = 46), with 24% ($n$ = 18) having a baccalaureate degree, 10% ($n$ = 7) having an associate's degree, and 4% ($n$ = 3) completing a doctoral program.

Finally, respondents were asked to indicate the length of time they had been at their current job. Overall, judges and counselors reported similar mean lengths of time, that is, seven years. Caseworkers reported considerably less time in their current job, with a mean of three years.

Because of the large number of items, factor analysis was conducted for data reduction purposes. Because it was not possible to conduct factor analysis on all the items at once, similar areas of functioning were combined. Within each category, only items with a factor loading of .70 or greater were retained. The categories were: (a) attitude, commitment, honesty, partner issues, self-esteem, and sincerity; (b) drug screens, mental health issues, recovery, relapse prevention, and substance abuse treatment; (c) housing, job, level of competency, reliability, self-care, and stress management; (d) caseworker, community resources, and connection; (e) interaction with children, interaction with temporary caregiver, and responsible parenting skills; and (f) court-related issues, other, and prior child welfare case issues.

Indicators in the areas of attitude, commitment, honesty, partner issues, self-esteem, and sincerity were largely concerned with motivation. The factor analysis identified eight factors, but two of these (Factors 5 and 7) had no item with a factor loading of .70 or greater and were omitted. Of the remaining six factors (see Table 1), Factor 1 concerned relational patterns of behavior. Factor 2 concerned a parent's attitude when initially engaging in services and a willingness to admit she or he currently was not prepared to parent. The third factor related to moving past the shame associated with a drug and prison history. The fourth was about the decision to stop using drugs and alcohol to regain custody of his or her children. The fifth involved moving past anger held toward the child welfare system. The final factor concerned willingness to ask for advice when confronted with not knowing what to do.

Combining the areas of drug screens, mental health issues, recovery, relapse prevention, and substance abuse treatment produced two factors that involved recovery (see Table 2). Factor 1 related to the process of recovering from substance use disorders, that is, initial treatment, early recovery, and relapse prevention. Factor 2 pertained to the drug screening process.

Respondents were also asked to identify the number of months of clean screens necessary for safe reunification. The median response was 8 months, but more than 30% of the respondents chose 6 months, and another 32% chose 12 months. When asked about the number of months of clean drug screens for both the client and a partner before reunification, a higher percentage of respondents chose 12 months (37%), 27% chose 6 months, and the median was 9 months. Respondents identified the median number of consecutive clean drug screens to be 12.

Table 3 displays the four factors that emerged from combining the areas of housing, job, level of competency, reliability, self-

## TABLE 1
**Motivation Items and Factor Loadings**

| *Factor/Items* | *Factor Loadings*[a] |
|---|---|
| *Factor 1* | |
| She leaves a substance-using partner to maintain recovery rather than relapsing. | .881 |
| She breaks away from an abusive relationship to maintain recovery rather than relapsing. | .869 |
| Her partner (paramour) is in treatment for domestic violence (if necessary). | .822 |
| She stands up for her children against her partner. | .809 |
| Her partner (paramour) is in treatment or otherwise following the care plan if required. | .764 |
| She adopts the attitude that her partner must participate in services or leave. | .758 |
| She stands up for herself against her partner. | .754 |
| They attend family therapy. | .746 |
| She demonstrates motivation to stay clean. | .710 |
| *Factor 2* | |
| When she started services, she said, "I can't be a mother right now." | .763 |
| When she started services she turned her children over to [the Department of Child and Family Services], showing readiness to work on herself. | .756 |
| When she started services, she said, "I need time out" (from the children). | .719 |
| *Factor 3* | |
| She no longer expresses shame talking about her prison time history. | .715 |
| She no longer expresses shame talking about her drug use history. | .712 |
| *Factor 4* | |
| She decided to stop using to get her children back. | .742 |
| *Factor 6* | |
| She no longer blames the system for her problems. | .829 |
| She has gotten past her anger towards the agencies that forced her into treatment. | .812 |
| *Factor 8* | |
| She asks for advice when she does not know what to do. | .717 |

Note: Factors 5 and 7 were not significant.
a. From the Rotated Component Matrix.

care, and stress management. Competency and reliability was the central theme. The first factor concerned using newly acquired, healthier coping skills. The second related to employment. The third had to do with behavioral reliability (i.e., not making excuses for or lying about one's behaviors). The final factor contained a single item about supportive family members living in close proximity.

When the areas of caseworker, community resources, and connection were combined, three factors with the theme of social support emerged (see Table 4). The first involved community support and resources. The second had to do with the client's relationship with the caseworker. The final factor contained a single item about the client's association with a church.

Table 5 presents the three parenting factors that were identified by combining the areas of interaction with children, interaction with temporary caregiver, and responsible parenting skills. The first factor had to do with responsible parenting skills, the second with interaction with their children, and the third with interaction with temporary caregivers.

Last, combining the areas of court-related issues, other issues, and prior child welfare case issues produced only one factor (see Table 6). This factor was about the legal aspects of child loss and reunification prospects.

## Discussion

This study has several limitations. The large number of items in this survey instrument required a fair amount of time and commitment to complete. It is possible that some respondents lost interest and did not consider each item carefully. The response rates were good, but the opinions of nonresponders are unknown. In addition, this study was conducted in one large midwestern state, which limited the ability to generalize the findings.

As might be expected due to the greater number of women in the field of social work and child welfare, more female than male

## TABLE 2

**Recovery Items and Factor Loadings**

| Factor/Items | Factor Loadings[a] |
|---|---|
| *Factor 1* | |
| She recognizes postacute withdrawal symptoms and states when they are occurring. | .866 |
| She is strong enough (prepared) to say, "Wait...I know what's happening here." | .849 |
| She has learned her relapse pattern from her own history. | .847 |
| She states it is about learning a more effective way of meeting a need. | .815 |
| She develops new friendships. | .804 |
| She...lets someone know she is in trouble. | .768 |
| She has a sponsor. | .751 |
| She gives constructive feedback in group therapy by applying situations to her own experiences. | .747 |
| She shares in group therapy without much prompting. | .742 |
| She works through new problems as they arise in substance abuse treatment. | .725 |
| She identifies her relapse triggers. | .718 |
| She takes responsibility for her recovery by going to extra meetings when needed. | .715 |
| She knows how to socialize without drugs or alcohol. | .714 |
| She knows how to seek intimacy without drugs or alcohol. | .707 |
| She goes to substance abuse counseling regularly. | .704 |
| *Factor 2* | |
| She has a significant period of time with clean drug screens. | .849 |
| She has given a number of consecutively clean drug screens. | .846 |
| She does not make excuses for missed drug screens. | .805 |
| Both she and her partner had clean urine drug screens. | .784 |
| She ultimately leaves drugs behind her. | .745 |
| She stays in substance abuse treatment through completion. | .738 |
| She never tries to get out of a drug screen. | .737 |

a. From the Rotated Component Matrix.

caseworkers responded to this survey. Female counselors also greatly outnumbered males who responded, similar to the results of a study by Harkness and Cotrell (1997). This response might be considered unusual because it has been suggested (Lott, 1989) that far more men than women, many of whom are in recovery,

**TABLE 3**

**Competency and Reliability Items and Factor Loadings**

| Factor/Items | Factor Loadings[a] |
|---|---|
| *Factor 1* | |
| She attends services she is referred to. | .759 |
| She completes treatment goals successfully. | .754 |
| She applies newly acquired coping skills learned in treatment to deal with stressors. | .748 |
| She exhibits positive problem solving skills without chemicals, frustration, or anger. | .728 |
| She exhibits newly acquired coping skills in her life. | .725 |
| She is taking care of her medical problems. | .709 |
| *Factor 2* | |
| She looks for work if unemployed. | .765 |
| She found a job. | .762 |
| She states her personal needs. | .750 |
| She starts working at the new job. | .739 |
| She asks for what she wants without being demanding. | .712 |
| She successfully completes job training. | .703 |
| She demonstrates improvement from program entry by holding a job and making a living. | .700 |
| *Factor 3* | |
| She does not make excuses for missing appointments. | .798 |
| She does not maker excuses for her behaviors. | .792 |
| She does not lie about her behavior. | .713 |
| *Factor 4* | |
| She has a supportive living environment with helpful relatives near by. | .712 |

a. From the Rotated Component Matrix.

become substance abuse counselors. Whether this response rate occurred because of a change in the gender distribution in the field of substance abuse or because women were more likely to participate in this study is unknown. The fact that more African American than Euro-American counselors responded was unexpected because most treatment programs are reportedly primarily managed and staffed by Euro-Americans. Consequently, many African Americans avoid getting help in traditional facilities (Rebach, 1992). Finally, the much lower average length of time

## TABLE 4
### Social Support Items and Factor Loadings

| Factor/Items | Factor Loadings[a] |
|---|---|
| *Factor 1* | |
| She builds and maintains positive personal relationships. | .824 |
| She has a community support system. | .816 |
| She engages agencies to help her with the children's needs and services. | .778 |
| She seeks out community resources. | .758 |
| She participates in the support system of women through relatives, friends, and church. | .748 |
| She has a support system of women. | .747 |
| She engages several community agencies to help her. | .716 |
| *Factor 2* | |
| She is cooperative with the caseworker. | .838 |
| She is open with the caseworker during unannounced visits. | .828 |
| She has a positive relationship with her caseworker and substance abuse counselor. | .808 |
| She maintains regular contact with the caseworker. | .776 |
| *Factor 3* | |
| She associates with a church. | .812 |

a. From the Rotated Component Matrix.

caseworkers reported working at their current job compared with responding judges and substance abuse counselors most likely reflects a high turnover rate in these agencies.

The purpose of this exploratory study was to identify indicators that judges who hear juvenile cases, child welfare caseworkers, and substance abuse counselors use to aid in the reunification decisionmaking process. From a preliminary list of 181 items generated by five focus groups, factor analysis was used to reduce the number of indicators to 97. This large number indicates the complexity of recovery and the reunification decisionmaking process. It also illustrates the many areas of functioning that a recovering woman must successfully address as well as the

## TABLE 5
**Parenting Items and Factor Loadings**

| Factor/Items | Factor Loadings[a] |
|---|---|
| *Factor 1* | |
| She makes arrangements for medical care for her children. | .879 |
| She makes sure physicals are done. | .868 |
| She makes sure dental appointments are made and kept. | .864 |
| She makes sure immunizations are up to date. | .862 |
| She makes sure the children are regularly going to school. | .858 |
| She attends all necessary appointments for the children. | .858 |
| She demonstrates ability to care for a child's special needs (if necessary). | .809 |
| She participates in school programs with and for the children. | .797 |
| She provides food, clothing, shelter, and medical exams for the children. | .776 |
| She plans for the children's future so they will be contributing members of society. | .747 |
| *Factor 2* | |
| She wants to make contact with the children. | .853 |
| She calls asking about the children. | .820 |
| She talks with the children. | .795 |
| She encourages the children. | .756 |
| The children respond positively to her. | .754 |
| She visits her children regularly and frequently. | .721 |
| The children want to be with her. | .717 |
| She honestly becomes interested in getting her children back. | .706 |
| *Factor 3* | |
| She takes suggestions from the parenting caregivers. | .782 |
| She goes to children's doctors' appointments with the temporary caregiver. | .781 |
| Temporary caregivers give positive feedback regarding reunification prospects. | .757 |

a. From the Rotated Component Matrix.

amount of knowledge the professional groups need to gather evidence of the woman's progress. Although these results have not been empirically linked to outcomes for victims of substance abuse or their children, they can be viewed as valuable practice wisdom to be used in further studies.

**TABLE 6**
**Legal Items and Factor Loadings**

| *Factor/Items* | *Factor Loadings*[a] |
|---|---|
| Factor 1 | |
| She addressed the issues and concerns that brought her other children into the system. | .847 |
| She asks things of the court and caseworker to better understand what is needed. | .840 |
| She makes reasonable progress versus reasonable efforts. | .827 |
| She is cooperative with the courts. | .826 |
| Service providers identify preventative chronic problems in mental health; emotional, physical, and dependency status; and domestic violence. | .823 |
| Service providers make every reasonable effort to gather all pertinent information for the judge to be able to make an informed decision. | .809 |
| She asks what her rights are. | .781 |

a. From the Rotated Component Matrix.

The central theme of motivation emerged when attitude, commitment, honesty, partner issues, self-esteem, and sincerity were combined. The resulting items were predominantly experiential and cognitive rather than reflecting behavioral changes. One factor had to do with both attitudinal and relational patterns of behavior.

The theme of recovery emerged when drug screens, mental health issues, recovery, relapse prevention, and substance abuse treatment were combined. The indicators were predominantly couched in behavioral changes, expanding on Larsen's (2000) reported criteria of "made striking progress towards recovery" (p. 3). The theme of competency and reliability emerged when housing, job, level of competency, reliability, self-care, and stress management were combined. As with the recovery theme, the items were predominantly behavioral in nature.

The combination of caseworker, community, and connections produced a theme of social support that was largely behavioral. The theme of parenting emerged when interaction with children, interaction with temporary caregiver, and responsible parenting skills were combined. Finally, combining court issues and prior child welfare case issues resulted in a central legal theme. It could be argued that these items expand on the criteria offered by Larsen (2000).

The results of this study suggest a need to identify what constitutes a significant number of consecutive months with clean drug screens of the parent, partner, or both and what is a sufficient number of consecutive clean drug screens. Of the respondents, one-half stated that eight months with clean screens were sufficient. These results were similar for both the individual parent as well as the parent-partner combination (median = 9 months). Of the respondents, one-half considered 12 months to be a sufficient number of clean drug screens. The optimal solution may be to randomly collect drug screens on a monthly basis with the goal of at least 12 consecutive clean screens.

## Implications

Research is needed to identify the most important factors that lead to positive outcomes for children in foster care. Replication of this study's findings might further reduce the number of indicators for safe reunification. In addition, comparisons between judges, caseworkers, and treatment professionals would be useful. The ultimate test of reunification indicators is research that relates them to actual reunification of children and their parents.

Greater dissemination of information about the number and complexity of the obstacles facing those with substance use disorders who lost custody of their children is required. For example, it is recommended that judges and child welfare workers be provided information about the intricacies of substance abuse, treatment, and recovery. Both groups need a greater understanding of this population's need to grow experientially and cognitively beyond demonstrating behavioral growth. This understanding includes a heightened awareness of the meaning of relapse as a normal cyclic phase of human intentional change (Prochaska et al., 1992). For their part, substance abuse treatment professionals need to understand the roles of judges and child welfare workers in the treatment and reunification process.

More important, increased communication and interaction between these professional groups are needed to identify and discuss specific characteristics indicative of a parent's readiness to reunify. One possible venue to accomplish this is through direct interaction. For instance, judges, caseworkers, and counselors may be invited to participate in joint educational and training programs, in which all groups would be responsible for presentations related to their needs, expectations, and experiences with this population.

## Conclusion

The increased recognition of parents with substance use disorders in the child welfare system has placed greater strain on an already over-burdened system. Policy changes that have shortened the time span during which this population has to demonstrate reasonable progress have affected the reunification process. The lack of education and expertise of the expectations and needs of the different professional groups involved with this population has also hindered the process. To serve this population more effectively in the time allotted, the judicial system, child welfare agencies, and substance abuse treatment agencies need to develop mechanisms to increase the contact and information shared among organizations. ◆

## References

Adoption and Safe Families Act, P.L. No. 105-89, 111 Stat. 2115 (1997).

Adoption Assistance and Child Welfare Act, P.L. 96-272, 94 Stat. 500 (1980).

Azzi-Lessing, L., & Olsen, L. J. (1996). Substance abuse-affected families in the child welfare system: New challenges, new alliances. *Social Work, 41*(1), 15–23.

Baker, P. L., & Carson, A. (1999). "I take care of my kids": Mothering practices of substance-abusing women. *Gender & Society, 13*(3), 347–363.

Black, C. (1981). *It will never happen to me!* New York: Ballentine.

Blume, S. B. (1997). Women and alcohol: Issues in social policy. In R. W. Wilsnack & S. C. Wilsnack (Eds.), *Gender and alcohol. Individual and social perspectives* (pp. 462–489). New Brunswick, NJ: Rutgers Center of Alcohol Studies.

Brown, S., & Lewis, V. (1999). *The alcoholic family in recovery. A developmental model.* New York: Guilford.

Chasnoff, I. J., Landress, H. J., & Barrett, M. E. (1990). The prevalence of illicit drug or alcohol use during pregnancy and discrepancies in mandatory reporting. *New England Journal of Medicine, 322*(17), 1202–1206.

Child Welfare League of America, North American Commission on Chemical Dependency and Child Welfare. (1992). *Children at the front: A different view of the war on alcohol and drugs.* Washington, DC: Author.

Copeland, J. (1997). A qualitative study of barriers to formal treatment among women who self-managed change in addictive behaviours. *Journal of Substance Abuse Treatment, 14*(2), 183–190.

Dore, M. M., & Doris, J. M. (1997). Preventing child placement in substance-abusing families: Research-informed practice. *Child Welfare, 72*(4), 407–426.

Freundlich, M. (1997). The future of adoption for children in foster care: Demographics in a changing socio-political environment. *Journal of Children & Poverty, 3*(2), 33–61.

Goldberg, M. E. (1995). Substance-abusing women. False stereotypes and real needs. *Social Work, 40*(6), 789–798.

Hanke, P. J., & Faupel, C. E. (1993). Women opiate users' perceptions of treatment services in New York City. *Journal of Substance Abuse Treatment, 10*, 513–522.

Harkness, D., & Cotrell, G. (1997). The social construction of co-dependency in the treatment of substance abuse. *Journal of Substance Abuse Treatment, 14*(5), 473–479.

Hollingsworth, L. D. (2000). Adoption policy in the United States: A word of caution. *Social Work, 45*(2), 183-186.

Kang, S.-Y., Magura, S., Laudet, A., & Whitney, S. (1999). Adverse effect of child abuse victimization among substance-abusing women in treatment. *Journal of Interpersonal Violence, 14*(6), 657–670.

Karoll, B. R. (2000). *A review of current alcoholism screening instruments and their appropriateness for women*. Manuscript submitted for publication.

Katz, R. S., & Ney, N. H. (1995). Preventing relapse. In S. Brown & I. D. Yalom (Eds.), *Treating alcoholism* (pp. 231–276). San Francisco: Jossey-Bass.

Larsen, J. (2000). Court strategies under ASFA to help substance-using families recover. *Juvenile and Family Court Journal, 51*(1), 1–8.

Loneck, B., Garrett, J., & Banks, S. M. (1997). Engaging and retaining women in outpatient alcohol and other drug treatment: The effect of referral intensity. *Health & Social Work, 22*(1), 38–46.

Lott, S. (1989). *Illinois department of alcoholism and substance abuse counselor training programs: An impact study*. Unpublished doctoral dissertation, Illinois State University, Normal.

Maluccio, A. N., Fein, E., & Davis, I. P. (1994). Family reunification: Research, findings, and directions. *Child Welfare, 73*(5), 489–504.

Miller, M., Gorski, T. T., & Miller, D. K. (1992). *Learning to live again. A guide for recovery from chemical dependency* (Rev. ed.). Independence, MO: Herald House/Independence Press.

Miller, W. R., & Cervantes, E. A. (1997). Gender and patterns of alcohol problems: Pretreatment responses of women and men to the Comprehensive Drinker Profile. *Journal of Clinical Psychology, 53*(3), 263–277.

National Institute of Drug Abuse. (1995). *The national household survey of drug abuse: Trends in substance use, 1979-1994*. Rockville, MD: U.S. Department of Health and Human Services.

Pagliaro, A. M., & Pagliaro, L. A. (2000). *Substance use among women. A reference and resource guide*. Philadelphia: Brunner/Mazel.

Poertner, J., & Garnier, P. (1998). *Outcomes report 1999*. Urbana: University of Illinois, Urbana-Champaign, School of Social Work, Children and Family Research Center.

Prochaska, J. O., DiClemente, C. C., & Norcross, J. C. (1992). In search of how people change. Applications to addictive behaviors. *American Psychologist, 47*(9), 1102–1114.

Rebach, H. (1992). Alcohol and drug use among American minorities. *Drugs & Society, 6*(1/2), 23–57.

Royce, J. E., & Scratchley, D. (1996). *Alcoholism and other drug problems*. New York: Free Press.

Salant, P., & Dillman, D. A. (1994). *How to conduct your own survey*. New York: John Wiley & Sons.

Semidei, J., Radel, L. F., & Nolan, C. (2001). Substance abuse and child welfare: Clear linkages and promising responses. *Child Welfare, 80*(2), 109–127.

U.S. General Accounting Office. (1994). *Foster care: Parental drug abuse has alarming impact on young children* [Report to the Chairman, Subcommittee on Human Resources, Committee on Ways and Means, House of Representatives]. Washington, DC: U.S. Government Printing Office.

U.S. General Accounting Office. (1998). *Foster care. Agencies face challenges securing stable homes for children of substance abusers* (GAO/HEHS-98-182). Washington, DC: Author.

Wegscheider-Cruse, S. (1989). *Another chance. Hope and health for the alcoholic family* (2nd ed.). Palo Alto, CA: Science and Behavior Books.

Wilke, D. (1994). Women and alcoholism. How a male-as-norm bias affects research, assessment, and treatment. *Health & Social Work, 19*(1), 29–35.

Wingfield, K., Klempner, T., & Pizzigati, K. (2000). Building bridges: Child protection/ alcohol and drug partnership. *Issues of Substance, 5*(2), 5, 13, 15.

Young, E. B. (1990). The role of incest issues in relapse. *Journal of Psychoactive Drugs, 22*(2), 249–258.

# Chapter 8

# Program Evaluation of the CREST Project: Empirical Support for Kinship Care as an Effective Approach to Permanency Planning

*Catherine A. Hawkins and Tammy Bland*

The number of children, especially from ethnic minority groups, in substitute care is growing rapidly even as the number of foster care homes is steadily decreasing. Kinship care has quickly become the permanency planning option of choice. This article describes a model kinship care project and the results of an extensive program evaluation. Results show that the project enhances functioning of relative caregivers and reduces the cost of care. Implications for contemporary permanency planning are presented.

*Catherine A. Hawkins, PhD, MSSW, is Associate Professor, School of Social Work, Southwest Texas State University, San Marcos, TX. Tammy Bland, LMSW, MSW, is Special Education Counselor, Hays Consolidated Independent School District, Buda, TX.*

Kinship care (the placement of children who are in state custody with their relatives) is a well-established, widely recognized, and generally accepted practice in child welfare. Kinship care emerged from a longstanding tradition of informal arrangements among kinship networks and reflects changing standards in the child welfare and legal systems (Dubowitz, 1994; Gleeson & Craig, 1994; Wilhelmus, 1998). Hegar and Scannapieco (1995) described the evolution of kinship care as one of family duty to family policy. According to Gleeson (1995), the movement toward kinship care represents a shift from viewing kinship care as an alternative to the child welfare system to a service encouraged and funded by that system.

Kinship care differs fundamentally from foster care. Kinship care has been described as a form of family preservation that maintains children in the extended family network (Berrick, Barth, & Needell, 1994; Cimmarusti, 1992). It is the fastest growing type of substitute care funded by child welfare, exceeding foster care in some states, and the number of kinship care placements is expected to continue to rise rapidly (Gleeson, 1995; Scannapieco & Jackson, 1996). Kinship care will become increasingly prevalent, because each year more children enter than exit government-supported care, whereas the number of foster care homes steadily declines (Barth, Courtney, Berrick, & Albert, 1994).

Despite the recognized advantages of kinship care and its subsequent growth, debate occurs over the nature and funding of these placements. Gleeson and Craig (1994) found evidence of inconsistent policies and services nationwide. Many states require care by relatives to be the first placement option considered, yet few states provide the same level of services to kinship families that they do to foster families. Kinship care policy has special implications for ethnic minority families, both because they are overrepresented in the child welfare system and because a larger proportion of ethnic minority children are placed in kinship care than in foster care (Berrick et al., 1994; Inglehart, 1994; Hornby, Zeller, & Karraker, 1996).

The complex needs of kinship caregivers present a unique set of challenges. Relatives are often unprepared for the demands of caring for their relatives' children, many of whom experience behavioral and psychosocial problems. Accepting these children into their homes can strain the caregivers' resources, both emotionally and financially. Relatives who are caregivers may be unprepared for the difficulties encountered as they confront the "larger system" of child protective services (CPS), schools, and the court. The stressors of caring for a relative's child can be particularly acute for elderly caregivers who confront health and financial problems of their own (Burton, 1992; Gleeson, O'Donnell, & Bonecutter, 1997). Nevertheless, these challenges are offset—and frequently overcome—by the relatives' commitment to care for these children and by their determination to succeed.

Kinship care also presents a unique set of challenges to CPS. Studies have found that children in kinship care receive fewer services than do children in foster care with nonrelatives (Gleeson, 1995). In one study, kinship caregivers reported overall satisfaction with their caseworker (CW), yet more than one-third stated that they wanted a higher level of contact (Scannapieco, Hegar, & McAlpine, 1997). Gebel (1996) also found that kinship caregivers had significantly lower income levels than foster parents and received lower levels of CW contact, yet they showed more positive perceptions about the children placed in their homes. Berrick et al. (1994) found some evidence that kinship providers are not adequately screened by child welfare agencies. Studies of the degree of risk for kinship placements and the level of supervision required to maintain them are inconclusive (Gebel, 1996; Rittner, 1995).

Principles of practice and guidelines specific to kinship care are needed. Currently, child welfare practice models are based on foster care and adoption services, although newer models are emerging (Berrick, Needell, & Barth, 1995; Bonecutter & Gleeson, 1997; Gleeson et al., 1997; Wilhelmus, 1998). Noting the mixed findings on risk factors in kinship care, Gebel (1996) posited the need for preservice training for CWs as well as CW support for kinship caregivers that is equal to support for foster caregivers. Given the high proportion of ethnic minority children in kinship care, these models also must be culturally sensitive and build on the inherent strengths of extended families (Scannapieco & Hegar, 1995).

Finally, more research on kinship care is needed. A survey of research priorities emphasized the following: effects on children, effects on caregivers, services to children and kinship families, and permanency planning (Dubowitz, 1994). The growing literature is limited, however, by methodological constraints resulting from the inability to conduct experimental or even quasiexperimental studies on these placements (Berrick & Barth, 1994; Goerge, Wulczyn, & Fanshel, 1994). Dubowitz (1994) has acknowledged the value of qualitative research in studying what factors influence the success of these placements.

## Program Description

The Comprehensive Relative Enhancement Support and Training Project (CREST), a three-year kinship care demonstration project, was located in Bexar County (San Antonio), Texas. This major urban center has a diverse population with a Mexican-American majority. In Texas, relatives who are caregivers are not reimbursed, except in the rare instance that they are either licensed foster parents or meet stringent criteria for a very limited one-time payment.

Furthermore, relatives do not receive any formal training or systematic social support. Before CREST, the case management needs of caregiving relatives were supposed to be addressed by the child's CW, who was often unavailable because of large caseloads and high turnover. CREST was established specifically to address the needs of these relatives and therefore strengthen these placements. The program goal of CREST was to "support and promote safety, permanency, and the well-being of children through care by relatives."

The CREST unit consisted of four kinship workers (KWs) and one supervisor. These staff were transferred from other units, and all KWs had many years of CPS experience. The supervisor position was provided by the agency. Two of the KWs were Caucasian, and two were Hispanic and bilingual in Spanish and English. CREST was first implemented from October 1997 through September 2000. (The program was continued at the end of the grant by Bexar County CPS.) The demonstration project was funded through the U.S. Department of Health and Human Services with a total budget of $600,000 ($200,000 for each of three years).

CREST provided three primary services to relative caregivers: formal group training, individualized case management, and limited financial assistance. The eight-week training, offered every quarter, consisted of a curriculum-based format and social support. Individualized case management was provided by the KWs who maintained direct contact with the relative caregivers. Case management—provided through telephone calls, home visits, and attendance at meetings (court, school, etc.)—included services such as ongoing emotional support, referrals, securing social services, and crisis management. As a part of case management, the KWs also coordinated the placement with the CWs. Financial assistance was limited to small stipends on an "as needed" basis to facilitate a placement. This service included, for example, medical care, utility assistance, household items, transportation, or child care. In addition, very limited in-kind assistance was available from local community agencies.

## Method

Both quantitative and qualitative data were collected by using multiple methods from multiple sources. The triangulation of data sources controlled for potential bias by respondents.

*Participants*

An available-subjects sample was used, consisting of relative caregivers, child CWs, KWs, and CW supervisors. Every relative entering the CREST program was asked to participate. A total of 416 relatives received CREST services in the three years of the project. Of these, 112 were eliminated from the evaluation, primarily because a child was never placed in the home or data on the case were completely missing. Thus, the sample size for the three-year evaluation consisted of 304 relatives providing care to 579 children (73% of the total number of families served). The cumulative number of relatives enrolled in CREST and included in the evaluation in Year 1 was 44 relatives caring for 106 children; in Year 2, 124 relatives caring for 236 children; and in Year 3, 136 relatives caring for 237 children. Families who carried over from one year to the next were counted only once to avoid duplication. Demographic data were reported on 247 of the 304 relatives studied (81%). Table 1 gives descriptive data from the sample of relatives. For relatives, one adult per household was designated as the primary provider; if spouses were present, the wife was so designated. This had the effect of inflating the gender and relationship to child category, but the distinction was necessary to avoid duplication in the sample size. In addition, over the three-year period, 142 CWs had responsibility for at least one case in which a child was placed in a relative's home. All these CWs were asked to participate in the evaluation. Finally, all four KWs provided substantial data.

*Procedures*

Data from relative caregivers were gathered by telephone interview regarding the placement, the child, and CREST services provided to them. At least three contact attempts were made. Relative interviews varied in length from 10 to 30 minutes. Feedback on the training groups was collected from relative participants at the end of each eight-week cycle. The KWs provided a record of ongoing CREST activities, responded to a written questionnaire on each placement and each child, and provided data for a cost-effectiveness analysis. The CWs responded to a written questionnaire pertaining to each placement and each child as well as CREST services provided both to the relative and to the CW. Follow-up telephone calls were made to increase the response rate. Completed questionnaires for the KWs and CWs were mailed directly to the evaluator. Each CW completed a referral form to indicate whether a placement was "marginal." Focus groups, conducted each year, included different stakeholders (relatives who were caregivers, child CW, and CW supervisors). Demographic information on relatives was collected through available CPS records provided by the KW; however, data were often missing or incomplete. The evaluator met regularly with the CREST staff to collect data as well as to ascertain the progress of the project.

*Measures*

**Formative (Process) Measures.** The nature and frequency of CREST activities were reported monthly on case management forms completed by the KWs. This form included data on cases opened, cases closed, and case management services provided. The six-item training group evaluation form contained open-ended questions asking participants to rate the group and to make suggestions for improvement. The eight-item schedule for interviews of relatives contained four open-ended questions asking about the placement, effectiveness of CREST services, and suggestions for improvement. The six-item KW questionnaire contained three open-ended questions about the effectiveness of CREST and about ideas for improving services. The seven-item CW questionnaire contained three open-ended questions about the effectiveness of services to the relative, services to the CW, and suggestions for improving the program.

**Summative (Outcome) Measures.** The project had six outcome measures: (1) number of placements opened; (2) number of placements disrupted, (3) number of placements closed, (4) child well-being, (5) customer satisfaction, and (6) cost-effectiveness.

### TABLE 1

**Characteristics of Relatives Served by the Comprehensive Relative Enhancement Support and Training Project (*N* = 247)**

|  | *Frequency* | *%* |
|---|---|---|
| *Gender* | | |
| Male | 32 | 13 |
| Female | 215 | 87 |
| *Marital Status* | | |
| Married | 135 | 54.70 |
| Single | 56 | 22.70 |
| Divorced | 35 | 14.10 |
| Widowed | 15 | 6.10 |
| Unreported | 6 | 2.40 |
| *Age* | | |
| <20 | 2 | 0.80 |
| 20-29 | 19 | 7.70 |
| 30-39 | 60 | 24.30 |
| 40-49 | 72 | 29.20 |
| 50-59 | 47 | 19.00 |
| 60-69 | 25 | 10.10 |
| 70-79 | 9 | 3.60 |
| 80-89 | 1 | 0.40 |
| Unreported | 12 | 4.90 |
| Median age = 45 | | |
| *Relationship to Child* | | |
| Great-grandparent | 13 | 5.30 |
| Grandmother | 92 | 37.30 |
| Grandfather | 18 | 7.30 |
| Great-aunt | 19 | 7.70 |
| Great-uncle | 2 | 0.80 |
| Aunt | 67 | 27.10 |
| Uncle | 8 | 3.20 |
| Cousin | 7 | 2.80 |
| Sibling | 7 | 2.80 |
| Stepmother | 1 | 0.40 |
| Unreported | 13 | 5.30 |
| *Education Level* | | |
| No formal | 2 | 1.00 |
| Grades 1–5 | 6 | 2.90 |
| Grades 6–8 | 25 | 12.30 |
| Grades 9–12 | 67 | 33.00 |
| General equivalency diploma | 15 | 7.40 |
| Vocational | 12 | 5.90 |
| Some college | 26 | 12.80 |
| Bachelors | 17 | 8.40 |
| Graduate | 3 | 1.50 |
| Unreported | 30 | 14.80 |

**TABLE 1 (CONTINUED)**
**Characteristics of Relatives Served by the Comprehensive Relative Enhancement Support and Training Project (N = 247)**

|  | Frequency | % |
|---|---|---|
| *Yearly Income* |  |  |
| <$10,000 | 30 | 12.20 |
| $10,000-19,999 | 93 | 37.70 |
| $20,000-29,999 | 34 | 13.80 |
| $30,000-39,999 | 27 | 10.90 |
| $40,000-49,999 | 21 | 8.50 |
| $50,000-59,999 | 6 | 2.40 |
| $60,000-69,999 | 9 | 3.60 |
| $70,000-79,999 | 1 | 0.40 |
| $80,000-89,999 | 0 | 0 |
| $90,000-99,999 | 0 | 0 |
| >$100,000 | 1 | 0.40 |
| Unreported | 25 | 10.10 |
| Median income = $17,688.00 |  |  |

**Number of Placements.** A comparison of the number of relative placements in Bexar County before and after CREST was not possible because these statistics were not available from CPS. The number of CREST placements was provided, however, on the KW case management forms. In addition, beginning in Year 2, a CW referral form was developed. This form specified whether a placement was marginal and contained a 10-item checklist indicating the reason (e.g., child behavior problems, large sibling group, insufficient resources, health problems of caregiver).

**Number of Placement Disruptions.** A comparison of placement disruptions in Bexar County before and after CREST was not possible because these statistics were not available from CPS. However, a qualitative item in the relative interview schedule, KW questionnaire, and CW questionnaire asked whether CREST had a substantial effect on maintaining the placement. In addition, the KWs reported disruptions on a form that gave the reason for removal.

**Number of Cases Closed.** The number of CREST closures was provided on KW case management forms. A closing summary form, to be completed by the KW, indicated the permanency plan and the reason for closure of each placement. The interview of the relative contained one item asking how CREST had helped with the placement. The CW questionnaire contained one item asking how CREST facilitated permanency for each child on the CW's caseload who was placed in the care of a relative. The KW questionnaire had one item asking how CREST facilitated permanency for each child.

**Child Well-Being.** This outcome was defined by CPS as "a child's adequate daily functioning, socially, educationally, and developmentally." Data were collected through relative interviews, CW questionnaires, and KW questionnaires. Respondents were asked to rate the functioning of each child placed in the home, using a scale of 1 (*low*) to 10 (*high*), and to provide a brief explanation of the rating. Three anchors for the scale were provided: 1 = *not able to remain in the home*, 5 = *ongoing problems but trying to maintain placement*, and 10 = *no problems*.

**Customer Satisfaction.** Data were collected from the two types of recipients of CREST services. First, relatives were asked in their interview to rate their overall level of satisfaction with CREST services, using a scale of 1 (*totally dissatisfied*) to 10 (*totally satisfied*) and to provide a brief explanation for their rating. Second, on their questionnaire, CWs were asked to give their level of satisfaction, using the same scale, and to provide a brief explanation. They were asked to rate both CREST services provided to relative caregivers, as well as CREST services provided to them as a CW.

**Cost-Effectiveness.** Because Texas does not provide regular financial assistance to relatives who are caregivers, the cost of the CREST Project was compared to what it would have cost the state to provide for these children if they had been placed in reimbursed foster care. For each year, a list was compiled of all children placed in homes that received CREST services. The total number of days that a child was placed was counted (or to the end of the project for those cases that remained open when the grant expired). The CPS level of care (LOC) was gathered for each child, based on an assessment of the child's level of functioning and the subsequent LOC required to maintain the child's safety and well-being. The LOC ranged from 1 (*highest functioning child requiring the least restrictive environment*) to 6 (*lowest functioning child requiring the most restrictive environment*). A child in each LOC is allocated a set amount of funding from CPS per day. In 2000, this funding ranged from $17 (foster home placement) to $200 (24-hour residential care). The equivalent cost to provide foster care was calculated on the basis of the daily reimbursement rate for the LOC assigned to each child multiplied by the number of days the child was placed in the care of a relative and CREST provided services.

## Findings and Discussion

### *Formative (Process) Measures*

**KW Activities.** KW caseloads steadily grew throughout the three years of the project, from 49 families served per month at the onset to 132 families at the end. This difference represented a net gain of 83 families or a 169% increase. At the onset, the average number of families served per KW ($n = 3$) was 19 per month; at the end, the average number served per KW ($n = 4$) was 30 per month. The average caseload increased 63%. This constituted sizeable growth, especially given that this percentage includes an additional KW in Year 3. The number of KW contacts with families per month also increased. At the onset, three KWs made 107 contacts each month, whereas four KWs made 384 contacts per month at the end of the project. This represented a 258% increase in the number of monthly contacts. Note that these data refer only to frequency and do not reflect duration or intensity. Furthermore, they do not include indirect activities, such as coordination with the CWs or documentation.

**Training Group for Relatives.** Of 304 relatives evaluated, 169 (56%) received training during the three-year project. Results were analyzed qualitatively. Participants were overwhelmingly positive about the group, both in terms of knowledge gained and social support received. They strongly stated a preference for more training.

**Interviews of Relatives.** Of the 304 relative caregivers who received CREST services, 144 (47%) were interviewed during the three-year project. Responses indicated that the program was very positively received and greatly appreciated. Respondents reported that all three services (training, case management, and financial assistance) were equally effective. One-half of the respondents reported satisfaction with the current level of services; the other respondents wanted more of the services already offered.

**Focus Groups.** Ten focus groups were conducted with relatives ($n = 104$), CWs ($n = 52$), and CW supervisors ($n = 27$). Groups may have included some of the same participants in different years. Relatives focused on how the program was helpful, and they identified no major omissions in services (other than wanting more of what they were already receiving). The CWs reported that CREST was effective in monitoring the placement, helping the family to align with CPS, and facilitating permanency. They stated that CREST was helpful to both relatives and CWs in this regard. The supervisors' feedback echoed that of the CWs. Both the CWs and their supervisors felt so strongly about the effectiveness of CREST that they advocated for more KW positions even though that would mean fewer CW positions and larger caseloads for them.

**KW Feedback.** The KWs reported that they viewed the project as beneficial both to the relatives and to the CWs. They identified all three components of the program as equally effective. They regarded ongoing coordination between the KW and CW as essential to program effectiveness. The KWs identified three important ways to improve services: (1) CREST should get involved as early in the placement process as possible, (2) kinship caregivers' attendance at the training group should be mandatory, and (3) caseloads should remain low (not to exceed current levels) so relatives can receive individualized attention.

**CW Feedback.** Questionnaires were sent to 133 CWs who had a child in their caseload placed in relative care; 110 (83%) responded. Their feedback pertained to 194 (64%) of the 304 relatives evaluated, because many CWs had several families their caseloads. Regarding overall program effectiveness, the CWs unanimously indicated that CREST was extremely helpful to the relatives and to themselves. They identified all three components of the program as equally effective. The CREST activity they identified as most helpful was the assistance from the KW in monitoring the placement and giving them more time to focus on the child. Furthermore, they identified that, by meeting the emotional and financial needs of the relatives, CREST strengthened the placement and in turn, the strengthened placement contributed to the well-being of the child.

*Summative (Outcome) Measures*

**Number of Placements.** CREST did not directly increase the overall number of placements with placements. This responsibility resides largely with the court and investigation units and, due to local and state initiatives, had been steadily increasing before CREST. Nevertheless, data showed a steady increase in the number of relatives served by CREST. The number of families evaluated from Year 1 ($n = 44$) compared to Year 3 ($n = 136$) increased 200%. As indicated previously, families served from one year to the next were counted only once to avoid duplication.

More important, the evaluation found that CREST likely increased the number of "marginal" placements opened. That is, the presence of CREST increased the confidence of the CWs to recommend (and the supervisor to approve) a placement with a relative when a placement might otherwise have been deemed too risky. This had the desirable effect of making kinship care available to more children. Marginal placements seemed to comprise a substantial number of placements, although the exact number cannot be reported because of the large number of missing forms. For Year 3, referral forms were received from the CWs on 84 of 136 relatives (62%). Of the 84 forms, 49 were indicated as marginal (58%) or an overall rate of 36% (49 of 136 total).

**Number of Disruptions.** KWs reported 39 placement disruptions (for evaluated families) involving 92 children in three years. In all cases, sibling groups placed in one home were removed together. The following explanations were provided: relative unable to manage child's behavior ($n = 10$), relative unable to provide adequate care ($n = 16$), physical abuse ($n = 8$), and other reasons ($n = 5$). This rate of disruptions (13%) was consistent with overall rates in the agency. Given the high number of marginal placements, however, this rate may actually be low. A comparison of disruption rates between marginal and regular placements was not possible because of missing data.

**Number of Cases Closed.** Of 304 families evaluated, closing summaries were received on 188 (62%). The resolution of these cases cannot be reported, however, because data are missing. Anecdotally, the most common resolution was permanent managing conservatorship (the child remained in the relative's home but the state retained custody). One-half of all Year 3 cases (including Year 2 ongoing) were closed in Year 3. The mean length of time that families received CREST services was 151 days (range, 11-365 days). Very rarely did a CREST case reopen. CPS does not track data on resolution of cases, so a comparison with non-CREST families is not possible. Therefore, although it is not clear that CREST led to quicker resolution of cases, CREST apparently was effective in closing cases in a timely manner without continued CPS involvement. In terms of whether CREST had an effect on maintaining placements, the KWs indicated "yes" on 221 of 295 placements (75%). The remaining 25% of placements were regarded by the KWs as "high functioning" and needing minimal assistance. The CWs reported that CREST was a factor in maintaining 90% of placements.

**Child Well-Being.** This measure was triangulated using three sources: relatives, CWs, and KWs. Cumulative ratings (on a scale of 10) were 8.9 for relatives ($n$ = 230 children), 8.7 for the CWs ($n$ = 312 children), and 7.5 for the KWs ($n$ = 528 children). KW ratings for all three years were consistently lower than ratings by the relatives and CWs. This result could be attributed to the higher KW response rate (91%) compared to the relatives (40%) and the CWs (54%), so that the KW sample may have included a far larger number of children functioning at a lower level. This difference is not attributed to lower ratings by the KWs overall, because when the KW's ratings were compared with the ratings by relatives and CWs by child (i.e., the subsample of 41 children in Year 3 for whom all three scores were available), the KWs rated the child as having an equal or higher well-being score. The low response rate of relatives and CWs may indicate a bias toward those who felt most favorable about the program.

**Customer Satisfaction.** A measure of customer satisfaction was gathered from relatives and CWs. First, of the 304 relatives evaluated, 136 (45%) responded to this item, yielding a weighted cumulative average score of 8.9 out of 10. Of these, 119 (87.5%) were satisfied or very satisfied with CREST services (score of 8 or more). Themes for the high ratings focused on the helpfulness of the KWs, especially regarding emotional support, advocacy, and securing resources, well as the usefulness of the training group. Several relatives stated that the placement would not have succeeded without CREST. Second, of 142 CWs, 99 (70%) responded to this item, yielding a weighted cumulative average score of 9.2 out of 10. Of these, 93 (94%) were satisfied or very satisfied with CREST services (score of 8 or above). Themes for the higher ratings focused on the quality of services provided to relatives as well as to the CW, especially in freeing up time to focus on the child's needs or giving them another point of view on the placement. The overall weighted cumulative average for both groups combined was 9.2 out of 10.

**Cost-Effectiveness.** Table 2 presents the findings of the cost-effectiveness analysis. Of the 579 children placed with evaluated relatives in the three years of the project, 42 were not included in the analysis because of missing data. The remaining 537 children were placed in a single budget year as follows: Year 1, $n = 81$; Year 2, $n = 219$; or Year 3, $n = 237$. In addition, 266 of these 537 children carried over into the next year as follows: Year 1 to Year 2, $n = 82$, and Year 2 to Year 3, $n = 184$. Thus, the analysis, calculated on a yearly basis, pertains to 803 children as follows: Year 1, $n = 81$; Year 2, $n = 301$; and Year 3, $n = 421$.

Table 3 shows the breakdown for the LOCs for these children for all three years: Level 1, $n = 494$; Level 2, $n = 172$; Level 3, $n = 89$; Level 4, $n = 38$; Level 5, $n = 9$; and Level 6, $n = 1$.

From 1999 through 2000, each LOC received a set amount of funding for substitute care per day as follows: Level 1 (primary) = $16.96, Level 2 (specialized) = $36.33, Level 3 (intermediate) = $62.15, Level 4 (therapeutic) = $88.42, Level 5 (intensive) = $106.66, and Level 6 (inpatient) = $200.98. Most children placed in relatives' homes receiving CREST services were designated as either Level 1 or Level 2. On the basis of the daily reimbursement rate for each LOC per child for total number of days placed, the cumulative cost to provide foster care services for these 803 children during all three years of CREST would have been $4,084,862. The median cost per child would have been $5,087 per year. If the entire three-year federally funded budget for CREST ($600,000) were deducted from this amount, the program would

## TABLE 2
### Equivalent Cost-Effectiveness for Children Placed in Relative Care (N = 537)

|  | Year 1 New | Year 2 New | Ongoing from Year 1 | Year 3 New | Ongoing from Year 2 | Total |
|---|---|---|---|---|---|---|
| Total Number of Children | 81 | 219 | 82 | 237 | 184 | 803 |
| Total Number of Ongoing Children | NA | NA | 82 | NA | 184 | 266 |
| Total Number of New Children | 81 | 219 | NA | 237 | NA | 537[a] |
| Cost of Level of Care ($) | 582,646 | 943,000 | 333,511 | 1,617,210 | 1,207,942 | 4,084,862 |
| Budget ($) | 200,000 | 200,000 | 200,000 | 600,000 | 3,484,862 | |

Note: NA = not applicable.
a. Actual number used in cost-effectiveness.

still have saved the state of Texas the equivalent of $3,484,862 in substitute care payments for Bexar County alone.

It should be noted that these are not actual savings, because care by relatives costs the state virtually nothing. Therefore, these savings cannot be attributed to CREST alone, because many of the placements would have occurred anyway. On the basis of the findings of the evaluation, however, a further analysis was conducted regarding "marginal" placements. Calculating the exact savings for marginal placements was not possible because of missing data. Nevertheless, the program essentially paid for itself when it maintained 45 children in marginal placements (15 children per year). That is, most of the children in marginal placements were Level 2, and the cost of Level 2 substitute care for one year is $13,260 ($36.33 per day, using year 2000 reimbursement rates). Thus, the care of 45 children at $13,260 a year is $596,700, which equals the $600,000 federally funded budget for CREST. In fact, the data confirm at least 55 marginal placements with relatives, involving 97 children, in Year 3 alone. The average length of placement for CREST families was 150 days. If these partial

TABLE 3

**Number of Children Placed in Care of Relatives by Level of Care (LOC) and Year**

| LOC | Year 1 New | Year 2 New | Ongoing from Year 1 | Year 3 New | Ongoing from Year 2 | Total |
|---|---|---|---|---|---|---|
| 1 | 14 | 150 | 51 | 151 | 128 | 494 |
| 2 | 43 | 35 | 22 | 50 | 22 | 172 |
| 3 | 19 | 22 | 4 | 21 | 23 | 89 |
| 4 | 3 | 10 | 4 | 12 | 9 | 38 |
| 5 | 2 | 2 | 1 | 2 | 2 | 9 |
| 6 | 0 | 0 | 0 | 1 | 0 | 1 |
| Total Children | 81 | 219 | 82 | 237 | 184 | 803 |

placements were combined into total number of days placed, they would equate 40 "marginally placed" children in Year 3. Even with these few data, with the number of marginal placements documented in Year 3 alone, it is reasonable to assume that the project certainly exceeded the number of marginal placements ($n$ = 45) needed to cover its total federally funded cost.

## Summary and Conclusions

Kinship care is the fastest growing child placement practice care in child welfare, yet limited research is available on its effectiveness. This article presents the findings of an evaluation of an innovative kinship care program and provides empirical evidence in support of the effectiveness of the CREST Project in achieving both formative and summative goals for three years of operation.

The CREST program is located in Texas, a state that does not provide reimbursement or training to relatives who are caregivers. Consistent with national norms, the CREST program serves economically disadvantaged, ethnic minority clients. The only program of its kind in this demographically large and politically conservative state, CREST was developed in response to the established practice in Texas of not providing systematic support to relative caregivers that resulted in inadequate recognition and services to this valuable group. Before this program, any services for relative caregivers were provided by the child's CW and were limited to meeting the needs of the child placed in the home. The CW was often unable to attend to the relatives, except during a crisis, because of exceedingly high caseloads.

KWs in the CREST program provided direct services to the relatives: individual case management, formal group training, and minimal financial assistance. In addition to providing direct services to the relatives, the KWs coordinated case management with the child's CW. This assistance was viewed as highly beneficial, because the KWs had greater knowledge about the home through their high level of contact with the relatives. Interestingly, the relatives valued the emotional support from the KWs as much as the formal services. Nevertheless, financial assistance was a particularly salient issue for these caregivers, because the typical relatives receiving CREST services were married, high school-educated, Mexican American grandparents, age 45, with a median household income of $18,000 a year.

The evaluation found that the project was universally respected and appreciated by all stakeholders. The findings clearly support the program's significance in increasing marginal placements and its high degree of cost-effectiveness. Placements with relatives were occurring at an increased rate in Bexar County and in Texas before CREST. This trend probably would have continued even if CREST had not been implemented. Thus, kinship care itself costs Texas virtually nothing, either with or without CREST. However, the evaluation clearly documents that CREST was a significant factor in increasing and maintaining the number of marginal placements. These placements probably would not have been approved without the availability of CREST services. Such at-risk placements were largely responsible for the program's cost-effectiveness, because most of these children otherwise would have gone into comparatively expensive, and arguably less desirable, foster care placements. In fact, the program more than paid for itself (i.e., saved more than the federally funded budget) by virtue of maintaining these at-risk placements.

The federally funded budget is not, however, a full picture of the program's cost. The budget does not include in-kind resources donated to CREST through the community. These resources were not an expense of the program, but successful replication in other regions may require a similar level of community support. The program actually may be more cost-effective than indicated, however, because many subjects in the evaluation reported the empirically unsubstantiated finding that CREST facilitated permanency. Finally, and perhaps most important, this analysis does not address the value to the individuals and families receiving CREST services and the potential long-term benefits to society of placing these children with their relatives.

This evaluation demonstrates that limited yet systematic support for an underserved population can result in a highly effective program. CREST provided a valuable service to a very needy group of relative caregivers, was recognized by all stakeholders as delivering high quality services, and essentially paid for itself. The cost-effectiveness analysis provided particularly strong support, not only for the continuation of the program in Bexar County, but also for its implementation in other regions in the state and the nation. Given the mission of child welfare, children in state conservatorship deserve the option of remaining with their relatives. In turn, relative caregivers warrant the quality of service provided by CREST, not only because they are a needy and underserved group, but because they provide a valuable service. Given the current political economy, child welfare will increasingly rely on kinship care, especially for ethnic minority children. Research into developing the most effective programs is more important than ever. It is especially important to provide empirical support for programs that redress social injustice. Vulnerable children and their relatives deserve nothing less.◆

# References

Barth, R., Courtney, M., Berrick, J., & Albert, V. (1994). *From child abuse to permanency: Child welfare services pathways and placements.* New York: Aldine de Gruyter.

Berrick, J., & Barth, R. (1994). Research on kinship foster care: What do we know? Where do we go from here? *Children and Youth Services Review, 16*(1/2), 1–5.

Berrick, J., Barth, R., & Needell, B. (1994). A comparison of kinship foster homes and foster family homes: Implications for kinship foster care as family preservation. *Children and Youth Services Review, 16*(1/2), 33–63.

Berrick, J., Needell, B., & Barth, R. (1995). *Kinship care in California: An empirically-based curriculum.* Berkeley, CA: Child Welfare Research Center.

Bonecutter, F., & Gleeson, J. (1997). *Achieving permanency for children in kinship foster care: A training manual.* Washington, DC: U.S. Department of Health and Human Services.

Burton, L. (1992). Black grandparents rearing children of drug-addicted parents: Stressors, outcomes, and social needs. *Gerontologist, 32*, 744–751.

Cimmarusti, R. (1992). Family preservation practice based upon a multisystems approach. *Child Welfare, 71*, 241–256.

Dubowitz, H. (1994). Kinship care: Suggestions for future research. *Child Welfare, 73*(5), 553–564.

Gebel, T. (1996). Kinship care and non-relative family foster care: A comparison of caregiver attributes and attitudes. *Child Welfare, 75*(1), 5–18.

Gleeson, J. (1995). Kinship care and public child welfare: Challenges and opportunities for social work education. *Journal of Social Work Education, 31*(2), 182–193.

Gleeson, J., & Craig, L. (1994). Kinship care in child welfare: An analysis of states' policies. *Children and Youth Services Review, 16*(1/2), 7–31.

Gleeson, J., O'Donnell, J., & Bonecutter, F. (1997). Understanding the complexity of practice in foster care. *Child Welfare, 76*(6), 801–826.

Goerge, R., Wulczyn, F., & Fanshel, D. (1994). A foster care research agenda for the 90s. *Child Welfare, 73*, 525–549.

Hegar, R., & Scannapieco, M. (1995). From family duty to family policy: The evolution of kinship care. *Child Welfare, 74*(1), 200–216.

Hornby, H., Zeller, D., & Karraker, D. (1996). Kinship care in America: What outcomes should policy seek? *Child Welfare, 75*, 397–418.

Inglehart, A. (1994). Kinship foster care: Placement, services, and outcome issues. *Child and Youth Services Review, 16*(1/2), 107–122.

Rittner, B. (1995). Children on the move: Placement patterns in child protective services. *Families in Society, 76*(8), 469–477.

Scannapieco, M., & Hegar, R. (1995). Kinship care: Two case management models. *Child and Adolescent Social Work Journal, 12*(2), 147–156.

Scannapieco, M., Hegar, R., & McAlpine, C. (1997). Kinship care and foster care: A comparison of characteristics and outcomes. *Families in Society, 78*(5), 480–488.

Scannapieco, M., & Jackson, S. (1996). Kinship care: The African American response to family preservation. *Social Work, 41*(2), 190–196.

Wilhelmus, M. (1998). Mediation in kinship care: Another step in the provision of culturally relevant child welfare services. *Social Work, 43*(2), 97–102.

# Chapter 9

# Engaging Families in Child Welfare Services: An Evidence-Based Approach to Best Practice

*Kari Dawson and Marianne Berry*

Successfully engaging clients in the helping process is a critical task for child welfare practitioners. Drop-out and noncompliance rates in child welfare services are high and lead to high rates of removal of children from their families and to eventual termination of parental rights. Although no known interventions guarantee treatment compliance, this review of the empirical literature delineates critical components of engagement in child welfare services. Effective engagement strategies, including service components and caseworker qualities and behaviors, are identified as contributing to the positive case outcomes of treatment compliance, family preservation, and placement prevention. The unique needs of neglectful parents are also examined, with recommendations for practice.

*Kari Dawson, MSW, is a recent graduate, and Marianne Berry, PhD, is Professor, School of Social Welfare, University of Kansas, Lawrence, KS. Support for this research was provided by a contract with the State of Kansas Department of Social and Rehabilitative Services, Division of Child and Family Policy.*

Child welfare programs cannot claim high success rates with current treatment populations. Rigorous experimental tests of intervention effectiveness are difficult, given many constraints on evaluations: High drop-out rates preclude posttests; mandated treatment prohibits the use of equivalent control groups; poorly specified treatment models are difficult to replicate; and standardized outcome measures are often developed and normed on populations unlike those beset by low income, inadequate housing, low literacy, and so forth. Contributing to the scarcity of effective public child welfare models is the absence of many controls often found in laboratory intervention research (Weisz, Weiss, & Donenberg, 1992). Effective models for the treatment of child maltreatment do exist (although models are better specified for child abuse than for child neglect), but they require strict adherence to model parameters (Cohn & Daro, 1987; Henggeler & Borduin, 1990; Kluger, Alexander, & Curtis, 2000).

Client drop out is problematic, not only for evaluators but for treatment itself. Client drop-out rates for therapeutic services range from 35% to 70% (Kazdin, 2000; Mueller & Pekarik, 2000), with higher rates among clients receiving involuntary or court-ordered services (Rooney, 1992). Because many child protective service agencies serve only court-ordered clients, referring voluntary clients to other agencies, client drop out and retention are significant issues, often ignored in the specification of treatment models.

For parents receiving child welfare services, the timely completion of treatment is part of a specified service plan. Noncompliance with that plan can result in the removal of children and their placement in foster care and, ultimately, termination of parental rights. Uncooperative parents may not be offered services (Jones, 1993), whereas cooperative parents are less likely to face court proceedings (Karski, 1999) or removal of their children and placement of their children in foster care (Atkinson & Butler, 1996; Jellinek et al., 1992).

Completing this picture is the recent shift to shorter time frames for serving families and their showing improvement, before moving on to the termination of parental rights. The Adoption and Safe Families Act of 1997 (ASFA; P.L. 105-89) reduced the amount of time agencies have (from 18 months [P.L. 96-272; 1980] to 12 months) to show a reduced likelihood of maltreatment in a family. If agencies cannot show family improvement by the 12th month of services, courts begin proceedings to terminate parental rights.

This reduction in the time the "treatment window" is open is intended to be a safeguard for children's healthy development in a permanent and family-like setting. The reduction is also intended to be sensitive to a child's developmental needs for safety and a timely and permanent disposition of his or her case. The reduction is furthermore intended to limit the amount of time during which agencies can intrude into the private lives of families. This reduction to a 12-month period to improve child safety was based on a small body of research on models that have achieved safety within 12 months with this population (Henggeler & Borduin, 1990). Those service models that have shown good outcomes for children and families often have voluntary clients, rather than families mandated by courts to public child welfare agencies. For instance, an effective home-based service model for troubled adolescents (Brunk, Henggeler, & Whelan, 1987) has had great difficulty in producing similarly good outcomes with families experiencing child maltreatment.

The majority of child welfare agencies across the country are currently operating under some form of settlement agreement or court disposition resulting from class action lawsuits regarding the poor oversight of child welfare cases. Most agencies have limits on the size of caseloads that child welfare caseworkers can carry. These limits can also, however, contribute to a reduced treatment window for helping an individual family, in that the number of case closures needs to match the number of incoming cases.

For caseloads to remain at a steady size, the number of case closures must be equal to the number of new cases in any given period. As new cases continue to come into the agency—and public agencies are not able to refuse serving families found to abuse or neglect their children—case closures must happen at a rate equal to case openings, regardless of the level of family difficulties. Treatment developments must therefore keep pace with the changing constraints on agencies and their service populations.

Research on intensive family preservation services has found program success to be predicted by a family's early cooperation and engagement in services (Berry, 1992; Kinney, Haapala, & Booth, 1991; Lewis, 1991). Given shortened time frames in which to involve families in services, and the importance of the family's engagement in contributing to positive case outcomes, a delineation of strategies that enhance family cooperation and engagement is an important task.

## Components of Services That Engage Families in Treatment

Services can only be effective when clients fully participate in them. Littell and Tajima (2000) distinguished between two constructs of client participation: collaboration and compliance. In collaboration, a client participates in both treatment planning and agreement with treatment plans; both can also be influenced by caseworkers and by agency practices. Client compliance consists of such behaviors as keeping appointments, completing tasks, and cooperating with caseworkers and others. Most literature in child welfare practice comments on client compliance, although we propose that client collaboration is the construct of most importance to client engagement.

For clarity, we have embraced the standard of effective intervention delineated by Carr and colleagues (1999), who stated that an intervention is deemed effective by stakeholders, including the agency, client, and policymakers, when it

- Helps to create changes in lifestyle, not just behavior;
- Includes practical and relevant interventions; and
- Strives for long-term changes.

Social service agencies and workers are responsible for embracing these standards. When these standards are implemented on every agency level, treatment collaboration and compliance are likely to increase. It should be emphasized, however, that many discrepancies exist in the literature regarding service structures as they relate to successful outcomes. Our purpose here is to outline briefly the strengths of various programs as they relate to effective client participation and collaboration.

### Immediate and Home-Based Interventions

Most social service agencies have an established system for service delivery. Many studies rule out other factors for successful outcomes, while finding that elements of the service structure affect treatment effectiveness. Widely cited intensive family preservation services programs have shown success in preventing out-of-home placement in 40% to 95% of participating families (Fraser, Pecora, & Haapala, 1991; Schuerman, Rzepnicki, & Littell, 1994). These home-based programs aim to provide alternatives to out-of-home placement, as well as to provide links to community supports, so that families can be self-sustaining for longer periods of time.

Conflicting research on the success of intensive family preservation services reveals that this service structure may not be effective for all families all of the time. As a system of service delivery, however, the home-based programs show great strengths in maintaining family participation in the intervention process (Fraser et al., 1991; Kinney et al., 1991). Intensive family preservation services, such as the Homebuilders program (Fraser et al., 1991; Kinney et al., 1991), claim that their successes directly relate to their service structure by:

- Contacting clients immediately (2 days or less) once a referral is made,

- Providing services in the home to teach practical skills in the setting where they will be used,
- Emphasizing skill building over therapeutic insight, and
- Emphasizing delivery of concrete services.

Studies of consumer satisfaction with services received have identified many of these same components as particularly helpful. A study of problem families with multiple problems (Benvenisti & Yekel, 1986) found consumers to rate caseworkers most helpful when they

- were willing to help and to be with the family,
- were supportive and nonpunitive,
- listened to clients and encouraged them, and
- provided concrete services.

Family preservation caseworkers seek to engage the family and to instill hope early in the intervention (Kinney et al., 1991). Workers provide understanding and emotional support by listening to and helping families define the problem and set their own goals for treatment. Huszti and Olson (1999) reinforced this practice. They emphasized the importance of educating families about the pending case issues during the initial interview process, in addition to modeling appropriate parent/child interventions during subsequent sessions.

Given the short duration of services, most family preservation programs do not emphasize the truly "soft services" of psychological individual or family counseling. For example, Whittaker, Schinke, and Gilchrist (1986) instead focused on the teaching of specific life skills. This form of soft services is especially applicable in short-term interventions, during which emotional support from agency workers is available only for a finite period, usually two to three months. The skill building that occurs will continue to support and reinforce positive family interaction in the long run, after formal services have ended.

Treatment in family preservation services focuses on modeling of life skills, such as teaching parenting and practicing with family members the constructive communication and negotiation skills that will contribute to a more positive and less abusive family environment. These positive communication skills foster a respectful and empathic working relationship, in addition to improving parenting skills. Workers assess parenting and communication skills, help parents and children to identify nonpunitive methods of interacting, and model and practice positive interaction. These skills apply not only to parent and child interaction. The same skills also help families to interact more productively with landlords, doctors, teachers, social workers, neighbors, relatives, and others who contribute to the support or stress in the family's social environment. The model is nonpunitive and nonblaming.

## Broadly Focused Case Management

Some studies show strong effects in areas of family need that can be met by flexible and concrete service delivery. For example, Huz, McNulty, and Evans (1996), in a study of intensive case management services in New York, showed declines in "unmet needs" when families received intensive case management services. Focused primarily on children, their study reported that children received significantly more recreational, medical, and educational services between baseline and discharge. Overall family functioning, however, showed few significant changes with intensive case management.

The family preservation model of services recognizes the important role of concrete resources in the support of families. First, families who improve their communication skills and increase the self-esteem of their members will continue to be stressed by their physical environment if they cannot provide for the basic needs of their children, such as housing, food, and medical care. A systems perspective recognizes the importance of these physical and environmental resources to family well-being. Therefore, assistance and the provision of concrete resources can reduce accumulation of stress, thereby positively affecting the ability to effectively participate in both services and family life.

Second, Kinney and colleagues (1991) indicated that provision of concrete resources helps to establish rapport between the caseworker and the family by showing an understanding of their concrete needs and then applying a direct and real solution. Caseworkers in intensive family preservation systems often help families to fix broken windows, shop for food, request furniture, access car repairs, and so forth. These "hard services" improve the impoverished circumstances of families as well as the physical environment. The assistance also provides an opportunity to model these repair, shopping, or negotiation skills so that families can learn to do them on their own. Indeed, in a study of the client and agency characteristics predicting client participation or collaboration in family preservation services program, Littell and Tajima (2000) found that programs that provided a wide range of concrete services had higher levels of client collaboration, as reported by their caseworkers.

A common criticism of social service agencies is that, to make difficult decisions easier, they simplify their services to a "single operating principle" (Besharov, 1998). This single operating principle often changes with child welfare trends. Service systems, however, have not "trended" to a system of flexible service delivery. Marcia Robinson Lowry is quoted as arguing, "Never have these systems acknowledged the fundamental principle that the circumstances of individual children and families vary, as should responses to those circumstances" (Besharov, 1998, p. 124). Broadly focused case management services should, therefore, be flexibly fashioned to meet the individual needs of the family.

### A Family Focus

Another form of service structure that has received much attention since the 1980s is the family-focused service agency. Many agencies are currently moving, or have recently moved, toward family-focused services, because of the long-term results more likely to be produced when the entire family system is affected. Agencies with a family focus target more needs within the client system than do services that focus primarily on the child.

Those therapeutic services for children that successfully engage parents as well as children are more likely to retain clients than those that do not engage the parents (Smith, Oliver, Boyce, & Innocenti, 2000).

Family group conferencing is a recent addition to many agencies' family-focused service repertoire. Research on family group conferencing emphasizes the inclusion of the entire family as the core component of intervention success (Connolly & McKenzie, 1999; Sieppert, Hudson, & Unrau, 2000; Swain & Ban, 1997). This research points to several themes common to successful family group conferencing programs:

- Use the strengths of a widely defined family group;
- Promote decisionmaking based on the family's needs, as well as the needs of children involved; and
- Allow for the cooperation of parents and workers in the planning process.

Anecdotal evidence indicates that these programs contribute to family engagement and cooperation in service planning and case dispositions (Jackson & Morris, 1999; Ryburn & Atherton, 1996; Thomas, 2000). More evidence must be gathered, however, before this approach is adopted with confidence.

## Caseworker Characteristics

Other factors in agency services also help result in the engagement and success of clients. These factors are embedded in the personality and professionalism of the therapist or worker. An agency's interventions and strategies must be flexible to target individual child and family needs, but an agency's caseworkers are the key reflection of the agency philosophy and approach to practice.

## Caseworker Qualities

Much research has coupled treatment success with the empathy, trust, and rapport established between a caseworker and his or her clients. These qualities are not typically factors inherent in the overall service structure of an agency; rather, they are found in the worker representing the social service agency (Lazaratou, Vlassopoulos, & Dellatolas, 2000; Menahem & Halasz, 2000).

## Caseworker Behaviors

A review of research on service effectiveness with involuntary clients (Rooney, 1992) identified caseworkers' behaviors, rather than their qualities, that are most successful in influencing the treatment adherence or compliance of clients. Rooney summarized the resulting treatment recommendations as follows:

- Make a specific request rather than a vague one,
- Seek overt commitments from clients to comply,
- Provide training in performing the task,
- Supply positive reinforcement of the task,
- Choose tasks that require little discomfort or difficulty, and
- Ensure client participation in the selection and design of tasks (p. 88).

These behaviors exemplify the qualities of empathy, trust, and respect noted above, as manifested in cooperative, mutually agreed on task design and completion. This mutual process is what helps to ensure the engagement of clients who are often mistrustful, having experienced little empathy and trust in their prior service history.

Research in this area reveals that a therapist/caseworker can influence the process of client engagement and compliance by increasing the amount of time spent in direct contact with clients. MacLeod and Nelson (2000) cited research in which a strong correlation was found between worker contact hours and family stability. They state that "interventions which were more intense, requiring a greater number of hours, resulted in fewer children being removed from their homes because of concerns about child maltreatment" (pp. 1130–1131). In a similar assessment of intensive case management services, Werrbach and Harrod (1996) showed a positive correlation between total case manager hours and a child's score on the function assessment inventory. Although the issue of contact hours might be seen strictly as an agency-level contributor to the engagement process, individual workers should consider how they structure services by integrating direct contact hours into the treatment plan.

Other factors, such as the type of treatment chosen and the clarity of goal setting, can be useful in the successful engagement and treatment of clients. For example, Littell and Tajima (2000) found fewer child removals and fewer recurrences of child maltreatment when parents were involved in treatment planning in intensive family preservation services. Traglia, Pecora, Paddock, and Wilson (1997) recommended the following practice principles in determining whether an intervention program is successful in engaging families:

- Are the goals and guidelines mutually agreed on by all involved parties, and are they clearly stated?
- Is the consumer making sound decisions and taking personal responsibility for the consequences for these decisions?
- Is the practice focus on expected results?
- Are the staff and clients committed to working together?

Most researchers agree that treatment goals should be met to consider an individual intervention successful. Few researchers, however, consider the elements of the treatment process themselves as important contributors to treatment compliance. In 1997, the U.S. Department of Health and Human Services (U.S. DHHS) issued a report that emphasized evaluation of change during the treatment process with neglectful families. Such evaluation should take place on two levels: changes in conditions and behaviors that originally caused maltreatment, and progress made by the client to achieve set tasks and goals. A formal evaluation in the midst of treatment, rather than at case closure, is also helpful in discussing familial perceptions of goal achievement (U.S. DHHS, 1997). A formal evaluation is not only empowering for families, it serves as a motivator for tasks and goals not yet achieved.

A study by Lazartou and colleagues (2000) examines the relationship between therapy type and compliance. The study results support previous research stressing the importance of family-focused services. Their study found greater compliance (77.8%) in parental counseling than in psychotherapy (38.8%) or specialized therapies (57.3%). Thus, their argument is that knowledge is power: i.e., through parental or family therapy, help and support are extended from the caseworker, and the direct result is treatment compliance. If these factors are combined with a caseworker's responsibility to offer clear goals (Traglia et al., 1997) and with cognitively, socially, and emotionally appropriate interventions (Huszti & Olson, 1999), engagement and successful outcomes increase.

## Caseworker Training and Credentials

Research findings are contradictory regarding the relationship between treatment compliance and the level of education and experience of individual clinicians and caseworkers. For instance, Mueller and Pekarik (2000) assessed the drop-out and satisfaction rates of 230 clients in private and public therapeutic clinics. Univariate tests were used for data collected from workers and clients, and the therapist's higher educational degree was found to be associated with the consistent attendance of clients. Of the responding caseworkers, 62% reported that they had a doctoral degree in psychology, and 25% reported that they had a master's degree in psychology or social work. Other research, however, has found that practitioners with bachelors degrees are effective in preventing out-of-home placement in home-based programs (Corcoran, 2000). Apparently, intervention location and technique may be at least as important as educational degree.

## The Special Problem of Child Neglect

According to the National Incidence Study of Child Abuse and Neglect, the incidence of physical abuse increased 45% from 1986 to 1993, whereas the incidence of neglect increased 100% in the same period (Sedlak & Broadhurst, 1996). Many service models, including the family preservation service models mentioned above, report much greater success with physical abuse than with neglect.

Given the time limitations in child welfare legislation and managed care, it is especially important to determine methods of quick engagement and treatment compliance for neglectful families. According to a 1997 report from the U. S. DHHS, nearly 41% of children in the child welfare system are in out-of-home placement for at least 18 months. Without quick engagement and effective treatments once families are engaged, these children experience unstable and lengthy care. The incidence of termination of parental rights among these families will likely increase significantly in the near future.

### Unique Needs of Neglectful Families

Of the interventions and treatment strategies available to parents who are served by child welfare agencies, many are targeted for both abuse *and* neglect. However, patterns of abuse and neglect are influenced by entirely different factors, and interventions should regard these differences appropriately.

**Substance Abuse.** No other factor causes more difficulty for treatment compliance than parents who are addicted to drugs and alcohol. The addictive nature of these substances is so powerful that poor parenting, unemployment, mental incapacitation, and homelessness become interconnected with the addiction itself. A national study (U.S. DHHS, 1997) found that substance abuse was the presenting problem in 26% of child neglect cases alone. In families that neglect children, alcohol and crack/cocaine are the primary drugs, followed by methamphetamines and mari-juana (Bartholet, 1999).

Engagement and retention of addicted mothers in substance abuse treatment programs are difficult at best (Eliason, Skinstad, & Gerken, 1995; Ingersoll, I-li, & Haller, 1995; Nelson-Zlupco, Kauffman, & Dore, 1995). Littell and Tajima (2000) found that substance-using parents in intensive family preservation services have significantly lower levels of collaboration with their caseworkers. These deficits are moderated, however, when the caseworker has a master's degree. Another program for substance-abusing mothers enhanced client participation by using a formal, signed treatment contract; goal setting; and a strength-based approach to encourage constructive relationships with caseworkers. A graduation ceremony was held to present certificates of completion (Plasse, 2000).

Most practitioners, policymakers, and researchers in the field passionately espouse one of two positions regarding parents who abuse substances. Either they advocate for amending legislation, such as ASFA, to account for the length of time it takes for parents and caretakers to recover from these addictions (Glisson, Bailey, & Post, 2000), or they advocate for speeding up the child placement process because of the high drop-out and relapse rates for parents in drug treatment programs (Besharov, 1998). Regardless of which position one takes, the issue remains: Until parents are capable of maintaining a substance-free and sober lifestyle, they are considered incapable of adequately parenting their children.

**Poverty.** Poverty is often associated with abuse and neglect for the obvious reason that impoverished environments create severe stresses for parents and caregivers (Besharov & Laumann, 1997; Lindsey, 1994; Pelton, 1989). Coupled with poverty, unemployment is the presenting problem for nearly 34% of neglecting caregivers (U.S. DHHS, 1997). In a rigorous study of out-of-home placement decisions for children, Rossi, Schuerman, and Budde

(1999) found that when families had some form of family income, family preservation services were more likely to be offered and/ or recommended. If families showed no family income, however, children were much more likely to be placed in out-of-home care.

One may argue that children are not removed from the care and custody of their parents strictly because they are poor or unemployed. If resources appear to be scarce, however, and the living conditions for children in poverty do not appear as if they will quickly change, then children are more likely to be placed out of the home (Lee & Goerge, 1999). Once children are removed, many social service agencies or courts require proof of consistent employment, among other things, for family reunification to occur. Employment is, therefore, considered a corollary parenting skill that should not be ignored in the treatment array of services. Thus, if joblessness is a reason for child placement, it must be a target of intervention.

**Mental Illness.** A study of five home-based programs in six different states revealed that nearly 56% of out-of-home placements for children involved both parental substance abuse and concurrent mental health needs/problems (Menahem & Halasz, 2000). For these families, not parental compliance but mental instability was the presenting problem for treatment (Menahem & Halasz, 2000). Mental illnesses are clearly a barrier to treatment compliance, especially considering that parents may or may not intentionally comply, given the severity of their mental illness.

### Effective Intervention Strategies

Current interventions are designed and implemented specifically for the treatment of neglectful families. Empirical support for these interventions might be limited to a single study, and some short- and long-term outcomes are missing from the data. Nevertheless, social service workers have found these techniques useful for their focus of service, and many offer successful outcomes; hence, they are included here.

**In-Home Services.** In Cohn and Daro's (1987) review of programs targeting child neglect, a combination of services was found to be the most successful in alleviating familial neglect. The services provided included family counseling, in-home casework and counseling, and skill development for jobs both in and out of the home. Given the range of problems in neglectful families, services must be more comprehensive and longer lasting than in physically abusive families.

Many in-home health programs are emerging as a preventative measure for treating families deemed to be at risk of child neglect (Gaudin, 1993; Holden & Nabors, 1999; Singer, Minnes, & Arendt, 1999). In-home services range from medical to clinical care, depending on the agency focus. Holden and Nabors (1999) examined one such program in New York for at-risk families with infants. This program combined in-home nurse visitation and case management for the first two years of the child's life. Long-term results from this program show that at 15-year follow up, the overall rate of child neglect was lower in the treatment group receiving in-home services.

Despite the success of this particular home health study, criticisms still exist of home-visiting programs used as the sole answer to the problem of neglect. Because the early intervention home health program is preventive in nature, it does not necessarily offer an appropriate response to current crises that might exist in a family that is abusing and neglecting children who are present in the home. Hence, families who chronically neglect their children, as much of the current research suggests, will need to be in multiple, intensive programs throughout their lifetime (Yuan & Struckman-Johnson, 1991).

**Early Intervention Through Early Childhood Programs.** Early childhood programs offer many of the same benefits, and often target the same populations, as in-home nurse visitation programs. These early intervention programs generally focus on the children at the developmental stages of ages 2 through 5. The programs may be offered through child care agencies, parenting classes, or in-home service agencies, although the majority are offered in day treatment centers. Gaudin (1993) reported that

> Child care programs for [maltreated] children with specially designed therapeutic activities to provide stimulation, cultural enrichment, and development of motor skills and social skills, have proven to have a significant impact on the child's functioning, and the prevention of repeated maltreatment by parents. (p. 42)

Examples of existing programs include Families First (Detroit), The Family Center (Philadelphia), The Center for the Advancement of Mothers and Children (Cleveland), and Head Start (nationwide).

**Concrete Services.** As noted above, meeting the immediate needs of families in the engagement process cannot be overemphasized. Families of neglect often experience a number of barriers to engagement, including inadequate housing, poverty, unemployment, and lack of transportation. Meeting these needs is of utmost importance if long-term behavioral change is expected. Research shows that families of all types who receive simple and effective services at the beginning of their treatment relationship are more likely to build and maintain a relationship with caseworkers (Lewis, 1991). Therefore, if treatment goals are quickly established, work progresses more quickly.

Concrete services should include, as standard in the intervention plan, both formal and informal helping resources. These services include alleviating the barriers to engagement, i.e., housing, employment, transportation, and childcare. Gaudin (1993) stressed that the "successful mobilization of outside resources to meet the family's identified priorities helps to overcome the family's hopelessness, resistance, and distrust of professional helpers" (p. 34). Any intervention that targets neglect and does not offer concrete services may miss the root of the problem. Other practitioners contend that programs claiming to work with children and families from backgrounds of neglect should openly address their intent to set long-term goals and to expect long-term treatment.

**Behavioral Parent Training.** Behavioral parent training focuses on teaching and reinforcing positive parental behaviors that will subsequently influence the children. This training may take place in a small group, in an agency setting, or in the home, but most of these behavioral strategies are concrete and problem-focused. Some multisystemic programs focus both on parental management of behavior and on appropriate responses to the child's needs (Corcoran, 2000). Criticism of this type of intervention is that behavioral parent training does not necessarily result in increased stimulation for the neglected child. Rather, the child's behavior, or the parent's behavior, is better *managed* by this training; nurturing and emotional bonding does not necessarily follow. Successful outcomes, however, are noted in some studies, e.g., an 83% reduction rate in out-of-home placement for families who participate in this training (Corcoran, 2000). Parent training that is especially effective with this population goes beyond parenting behaviors to address parental coping with multiple forms of family stress, including financial and other adult problems (Griest & Forehand, 1982; Patterson, Chamberlain, & Reid, 1982).

**Family-Focused Approaches.** Family preservation strategies have come under intense scrutiny. Research reveals poor results in effectiveness of this approach with neglectful families (Berry, 1994). Gaudin (1993) asserted that traditional, one-on-one counseling, in a formal office setting, is typically ineffective with families of neglect. He cites studies by Polansky and colleagues (Polansky, Ammons, & Gaudin, 1985; Polansky, Gaudin, Ammons, & Davis, 1985; Polansky, DeSaix, & Sharlin, 1972) advising, instead, assertive interventions that emphasize:

- Reassigning role tasks within the family,
- Establishing of better parent/child boundaries,
- Improving in clear communication between family members, and
- Reframing dysfunctional perceptions by parents and children.

**Strengthening Support and Community Networks.** Many interventions mentioned above are most effective when caseworkers establish a trusting and empathetic relationship with their clients. Although these skills are important, they do not necessarily help families to become self-sufficient in the long run (DePanfilis, 1999). Equally important, therefore, is helping families to build and to maintain support networks outside the professional working relationship.

Formal, community-based practices differ in the connections that they provide. Typically, support networks include key stakeholders from public and private agencies, schools, clergy, universities, as well as children and their families. A support team might also be created or strengthened by using members of the client's family and close neighbors or friends (VanDenBerg & Grealish, 1996).

An example of this type of community-based intervention is the Social Network Intervention Project developed by Gaudin, Wodarski, Atkinson, and Avery (1997) in Georgia. The Social Network Intervention Project comprises a four-step process of case management:

- Making assessments and targeting existing needs/supports;
- Identifying barriers to involvement, such as the lack of a phone, transportation, or childcare;
- Setting goals (e.g., facilitating needed concrete services, enhancing parenting and professional skills, and increasing social networks); and
- Intervening on various levels: personal, mutual, volunteer, neighborhood, and social.

Program evaluation revealed that the Social Network Intervention Project improved both parenting adequacy and overall attitudes about parenting. The Social Network Intervention Project also aided in increasing support systems, while decreasing unrealistic parental expectations of children (Gaudin et al., 1997).

## Conclusions and Recommendations

This review of engagement strategies and behaviors that contribute to positive case outcomes has identified several promising practices in child welfare. Most notably, caseworker and agency behaviors, rather than qualities, appear to be the most important in the engagement of clients in child welfare services. Although empathy and respect are certainly important in building a working relationship, these qualities are best communicated through clear and concrete behaviors between the caseworker and client. These behaviors include: setting of mutually satisfactory goals, providing services that clients find relevant and helpful, focusing on client skills rather than insights, and spending sufficient time with clients to demonstrate skills and provide necessary resources. These practices, when applied in a supportive and nonpunitive manner, help to engage clients in treatment and, perhaps, decrease the number of families experiencing the termination of parental rights because of noncompliance with agency goals. These practices may also prevent the placement of children in out-of-home care and may promote family reunification when such placements occur.◆

## References

Atkinson, L., & Butler, S. (1996). Court-ordered assessment: Impact of maternal noncompliance in child maltreatment cases. *Child Abuse and Neglect, 20,* 185-190.

Bartholet, E. (1999). *Nobody's children.* Boston: Beacon Press.

Benvenisti, R., & Yekel, H. (1986). Family intervention: A description and evaluation. *Society and Welfare, 7*, 142-155.

Berry, M. (1992). An evaluation of family preservation services: Fitting agency services to family needs. *Social Work, 37*, 314-321.

Berry, M. (1994). The relative effectiveness of family preservation services with neglectful families. In E. S. Morton and R. K. Grigsby (Eds.), *Advancing family preservation practice* (pp. 70-98). Newbury Park, CA: Sage.

Besharov, D. (1998). Four commentaries: How we can better protect children from abuse and neglect. *Protecting Children from Abuse and Neglect, 8*(1), 120-132.

Besharov, D. J., & Laumann, L. A. (1997). Don't call it child abuse if it's really poverty. *Journal of Children and Poverty, 3*(1), 5-36.

Brunk, M., Henggeler, S. W., & Whelan, J. P. (1987). Comparison of multisystemic therapy and parent training in the brief treatment of child abuse and neglect. *Journal of Consulting and Clinical Psychology, 55*, 171-178.

Carr, E., Levin, L., McConnachie, G., Carlson, J., Kemp, D., Smith, C., et al. (1999). Comprehensive multisituational intervention for problem behavior in the community: Long-term maintenance and social validation. *Journal of Positive Behavior Interventions, 1*(1), 5-25.

Cohn, A. H., & Daro, D. (1987). Is treatment too late? What ten years of evaluative research tell us. *Child Abuse & Neglect, 11*, 433-442.

Connolly, M., & McKenzie, M. (1999). *Effective participatory practice: Family group conferencing in child protection.* New York: Walter de Gruyter.

Corcoran, J. (2000). Family interventions with child physical abuse and neglect: A critical review. *Children and Youth Services Review, 22*, 563-591.

DePanfilis, D. (1999). Intervening with families when children are neglected. In H. Dubowitz (Ed.), *Neglected children* (pp. 211-236). Newbury Park, CA: Sage.

Eliason, M., Skinstad, A., & Gerken, K. (1995). Drug-alcohol addictions and mothering. *Alcoholism Treatment Quarterly, 12*, 83-96.

Fraser, M., Pecora, P. J., & Haapala, D. A. (1991). *Families in crisis: The impact of intensive family preservation services.* Hawthorne, NY: Aldine de Gruyter.

Gaudin, J., Wodarski, J., Atkinson, M., & Avery, L. (1997). Remedying child neglect: Effectiveness of social network interventions. *Journal of Applied Social Sciences, 15*(1), 97-123.

Gaudin, J. M. (1993). *Child neglect: A guide for intervention.* Washington, DC: U.S. Department of Health and Human Services, Administration for Children and Families.

Glisson, C., Bailey, J. W., & Post, J. A. (2000). Predicting the time children spend in state custody. *Social Service Review, 74,* 253-280.

Griest, D. L., & Forehand, R. (1982). How can I get any parent training done with all these other problems going on? The role of family variables in child behavior therapy. *Child and Family Behavior Therapy, 4,* 73-80.

Henggeler, S. W., & Borduin, C. M. (1990). *Family therapy and beyond: A multisystemic approach to treating the behavior problems of children and adolescents.* Belmont, CA: Brooks/Cole.

Holden, E. W., & Nabors, L. (1999). The prevention of child neglect. In H. Dubowitz (Ed.), *Neglected children* (pp. 174-190). Newbury Park, CA: Sage.

Huszti, H., & Olson, R. (1999). Noncompliance. In S. D. Netherton, D. Holmes, & C. E. Walker (Eds.), *Child and adolescent psychological disorders* (pp. 567-581). New York: Oxford University Press.

Huz, S., McNulty, T., & Evans, M. (1996). *Child and family outcomes from intensive case management for children with serious emotional disturbance in New York State.* Paper presented at the 8th Annual Research and Training Center Conference Proceedings, University of South Florida, Department of Child and Family Studies, Florida Mental Health Institute.

Ingersoll, K., I-li, L., & Haller, D. (1995). Predictors of in-treatment relapse in perinatal substance abusers and impact on treatment retention: A prospective study. *Journal of Psychoactive Drugs, 27,* 375-386.

Jackson, S., & Morris, K. (1999). Family group conferences: User empowerment or family self-reliance? *British Journal of Social Work, 29,* 621-630.

Jellinek, M. S., Murphy, M., Poitrast, F., Quinn, D., Bishop, S. J., & Goshko, M. (1992). Serious child mistreatment in Massachusetts: The course of 206 children through the courts. *Child Abuse and Neglect, 16,* 179-185.

Jones, L. (1993). Decision-making in child welfare: A critical review of the literature. *Child and Adolescent Social Work, 10,* 241-262.

Karski, R. L. (1999). Key decisions in child protective services: Report investigation and court referral. *Children and Youth Services Review, 21*, 643-656.

Kazdin, A. E. (2000). Perceived barriers to treatment participation and treatment acceptability among antisocial children and their families. *Journal of Child and Family Studies, 9*, 157-174.

Kinney, J., Haapala, D. A., & Booth, C. (1991). *Keeping families together: The Homebuilders model*. Hawthorne, NY: Aldine de Gruyter.

Kluger, M. P., Alexander, G., & Curtis, P. A. (2000). *What works in child welfare?* Washington, DC: Child Welfare League of America.

Lazaratou, H., Vlassopoulos, M., & Dellatolas, G. (2000). Factors affecting compliance with treatment in an outpatient child psychiatric practice: A retrospective study in a community mental health center in Athens. *Psychotherapy and Psychosomatics, 69*, 42-49.

Lee, B. J., & Goerge, R. M. (1999). Poverty, early childbearing, and child maltreatment: A multinomial analysis. *Children and Youth Services Review, 21*, 755-780.

Lewis, R. E. (1991). What elements of service relate to treatment goal achievement? In M. W. Fraser, P. J. Pecora, & D. A. Haapala, *Families in crisis: The impact of intensive family preservation services* (pp. 225-271). Hawthorne, NY: Aldine de Gruyter.

Lindsey, D. (1994). *The welfare of children*. New York: Oxford University Press.

Littell, J. H., & Tajima, E. A. (2000). A multilevel model of client participation in intensive family preservation services. *Social Service Review, 74*, 405-435.

MacLeod, J., & Nelson, G. (2000). Programs for the promotion of family wellness and the prevention of child maltreatment: A meta-analytic review. *Child Abuse and Neglect, 24*, 1127-1149.

Menahem, S., & Halasz, G. (2000). Parental non-compliance—A paediatric dilemma: A medical and psychodynamic perspective. *Child: Care, Health and Development, 26*(1), 61-72.

Mueller, M., & Pekarik, G. (2000). Treatment duration prediction: Client accuracy and its relationship to dropout, outcome, and satisfaction. *Psychotherapy, 37*(2), 117-123.

Nelson-Zlupco, L., Kauffman, E., & Dore, M. M. (1995). Gender differences in drug addiction and treatment: Implications for social work intervention with substance abusing women. *Social Work, 40*, 45-54.

Patterson, G. R., Chamberlain, P., & Reid, J. B. (1982). A comparative evaluation of a parent training program. *Behavior Therapy, 13*, 638-650.

Pelton, L. (1989). *For reasons of poverty: A critical analysis of the public child welfare system in the United States.* New York: Praeger.

Plasse, B. R. (2000). Components of engagement: Women in a psychoeducational parenting skills group in substance abuse treatment. *Social Work with Groups, 22*, 33-50.

Polansky, N. A., Ammons, P. W., & Gaudin, J. M. (1985). Loneliness and isolation in child neglect. *Social Casework, 66*, 38-47.

Polansky, N. A., DeSaix, C., & Sharlin, S. A. (1972). *Child neglect: Understanding and reaching the parent.* New York: Child Welfare League of America.

Polansky, N. A., Gaudin, J. M., Ammons, P. W., & Davis, K. B. (1985). The psychological ecology of the neglectful mother. *Child Abuse and Neglect, 9*, 265-275.

Rooney, R. H. (1992). *Strategies for work with involuntary clients.* New York: Columbia University Press.

Rossi, P. H., Schuerman, J., & Budde, S. (1999). Understanding decisions about child maltreatment. *Evaluation Review, 23*, 579-598.

Ryburn, M., & Atherton, C. (1996). Family group conferences: Partnership in practice. *Adoption and Fostering, 20*, 16-23.

Schuerman, J. S., Rzepnicki, T., & Littell, J. (1994). *Putting families first.* Hawthorne, NY: Aldine de Gruyter.

Sedlak, A. J., & Broadhurst, D. D. (1996). *The third national incidence study of child abuse and neglect.* Washington, DC: U.S. Department of Health and Human Services.

Sieppert, J., Hudson, J., & Unrau, Y. (2000). Family group conferencing in child welfare: Lessons from a demonstration project. *Families in Society, 81*(4), 382-391.

Singer, L., Minnes, S., & Arendt, R. E. (1999). Innovations for high-risk infants. In P. Biegel & A. Blum (Eds.), *Innovations in practice and service delivery across the lifespan.* New York: Oxford University Press.

Smith, T., Oliver, M., Boyce, G., & Innocenti, M. (2000). Effects of mothers' locus of control for child improvement in a developmentally delayed sample. *Journal of Genetic Psychology, 161*(3), 307-313.

Swain, P., & Ban, P. (1997). Participation and partnership: Family group conferencing in the Australian context. *Journal of Social Welfare and Family Law, 19*, 35-52.

Thomas, N. (2000). Putting the family in the driving seat: Aspects of the development of family group conferences in England and Wales. *Social Work and Social Sciences Review, 8*, 101-115.

Traglia, J. J., Pecora, P. J., Paddock, G., & Wilson, L. (1997). Outcome-oriented case planning in family foster care. *Families in Society, 78*, 453-462.

U.S. Department of Health and Human Services. (1997). *National study of protective, preventive, and reunification services delivered to children and their families.* Washington, DC: Author.

VanDenBerg, J., & Grealish, E. (1996). Individualized services and supports through the wraparound process: Philosophy and procedures. *Journal of Child and Family Studies, 5*(1), 7-21.

Weisz, J. A., Weiss, B., & Donenberg, G. R. (1992). The lab versus the clinic: Effects of child and adolescent psychotherapy. *American Psychologist, 57*, 741-746.

Werrbach, J., & Harrod, J. (1996). *Providing intensive child case management services: What do case managers do with their time?* Paper presented at the 8th Annual Research and Training Center Conference Proceedings, University of South Florida, Department of Child and Family Studies, Florida Mental Health Institute.

Whittaker, J. K., Schinke, S. P., & Gilchrist, L. D. (1986). The ecological paradigm in child, youth, and family services: Implications for policy and practice. *Social Service Review, 60*, 483-503.

Yuan, Y. Y., & Struckman-Johnson, D. L. (1991). Placement outcomes for neglected children with prior placements in family preservation programs. In K. Wells & D. E. Biegel (Eds.), *Family preservation services: Research and evaluation* (pp. 92-118). Newbury Park, CA: Sage.

# Chapter 10

# Culture Loss: American Indian Family Disruption, Urbanization, and the Indian Child Welfare Act

*Kelly Halverson, Maria Elena Puig, and Steven R. Byers*

This study examined the perceptions and views of urban American Indian parents regarding foster care and American Indian family issues. Findings highlight four themes: (1) discouragement from working with the current foster care system, (2) the role of culture in caregiving, (3) differing definitions of family and relatedness, and (4) the effects of historical pain due to past family disruption. These themes are used to formulate guidelines for the development of an American Indian foster care and child welfare program.

*Kelly Halverson, MSW, is Child Protection Caseworker, Boulder County Department of Social Services, Boulder, CO. Maria Elena Puig, MSW, PhD, is Assistant Professor, Colorado State University School of Social Work, Fort Collins. Steven R. Byers, PhD, is Assistant Professor, University of Colorado at Denver.*

Until 1978, the forced removal and attempted assimilation of American Indian children were among the most devastating U.S. federal policies forced on Indian families. These policies, although allegedly prohibited by the passage of the Indian Child Welfare Act (ICWA) of 1978, continue to affect a high percentage of American Indian families residing in urban areas. American Indians encounter family disruption caused by the persistent removal of their children. Currently, child welfare statistics confirm that Indian children are not doing much better than during the years before passage of ICWA. Indian children are still being removed at a disproportionate rate that is three times greater than in the general population (California Indian Legal Services, 1998).

Along with questioning the continued removal of American Indian children from their families, all child welfare professionals should ask why there is a continued shortage of Indian foster families. Oftentimes, Indian children continue to be placed with non-Indian families because public child welfare agencies fail to recruit and retain native foster and adoptive homes. The reality is that most American Indians live in urban areas away from families and tribal members, and most lack the resources necessary to secure services. Others have had extremely negative experiences with the child welfare system, and they have watched social services remove children from family members and friends.

Compounding the problem is the fact that, in urban areas, great variance occurs in availability and accessibility of culturally responsive services and advocacy for Indian families. In part, this results from the bias that exists, i.e., many of these families have been the source of child abuse and neglect. This bias extends to using other family members for kinship placements. Ultimately, when ICWA and Indian cultures are not respected or assessed, family malfunctioning as well as cultural loss and its devastation continue.

## Literature Review

By the start of the 20th century, American Indians who had survived contact with Europeans had been redistributed. Much of this reallocation occurred during the 19th century with American Indian "removals," the establishment of the reservation system, and the subsequent eradication and apportionment of some reservations (Thornton, 2001). In both the United States and Canada, redistribution of American Indians also occurred through urbanization.

According to the U.S. Bureau of the Census (2000), as of November 1, 1999, there were 2,410,000 American Indians and Alaska Natives in the United States. Often, it is believed that American Indians live in isolation on reservations. Actually, most American Indian people live in urban centers; more than twice as many live in urban centers than on reservations. The five urban areas with the largest American Indian populations are Los Angeles (87,487); Tulsa, Oklahoma (48,196); New York (46,191); Oklahoma City (45,120); and San Francisco (40,847). Census figures indicate that 51% of American Indians reside in urban communities, and 25% live on reservations. The urbanization of American Indians, through migration to cities and towns, began in the 1950s and has continued since (Thornton, 2001). Urbanization has created new problems for American Indians, including the accelerated numbers of intermarriage with non-Indians, a decrease in a sense of tribal identity, a decrease in the number of American Indians who speak a tribal language at home, and increases in those who have no reported tribal affiliation and little, if any, participation in cultural activities (Thornton, 2001). These trends have affected both the genetic and tribal distinctiveness of the American Indian population; they have also contributed to the development of unstable family functioning.

Among American Indians, family functioning generates from a cultural context that emphasizes the importance of childhood socialization within two distinct but interrelated systems. For example, research on American Indian childrearing values and practices indicates that Indian children are socialized through the nurturance and teaching provided by the birthfamily and by the extended kinship network. The key is to ensure that neither system has primacy over the other (Blanchard & Barsh, 1980).

Before the passage of federal legislation requiring assimilation, American Indian and Alaska Native children were raised within a cultural context that emphasized the participation of the entire community or tribe in day-to-day childrearing responsibilities. These culturally based values, and the resulting behavioral practices derived from them, imply that children are sacred to and highly valued by their birthparents and all tribal members (Cross, 1996).

Closely related to these cultural values and maxims of socialization, nurturance, and teaching, the American Indian concept of "relatedness" emphasizes that children are embedded within a complex and dynamic set of relations that include self, kin, and universe. This spiritual and cultural value, foreign to most members of the culturally dominant group, has been considered an impediment to the assimilation of American Indians into U.S. culture.

In the dominant culture, members interpreted American Indian family values and behavior practices as alien and incongruent with the advancement of U.S. values. In addition, American Indians were considered a barrier to the dominant groups' desire to expand their acquisition of territory throughout the North American continent. Given these two prevalent sentiments, American Indians logically were targeted for extermination and assimilation (Burger, 1995).

For American Indians, the development of unstable families and disrupted childrearing practices have been in the making for hundreds of years. Because transmission of cultural values, behaviors, and identity development rely on cross-generation parenting and socialization, U.S. federal policies and practices were designed to disrupt family childrearing customs among Indians. Although they are not often acknowledged and little research has been done on their effects, these federal policies have resulted in major intrusions into American Indian family life.

From 1789 through 1871, the Pre-Reservation Era included policies that were intended to extermination the "Indian problem." During this period, most Indians began to be forced onto reservations, and the education and well-being of Indian children were of no consequence to the government. In the Early Reservation Era, from 1871 to 1928, policies toward Indians changed from extermination to assimilation and dependency. During this period, federal policies further diminished the Indian land base. The Bureau of Indian Affairs (BIA) and the Indian Health Services were established; Indians became U.S. citizens. During this time, federal policies included the destruction of Indian families through the removal of Indian children from their tribal homes.

Simultaneously, federal policies from the 1880s through the 1950s incorporated the creation of boarding schools, where the Indian problem was addressed by the removal of Indian children from their families and their placement in government-run boarding schools and Christian mission schools. From the 1950s through the 1970s, the Indian Adoption Era occurred. A collaborative agreement between the BIA and the Child Welfare League of America (CWLA) established a "clearinghouse for the interstate placement of Indian children with non-Indian families" (George, 1997, p. 169). This policy was considered a "success," because 25% to 35% of all Indian children were removed from their families (Paulson, 1999).

The right of Indians to remain Indian was reaffirmed during the late 1960s to the early 1980s, with the passage of ICWA in

1978. ICWA provided Indian parents and tribes the right to decide what was best for their children and affirmed the cultural needs of Indian children. ICWA also recognized the notion of "groupness" and the understanding that Indian people placed a high value on the support and well-being of the tribe and extended family (Paulson, 1999).

From the outset, the aim of federal policy had always been to deal with the Indian problem. The goal of federal legislation was to separate American Indian children from their families and to eradicate communally based child socialization. It was reasoned that curtailing, if not totally stopping, the transmission of American Indian socialization and family practices would result in assimilation of American Indians into the fabric of the dominant social structure. It was believed that this absorption would cause American Indian children to develop autonomy (Deloria, 1985). What followed, however, was almost 100 years of deliberate family separation as a method of "deculturation" (Burger, 1995).

Another corollary to deculturation and family disruption was the belief in "child rescue," a policy whereby the removal of American Indian children was promoted and supported (Mannes, 1993). By removing these children from their families and facilitating their adoption by non-Indian families, social services aided in the assimilation of thousands of Indian persons (Byler & Unger, 1974-1979). As a result, many American Indian children in this century have grown up separated from their families of origin, away from their tribal localities, and outside their culture (Coontz, 1988).

## A Change in U.S. Policy: The Indian Child Welfare Act

In 1978, ICWA (P. L. 95-608) attempted to suspend the continued out-of-home placement of American Indian children by returning to their respective tribes the majority of placement and adoption decisions regarding Indian children. ICWA is said to have "revolutionized" the best interest test in the context of Indian children. The best interest of the child standard in child custody proceedings is generally defined by looking at interest as being a stable placement with an adult who becomes the psychological parent. Under ICWA, however, federal standards define the best interests of Indian children as those served by protecting the rights of each child as an Indian and the rights of the Indian community and tribe in retaining the children in its culture. Generally, the federal policy attempts to protect the best interest of Indian children by preserving Indian families as well as the connection between tribes and their children. ICWA has not, however, been able to change "the bitter feelings toward foster care and the agencies and staff associated with foster care," as well as a "genuine and deep-seated fear of government agencies that have the power to place children" (Horejsi, Heavy Runner Craig, & Pablo, 1992).

Cross (1996) corroborated these beliefs by reporting that child welfare agencies intent on recruiting American Indians as foster care and adoptive families must address these feelings by "going to the community and asking elders, community leaders, and other Indian foster parents" (p. 66) for assistance. Cross further stated that this must happen because Indians must be convinced of the agency's goodwill and concern for the children and families involved.

## Theoretical Framework of the Study

Narrative and constructivist theories, with respect to cross-cultural research, were used to describe the development and foundation of this qualitative research study. Both theories allow for a more ecologically and culturally valid method for engaging in research with ethnic communities. Narrative theory incorporates the use of storytelling, a traditional American Indian method used to provide contextual information for community members. Sheafor, Horejsi, and Horejsi (1997) described the narrative approach as "focusing on personal stories and anecdotes and the stories of a community or culture...that people use as frames of reference to describe their situation and create meaning and purpose" (p. 110). Narrative theory allows people to assemble their own reality, and, as Cross (1996) stated, "it promotes meaning and recognizes the nuances of expression" (p. 24).

Constructivist theory proposes that people, through their interactions with others and their environments, continuously build reality. Babbie (1994) noted that, in this paradigm, all people are "acting like social scientists because they are trying to make sense of the life they experience" (p. 44). Similarly, Howard (1991) stated that "science represents a case of meaning construction through storytelling" (p. 187), as all mental images are products of human creativity. Constructivists know that they actively create reality by documenting their own views of the world they observe, conceive, and create. By combining the use of narrative and constructivist theory, research then "shifts from notions of truth to notions of significance or meaning" (Howard, 1991).

## Method

As a method for gathering data, the qualitative interview dates back to field research techniques used earlier in the 20th century (Babbie, 1994). By combining the two theoretical frameworks mentioned above, the present study based its research strategy on the works of Tashima, Crain, O'Reilly, and Elifson (1996), called the Community Identification Process (CID).

The CID process starts with the premise that, when community input is not included in exploratory research, key concepts and dynamics relevant to the topic are often omitted. Including members of the target community in the design and execution of a cross-cultural research effort enhances the cultural efficacy and ecological validity of the project.

The CID process seeks to uncover how people view themselves and their world, as a means to discover how best to embody key views and concepts in a research project (Tashima et al., 1996).

The CID process begins with a review of information in the research agency and discussions between the researchers to determine how the target population can be defined. Basically, it allows researchers to move "from a distant position, with little or no information about the target population, to direct proximity, and providing the target population with direct access to those creating the research" (Tashima et al., 1996, p. 33). In this study, it also allowed key members of the American Indian community to be identified and then to advise the researchers regarding methodology, subject recruitment, and instrumentation.

Figure 1 illustrates the basic components of the CID process.

Use of the CID process led to identification of key American Indian informants within urban neighborhoods. Key community informants (as identified by tribal members) were interviewed regarding: (a) the feasibility of a research project focused on American Indian foster parents, (b) identification of research methods with which community participants would be comfortable, and (c) identification of subjects and the development of sampling strategies.

During these interviews, key informants indicated that a viable method of collecting data was through storytelling and soliciting responses to storied accounts of the issues affecting American Indians involved with the foster care system. Storytelling plays a special role in Indian culture because it avoids the appearance of personal criticism while teaching culturally congruent values and behaviors (Red Horse, 1980). Key informants also suggested contacting American Indians who had personal knowledge of foster care and adoptions, because they themselves were caring for American Indian children. All informants emphasized the need for conducting such a study, particularly one that would examine American Indian foster care in an urban setting.

On the basis of the interviews with key informants, the researchers wrote a "near experience" or hypothetical story that developed a narrative account of a prototypical Indian child welfare case. This account was presented to each respondent, along with a structured questionnaire that corresponded to the hypo-

**FIGURE 1**
**Community Identification Process**

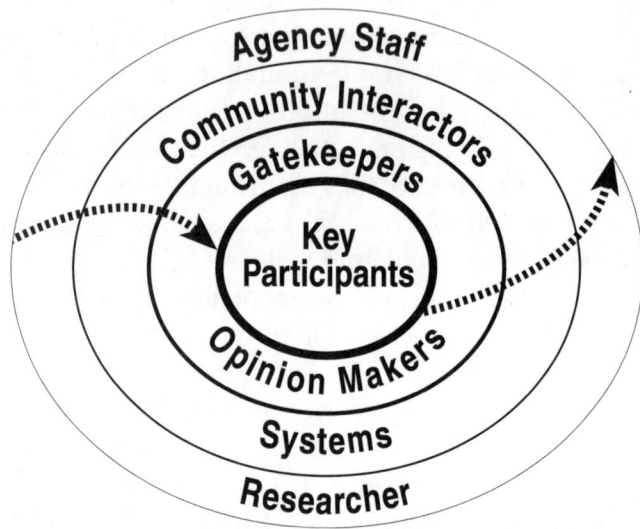

thetical story. The narrative account and the corresponding structured questionnaire were used as the basis for the interview schedule. The structured questionnaire, in particular, was developed to tap into attributions and viewpoints germane to the cultural and contextual dynamics that key informants deemed critical to Indian family and child welfare issues. Responses were collected from the structured questionnaires and from the open-ended answers to the near experience or hypothetical story.

*Sample*

Study participants were recruited through identification by key informants. After being categorized, potential participants were contacted by telephone. Nine American Indian foster parents were identified; seven agreed to participate in the study. All participants were members of tribes recognized by the federal government, as verified through their tribal enrollment. All participants resided in the Rocky Mountain Front Range area of Colorado, and all were current providers of kinship or foster care to American Indian children. Participants, all women, ranging from age 18 to 65, were members the Apache, Chippewa, Navajo, Pueblo, and Sioux tribes.

## Design

This qualitative study explored the child welfare experiences and ideas of Colorado-based American Indian foster parents. Qualitative data were collected through key participant interviews, using a near experience story about a hypothetical child welfare case involving an American Indian child. The case served as a springboard for related scenarios and comments from participants.

A letter, sent to participants, explained the study in detail. A copy of the story used in the interview process was enclosed. Later, participants were contacted by telephone to schedule personal interviews, either in their homes or in a local social service agency that provided services to American Indian clients.

The interviews were audiotaped, and all questions were written on large sheets of papers mounted on an easel. Notes were taken as participants answered each question. Participants were then asked to correct any answers that they felt did not accurately reflect their responses. All interview questions were related to the hypothetical child welfare case in which the research questions were embedded.

This method made it possible for participants to answer all questions, as well as to elaborate more fully on specific responses. All participants were asked what type of foster care services they had provided (e.g., kinship care, nonrelative foster care, group home care).

Audiotapes were transcribed by the investigators, and written notes were examined for accuracy of recording of participants' responses. A coding scheme was developed by cataloging into common themes and categories the responses to each question.

## Findings and Discussion

Once the interviews were completed, the information was analyzed. Key informants were contacted again and asked to review and sort the statements into principal themes. Disagreements and rationales were discussed. The following list outlines the principal themes derived from the responses.

### Theme 1. Discouraged from Working with the Present Foster Care System

All respondents noted the first theme as a prominent issue. Participants emphasized that the problems between American Indians and the public child welfare system stemmed from discrimination and from negative perceptions of American Indians as being either poor or problematic as caregivers. All reported feeling discouraged by the lack of support they had received from child welfare staff. This factor may be a primary reason for the lack of American Indian foster parents in the system.

### Theme 2. Role of Culture in Caregiving

American Indians view themselves as members of a unique cultural group. They have a responsibility to carry their cultural norms with them and to impart their values, customs, and traditions to successive generations. They see themselves as both part of and purveyors of American Indian culture for Indian children in foster care. Respondents indicated that they must socialize their children through American Indian practices. According to the respondents, foster and adoptive care systems typically do not acknowledge or have programs to help Indian parents and caregivers sustain Indian values and socialization practices.

### Theme 3. Different Definition of Family and Relations

This theme pertained to the value and cultural belief of "kin." American Indians consider themselves as actual kin to other

American Indians who may or may not be direct biological relations. All respondents emphasized the concept of relatedness,
being connected to all American Indian people regardless of tribe
or the status of families. This theme underscored the cultural value
of shared responsibility, as many participants hold the traditional
belief that all American Indians are related to one another. Therefore, they naturally assume the role of mentors and supporters of birthparents, even when such a role is not formalized or
conceptualized.

This point is an important consideration when working with
families who are at risk of losing a child. Respondents indicated
that they are responsible for all children in their community and
nationwide. Placement of an Indian child from one family into
another should be considered within the context of cultural continuance and relatedness. Westernized concepts, such as the
nuclear family and birthfamily, are not as important to American
Indian foster parents.

### Theme 4. Historical Pain Due to Past Family Disruption

This theme stressed the pain of losing children or having families disrupted through the removal and out-of-home placement
of American Indian children. All respondents noted that many, if
not all, American Indian families have histories that include the
forced removal of children from their homes. This history has
caused many painful memories and "hurts" in the lives of American Indians, some of whom would and could be foster or adoptive parents. Respondents also reported painful memories associated with boarding schools; these institutions played a significant,
and oftentimes traumatizing, role in their lives. Respondents repeatedly underscored the need to address these hurts, so that parents and family members in American Indian communities can
heal from the past and become the best parents and caregivers
possible. This healing, they felt, could be the best motivator American Indians have to participate in the foster care system.

## Discussion and Recommendations

Although limited in scope, this study shows that barriers exist between Indian communities and the child welfare system, particularly in relation to the recruitment and retention of American Indians as foster or adoptive parents. The lack of attention given by the child welfare system to the cultural traditions and values of American Indians continues to alienate and reduce their numbers as foster care providers.

Foster care, under any circumstance, is a very demanding and complex undertaking. Foster care in urban American Indian families is even more so. Efforts must be made to assist American Indians who live in urban communities to interact with the child welfare system in ways that are not always adversarial or confrontational. American Indians, along with child welfare providers, must recognize and work through the remnants of historical pain and distrust that for years have afflicted this population. Continued strained relations and cultural misunderstandings may help to explain why child welfare services for this indigenous group are generally not provided in culturally appropriate ways.

## Conclusion

This study is an initial effort to examine how urban American Indians think and feel about the foster care system. Interpretations are based on indigenous cultural values and historical issues. For example, respondents emphasized a more holistic approach to foster care, such as taking into consideration the needs of both the foster parents and birthparents, rather than severing ties between parents and kin. Cultural orientation also points to the need for child welfare workers to take a less Western view of many social and economic standards. For instance, when considering adequate housing for families, values differ on the space and layout of homes. American Indian foster parents who participated in this study believed that it was more important to nurture their children culturally than to show great concern for how their living spaces were furnished and whether they met foster care licensing regulations. The latter middle-class values are indicative of cultural differences that reflect continued lack of awareness and understanding by the system charged with the responsibility to assist at-risk American Indian families.

Foster care, adoption, and other recruitment and retention efforts among American Indians should also involve a reexamination of how home studies for potential families take place. The authors of this article have personally experienced how intimidating such a process can be, particularly when representatives of the child welfare system exhibit cultural bias and distrust. In many instances, these interactions were stilted and unnatural, making the situation quite tense. In other cases, when the home studies were conducted by an American Indian, surprise and relief were followed by much discussion by all involved. Future efforts in this area are needed to be more respectful and less prejudicial toward American Indians potentially interested in becoming foster or adoptive parents.

The study's findings support the conclusion that decades of assimilative and genocidal federal policies thrust on American Indians have resulted in a group of people who continue to experience multiple problems and stressors. The longstanding federal policies and practices have taken a toll on all American Indian families. This study supports the belief that child welfare agencies do not customarily address the complexities and diversity of urban Indians' histories. Much needs to be done by child welfare practitioners to engage and partner with urban Indian communities and families to achieve culturally appropriate family preservation and reunification services. The key to achieving these goals is the culturally based socialization of American Indian children. To accomplish this, Native American families must be permitted to rear their children in a healthy and culturally competent context. Current foster care and adoption programs do not usually function in ways conducive to safeguarding ICWA.

Based on the findings of this study, the following policy and programmatic recommendations are made:

- More education and support are needed for American Indian foster parents. A foster parents' training curriculum should openly address intergroup cultural conflicts, as well as bicultural socialization concerns that child welfare staff may have.
- The perception of discrimination experienced by American Indian foster and adoptive parents must be addressed. Possible methods may include forums, where American Indians service providers have the opportunity to share their views and concerns with social workers, juvenile and family court judges, attorneys, guardians ad litem, and non-Indian foster and adoptive parents. More open and honest communication between all parties is greatly needed.
- Although initial foster parent training could be done in groups, individualized support is necessary to address American Indian families' many complex issues and needs.
- The use of support groups, modeled after Indian cultural traditions such as the "talking circles," should increase the likelihood of greater foster and adoptive parent participation.
- American Indian foster and adoptive parents can be mentors and trainers of potential and newer Indian foster and adoptive parents. They can also be used as mentors for American Indian families who have been reunified with their children or for children placed in kinship care.
- Elders and respected American Indian community members can be used more to help non-Indian foster and adoptive parent learn and understand the culture and the community. Elders can also help these foster and adoptive parents to work more effectively with American Indian families to achieve family reunification.

- More tangible assistance should be provided to American Indian foster and adoptive parents, including transportation and childcare during training sessions. Help is also needed with the costs associated with the completion of the foster and adoptive parent application material, such as costs of medical physicals, fingerprinting, etc.
- Social workers should telephone the foster parents at least once each week and should use home or school visits to call on American Indian foster children. This support would also help to retain foster parents and provide the emotional support American Indian children need.

Successful foster care programs for American Indians are possible, but problems continue to exist between the child welfare system and the American Indian community. Obviously, more research needs to be conducted to explore further the findings of this study. More field work that embodies both qualitative and quantitative analyses would enhance this preliminary description of urban and nonurban American Indian families, parenting practices, and children's needs.◆

## References

Babbie, E. (1994). *The practice of social research*. Boston: Wadsworth.

Blanchard, E. L., & Barsh, R. L. (1980). What is best for tribal children: A response to Fischler. *Social Work, 25*, 350-357.

Burger, R. A. (1995). *Effects of the boarding school experience on American Indian families: Practice guidelines*. St. Paul, MN: Augsburg College.

Byler, M. G., & Unger, S. (1974-1979). *Indian Family Defense*. Bulletin Nos. 1-11. New York: Association on American Indian Affairs.

California Indian Legal Services. (1998). *California judges benchguide: The Indian Child Welfare Act* (pp. 42-43). Eureka, CA: Author.

Coontz, S. (1988). *The social origins of private life: A history of American Indian families, 1600-1900*. New York: Verso.

Cross, T. (1996). *Cross-cultural skills in Indian child welfare: A guide for the non-Indian*. Portland, OR: National Indian Child Welfare Association.

Deloria, V. (1985). *American Indian policy in the twentieth century*. Norman: University of Oklahoma Press.

George, L. J. (1997). Why the need for the Indian Child Welfare Act? *Journal of Multicultural Social Work, 5*(3/4), 165-175.

Horejsi, C., Heavy Runner Craig, B., & Pablo, J. (1992). Reactions by Native Americans to child protection agencies: Cultural and community factors. *Child Welfare, 17*(4), 329-342.

Howard, G. S. (1991). A narrative approach to thinking, cross-cultural psychology, and psychotherapy. *American Psychologist, 46(3)*, 187-197.

Mannes, M. (1993). Seeking the balance between child protection and family preservation in Indian child welfare. *Child Welfare, 72*(2), 141-152.

O'Brien, S. (1989). *American Indian tribal governments*. Norman: University of Oklahoma Press.

Paulson, S. (1999). *Would we still be Indian without our parents?* [Training brochure]. Bismark, ND: Native American Child and Family Services Training Institute.

Red Horse, J. (1980). American Indian elders: Unifiers of Indian families. *Social Casework, 61*, 490-493.

Sheafor, B. W., Horejsi, C. R., & Horejsi, G. A. (1997). *Techniques and guidelines for social work practice* (4th ed.). Boston: Allyn and Bacon.

Tashima, N., Crain, C., O'Reilly, K., & Elifson, C. S. (1996). The community identification (CID) process: A discovery model. *Qualitative Health Research, 6*(1), 23-48.

Thornton, R. (2001). *Studying Native America: Problems and prospects*. Madison: University of Wisconsin Press.

U.S. Bureau of the Census. (2000). *Statistical abstract of the United States*. Washington, DC: U.S. Government Printing Office.

# Chapter 11

# Transracial Adoption and Foster Care Placement: Worker Perception and Attitude

*Jan Carter-Black*

This study explores black child welfare workers' perceptions of transracial adoption (TRA) and foster care placement (FCP). Informants were asked to discuss their attitudes toward the placement of black children with white families, as well as their perception of the Multiethnic Placement Act of 1994 and the supplemental Interethnic Adoption Provision of 1996. This study expands existing research regarding the viability of TRA and FCP by incorporating the previously ignored perceptions of social service professionals who are charged with the responsibility of providing child and family services. Findings illuminate the significant role that prioritization of client need plays in the perceptions of workers.

*Jan Carter-Black, MSW, is Doctoral Student, School of Social Work, University of Illinois at Urbana-Champaign, Urbana, IL.*

T he adoption of children of color by Caucasian parents looms larger than ever over the child welfare policy agenda....The debate leading up to the passage of P.L. 103-382, the Multiethnic Placement Act (MEPA),...reflect the fierce emotions and high hopes pervading transracial adoption (TRA). There is scant middle ground in this debate. (Courtney, 1997, p. 750)

## "We Know *Their* Position on Transracial Adoption"

MEPA and the subsequent supplemental Interethnic Adoption Provision (IEP), were signed into law by President William J. Clinton on October 20, 1994, and August 20, 1996, respectively (Hollinger, 1988a, Rel. 9-12/97). MEPA was enacted to redress several social issues that had come to the attention of the U.S. Congress. First, the numbers of children entering the public child welfare system had reached record levels. Second, black children were disproportionately represented in out-of-home placements. Third, thousands of children were waiting a median of three years—five years in the case of black children—for adoptive homes. Finally, reports indicated that white families were routinely being denied the opportunity, solely on the basis of race and ethnicity, to become foster parents or to adopt children of color (Brooks, Barth, Bussiere, & Patterson, 1999).

The enactment of MEPA-IEP refueled the longstanding and persistent controversy surrounding TRA—more pointedly, the adoption of black children by white parents. TRA has remained a highly charged and conflictual issue since the 1960s, when more than 10,000 black children were adopted by white families between 1967 and 1972 (Curtis, 1996; Curtis & Alexander, 1996; Hollingsworth, 1997; Kallgren & Caudill, 1993).

## "There's Something Missing Here"

Unfortunately there is no reliable evidence regarding the magnitude of any bias against TRA that might exist within child welfare and adoption agencies. (Courtney, 1997, p. 763)

Copious research conducted by various national and international organizations, social science researchers, and professional associations has addressed the viability of TRA and foster care placement (FCP). However, the perceptions of workers charged with the day-to-day responsibility of providing direct client services to children and their families generally have been ignored. Furthermore, empirical data are lacking that identify the individual views of contemporary child welfare professionals concerning MEPA-IEP.

Research has established that the administration of social welfare policies and programs is realized at the local level. Front-line workers exert considerable influence over the implementation of policies and procedures, and these workers frequently wield considerable power by virtue of their immediate and consistent contact and communication with clients and other consumers of services.

> Street-level bureaucrats play a critical role in these citizen entitlements....The poorer people are, the greater the influence street-level bureaucrats tend to have over them. (Lipsky, 1980, p. 6)

This study explores child welfare workers' perceptions of TRA and FCP by asking them to discuss their attitudes about the placement of black children with white families, as well as their views of the accompanying legal mandates found in the MEPA and IEP. Exploration of these issues with workers contributes to filling the current void in the literature: the omission of experientially based practice wisdom regarding TRA and FCP.

One premise of this study is that individuals and organizations at the macro level of child welfare are far removed from clients. Conversely, workers who interact with children and families on a daily basis do so on a micro level. The workers in the latter category are responsible for policy and program implementation (Brodkin, 1997; Lipsky, 1980). These direct interactions result in these workers' unique experiences, which can affect the way they implement the mandates of adoption and permanency laws (Brooks et al., 1999). Highlighting child welfare workers' perceptions regarding the efficacy and viability of TRA and foster care, if brought to the forefront of the controversy, could aid in resolving the longstanding debate.

This article addresses two key research questions: (1) What are child welfare workers' perceptions and attitudes toward TRA and FCP? and (2) What are their views of MEPA-IEP, as it affects black children and their families. Three research objectives were established to facilitate and guide this study: (1) to ascertain whether child welfare workers perceive the placement of black children with white families as harmful to the children and, if so, why; (2) to address the effect of TRA or FCP on the racial identification and socialization of black children, as well as knowledge and acceptance of their cultural heritage; (3) and to explore the extent to which MEPA-IEP might be deleterious to black children and their families and, if so, how?

It is important to understand workers' attitudes regarding TRA and foster care, regardless of their race. The National Association of Black Social Workers (NABSW), however, played a key role in adoption agencies' decisions to minimize the number of adoptions and foster home placements of black children with white families from the late 1970s to 1994 and the passage of MEPA (Jones & Else, 1979). It seemed quite likely that the position held by some individual members of NABSW may differ from that of the professional organization. Therefore, the focus here is on the stance taken by individual black child welfare workers.

This article is divided into four sections. The first section presents a review of the literature on TRA and the foster care system, including a comprehensive historical overview. The second section describes the process of in-depth interviews with black child welfare workers who participated in this study as key informants. Section 3 presents the findings on workers' perceptions, as derived from the interviews. In addition, three thematic conceptualizations are discussed. These emerged from the data and are related to TRA and FCP (1) prioritization of children's needs, (2) unresponsiveness of the child welfare system, and (3) potential harm of MEPA-IEP. Excerpts from the interviews are included to facilitate a comparison between the research literature and the findings of this study. Finally, Section 4 considers the contribution of findings derived from the interviews, including implications for development of future adoption and permanency legislation, the formulation and implementation of child welfare policies and procedures, and social work "best practice" strategies. Implications for further research are considered.

## Review of the Controversy

In 1999, approximately 568,000 children were in foster care nationwide; an estimated 118,000 of these children were waiting to be adopted. Of the total number of children in foster care at that time, 239,500 were black. More than 58,000 black children were waiting to be adopted. More than 187,000 children remain in the foster care system for three to five years or more (U.S. Department of Health and Human Services, 2000). In 2001, funding for foster care was $5.1 billion and $1.2 billion dollars for adoption assistance programs (U.S. Department of Health and Human Services, 2001).

Although these numbers indicate how many children are in foster care, how many of them are waiting for adoptive and permanent homes, and the cost to the American public, the data do not explain the controversy that swirls around the issues of TRA and FCP. The historical background of the practice helps to establish the context of the debate.

### Historical Overview

There wasn't no Department of Children and Family Services for black kids when we were growing up—at least not in Mississippi. We just did what we had to do to take care of those children. Say a mother died in childbirth and the daddy wasn't able to take care of the kids. The people, usually through the church, would just take the kids home to live with them. If there was a whole lot of kids and one family couldn't take them all, then they'd be split up between several families. But they always knew who their family was and where they lived. They'd see them all the time in church, at the school, in town, even in the fields chopping cotton. So if that's what you call "informal adoptions," then that's what we did. (Pearlie M. Hill, personal communication, September 19, 1999)

Historically, the adoption of black children rested in the hands of the black community with little or no assistance provided by any public social welfare policy or program. The personal communication above was provided by an 85-year-old black woman, born and raised on the Mississippi Delta, who remembers quite clearly the response of the black church community to children who needed homes and families.

As early as the 1920s, the purpose of private adoption agencies was to place healthy white babies with white adoptive parents. A commonly held belief among adoption specialists at that time was that similarities in physical attributes, intellectual potential, nationality, and temperament of the adoptive parents and the adoptee were vital in the search for an optimal match. Of course, religion and race was paramount to the proper match (Simon & Altstein, 1992). In 1959, the Child Welfare League of America (CWLA) published its first Standards for Adoption Service. These standards publicly proclaimed racial matching as a necessary professional obligation for child welfare practitioners.

Until the 1930s, child welfare services were primarily provided by private, nonprofit agencies that exercised "policies of racial exclusion." Along with other forms of unequal treatment, adoption and institutional care were typically unavailable to black children (McRoy, 1989). Despite the detrimental effect such racist policies had on these children, the cultural practice of informal adoptions throughout the black community worked sufficiently well for many generations. Were it not for the continued operation of informal adoptions, once the foster care system began to provide services to blacks, many more of these children would have become the responsibility of public child welfare.

The demands placed on the child welfare system increased as the number of dependent children, including racial minority youth, continued to rise. Many of the private agencies that had traditionally provided adoption services to the white community offered only foster care to black children. Consequently, the numbers of black children in the foster care system expanded significantly over the next 20 years (McRoy, 1989).

The trend of transcultural adoptions of foreign-born refugee children began in the 1950s. Significant numbers of Japanese, Chinese, and Korean children—many left without families as a result of World War II and the Korean War—were adopted by white American families. At that same time, CWLA joined forces with leaders of the U.S. Bureau of Indian Affairs to encourage and facilitate the adoption of hundreds of American Indian children by white families (Jones & Else, 1979).

Changes in the social, political, and economic climate during the 1960s in this country were accompanied by dramatic upheavals that altered the face of America. These changes included the approach to the adoption of children. Social changes, such as legalized abortion, contraception, and less stigma attached to out-of-wedlock childbirth, have been cited as significant factors that have led to a decrease in the numbers of healthy white babies available for adoption (Hollingsworth, 1998b, 1999; Howard, Royce, & Skerl, 1977). Consequently, agencies began to fill the gap in the "supply and demand" for adoptable babies with non-white infants. TRAs began to occur in noticeable numbers during that same time period, signaling a major shift in traditional adoption practices (Simon & Altstein, 1987). For example, in 1969, the Chicago Child Care Society began to place black infants and toddlers in nontraditional (single parent and transracial) adoptive homes. Within 5 years, an estimated 10,000 black children were adopted by white families. Furthermore, 10 years after publication of its original Standards for Adoption Service, CWLA reversed its opinion and actually advocated for TRAs (McRoy, 1989).

Controversy over the issue occurred in 1972 when NABSW took an explicit position in opposition to TRA and FCP. NABSW launched a strong attack against the adoption of black children by white families.

> Black children belong physically and psychologically and culturally in black families where they receive the total sense of themselves and develop a sound projection of their future. Only a black family can transmit the emotional and sensitive subtleties of perceptions and reactions essential for a black child's survival in a racist society....Black children in white homes are cut off from the healthy development of themselves as black people. (as cited in McRoy, 1989, p. 150)

Well-respected and traditional leaders of the black community joined the NABSW's protest against TRA. In 1974, the Black Caucus of the North American Conference on Adoptable Children announced "that every possible attempt should be made to place black and other minority children in a cultural and racial setting similar to their original group." Black social workers were extremely vocal in their opposition to TRAs, referring to the practice as a "diabolical trick" and a "lethal incursion on the black family" (Jones & Else, 1979). American Indian leaders also joined the protest against TRAs. Consequently, in 1978, Congress passed the Indian Child Welfare Act (ICWA) to prevent the disintegration of families by TRAs of American Indian children (Gaber & Aldridge, 1994).

CWLA found itself in the awkward position of having to modify its position on TRA once again as a result of the pressures brought to bear on the organization by the NABSW, black leaders, the American Indian community, and other constituent groups. In 1973, the Standards for Adoption Services indicated preference for same race adoptions as a means towards easier "integration" into the adoptive family (McRoy, 1989).

TRAs declined almost immediately. The opposition to TRAs was powerful enough that state agencies such as the Illinois Department of Children & Family Services adopted a policy that prohibited TRAs of black children (Jones & Else, 1979). The result of this policy, coupled with the disproportionate number of black children removed from their homes, had an unfortunate consequence, i.e., black children lingering in foster care or "foster care drift" (Curtis, 1996). To address the problem, permanency planning was decreed in both the Adoption Assistance and Child Welfare Act of 1980 (Mannes, 1998), and the Adoption and Safe Families Act of 1997 (Public Law 105-89, 1997).

MEPA, in 1994, was a legal injunction created to facilitate moving children out of the child welfare system and into permanent living arrangements as well as to ensure the elimination of discriminatory practices in approving potential foster and adoptive parents. MEPA granted additional support to permanency for children by providing legal ratification for TRAs and FCPs (Hollinger, 1988a, Rel. 9-12/97). The aftermath of MEPA, however, was both extensive and convoluted.

Those who opposed TRA rejected MEPA on the basis that black children who were adopted transracially would not learn critical strategies for living and surviving in racist America. They also suggested black children raised in white families and living in predominately white communities would be more likely to develop racial identity problems and poor self-esteem (Curtis, 1996).

Proponents of TRA also objected to MEPA. Under the original act, child welfare agencies were given permission to consider culture, race, and/or ethnicity in foster or adoption placement decisions.

Permissible consideration: An agency or entity...may consider the cultural, ethnic, or racial background of the child and the capacity of the prospective foster or adoptive parents to meet the needs of a child of this background as one of a number of factors used to determine the best interests of a child. (Hollinger, 1988a, Rel.9-12/97)

The insinuation was that, on the basis of the "permissible consideration" language, the alleged discriminatory practice of routinely denying and/or delaying the placement of black children with white families to place them with racially similar families could easily be justified, thereby negating the effects of the act altogether (Hollinger, 1988a, Rel.9-12/97; Hollingsworth, 1998b). In addition, TRA supporters were displeased with the absence of legal enforcement for violations of MEPA mandates (Courtney, 1997).

On August 20, 1996, the IEP was signed into law. As a response to the tremendous controversy and confusion created by MEPA, IEP was an attempt to clarify the intent of Congress to eliminate delays in the placement of children for foster care and adoption in several ways. First, IEP indicates that agencies cannot routinely assume that children have needs related to their racial, color, or national origin. (Hollinger, 1988b, Rel. 11-12/98). Second, agencies may not routinely evaluate the ability of prospective foster or adoptive parents to meet the racial, color, or national origin needs of a child. Third, IEP confirms the fact that these statutes fall under the rubric of civil rights law. Fourth, provisions are clearly designated for aggrieved individuals to bring legal action against a state, agency, or other federally funded entity for violation of the mandates. Finally, sanctions for noncompliance or violation of MEPA-IEP were established, including fiscal penalties (Hollinger, 1998).

Despite the intent of Congress to eliminate delays in the placement of children and redress the negative reactions to MEPA, the confusion and controversy remained quite high (Brooks et al., 1999). Crucial to the debate was the emotionally weighted dispute regarding the appropriateness and efficacy of TRA in general.

Opponents of TRA who have strongly held views have claimed that TRA, as a form of child care, is inadequate in preparing a black child for life in a racist society. Others have alleged that black children raised in white families and communities will be moderately to severely deficient in terms of self-identity and self-esteem. Still others propose that transracial adoptees will find themselves ostracized from both the black and white social worlds, unable to really find a "fit" in either environment. Perhaps most impressive of all these concerns is that the black transracial adoptees will not be able to develop a healthy racial identity (Curtis, 1996; Hollingsworth, 1998a; McRoy, 1994). In 1994, the NABSW modified its original 1972 stance on TRA to read:

> In conclusion, family preservation, reunification and adoption should work in tandem toward finding permanent homes for children. Priority should be given to preserving families through the reunification or adoption of children with/by biological relatives. If that should fail, secondary priority should be given to the placement of a child within his own race....Under no circumstance should successful same race placements be impeded by obvious barriers. (NABSW, 1994, as cited in Hollingsworth, 1998b)

Courtney (1997) suggested that, rather than all the debate over the effects TRA has on the self-esteem, racial identity, or psychological adjustment of black children (child- and family-focused), attention should be on the much larger issue of the inadequacy and the failure of the national child welfare system. Clear and sufficient evidence is available that, at times, the public child welfare system is less than effective and efficient (Courtney, 1997; Hollingsworth, 1998b; Kallgren & Caudill, 1993).

Proponents of TRA who have strongly held views contend that studies most frequently indicate no significant effects on the self-esteem, self-identity, intellectual or behavior development, or even the racial identity development of transracial adoptees (Hayes, 1993; Simon, Altstein, & Melli, 1994; Vroegh, 1997). In response to the stance taken by the NABSW and American Indian councils in the 1970s, the parents in a longitudinal study claimed that the position taken by various groups, such as NABSW, conflicted with the best interest of the child, and "smacked of racism." Offended by the allegation that white families could not properly parent black children, they felt betrayed by the very organizations they thought would support them (Simon et al., 1994).

Hayes (1993) pointedly suggested that opponents of TRA wrongly insist that black children have both a need and a right to the racial and ethnic cultural heritage into which they were born. To this assertion he adds that the concept is simply "the more radical aim of African American [separatists]," who place unreasonable responsibilities on black children to be a resource for the community. He further claims black separatists expound the belief that every black person has a "duty" to maintain a unique race-based culture rather than be assimilated into the "Caucasian society" (Hayes, 1993). In a final declaration, Hayes acknowledged that, although it was probably valid during the 1960s and 1970s to say adoption agencies were slanted toward white adoptive parents, by the 1990s the trend had shifted in favor of black adoptive parents. "The importance attached to finding minority parents is such that they are actively screened in" (Hayes, 1993, p. 304). He further commented that the search for black adoptive parents extends to "canvassing bars, pool halls, speaking to ministers and their church groups, women's clubs, and simply stopping people in the street" (Ladner, 1977, as cited in Hayes, 1993, p. 304).

The controversy, conflict, and subsequent debates over TRA has persisted for almost 40 years. The absence of a resolution to this conflict contributes to the expenditure of valuable resources in launching offensive and defensive actions rather than in pursuing strategies to enhance the successful outcomes for adoptive families and their children. Therefore, one goal of this study is to provide information that will augment pertinent research and contribute to the resolution of the TRA debate.

## Method

Ethnographic research was chosen as the method for this study. Because it facilitates and encourages in-depth discussions through individual interviews, an ethnographic research method enabled workers to provide a richly textured quality of information. With a limited number of participants involved, however, the ability to generalize is diminished. Nonetheless, this methodology was particularly appropriate for this study because previous research did not give much attention to the views of child welfare workers who deal with the issue of TRA/FCP in their everyday work.

### *Participants: "The Professional Child Welfare Community"*

Ten black child welfare workers participated in this study. Each was purposely selected or was referred by other informants. Purposive sampling guaranteed that each participant had at least one year of direct practice experience in the field of child welfare and had participated in child placement decisionmaking processes in their respective agencies. Snowball sampling allowed knowledgeable participants to refer other potential informants. It should be noted, however, that only one informant made referrals and only one of the referrals was ultimately selected as a participant.

The workers were recruited from a mid-Western child welfare community. The ratio of 9 women to 1 man reflects the preponderance of women to men in child welfare nationally. Workers were selected, through personal contact by the primary researcher, from a pool of 4 distinct private agencies. The workers' years of experience in the field of child welfare ranged from 5 to more than 15 years. All had succeeded in establishing a credible reputation in their professional community.

### *Procedures: "Just Between You, Me and the Lamp Post"*

Data were obtained over a two-month period in 2000 through open-ended, semistructured, face-to-face interviews, each lasting 1 to 2 hours. Five interviews were conducted at workers' agencies; one took place in a participant's home. Because of scheduling issues, three separate interviews were conducted in public settings.

Fourteen questions were developed to facilitate discussion pertaining to predetermined general topic areas. Examples of the nature of the facilitative questions asked of each participant are the following: "Discuss the current foster care system from your perspective as a veteran child welfare worker." "Tell me how TRA or FCP affects the racial identity development of black children." "How do you think MEPA/IEP will affect black children and their families?"

### *Data Analysis: "Emerging Patterns of Realities and Meanings"*

An inductive analysis of the interview data was facilitated through the emergence of patterns and themes typical of ethnographic research. Analysis continued as an on going process throughout data collection. Each interview was audiotaped, reviewed, and transcribed by the primary researcher. Coded categories were constructed to organize and manage data, promote content analysis of transcriptions, and aid in the development of conceptual themes. Identification of categories was based on themes and patterns as they emerged from the data by using a constant comparative method of analysis. Categories were then further defined, their properties were delineated, and both the causes, as well as the conditions under which they operated, were identified as suggested by Charmaz (1983).

## Findings

### *"But What Do You Think; We Need to Hear from You"*

The purpose of this research is to identify the perceptions of black child welfare workers about TRA and FCP, as well as the effect of the MEPA of 1994 and the IEP of 1996 on black children and their families. This inquiry first explored the two major competing arguments concerning TRA and FCP then proceeded to the perceptions obtained from the workers' interviews. Comparing the pros and cons of TRA/FCP (as posited by national and international organizations, social science researchers, and the professional associations) against the perceptions and attitudes of direct service practitioners permitted the illumination of assonance and dissonance between the two. As a result of the inquiry and subsequent comparison, three thematic concepts emerged from the analyzed data: (1) prioritization of children's needs, (2) unresponsiveness of the child welfare system to the needs of these children, and (3) potential harm of MEPA-IEP.

### Prioritization of Children's Needs: "The Family [Has] to Make That Commitment"

The workers who participated in this study consistently declared that the most important determinant in making FCP and adoption decisions on behalf of any child is to ensure that the family is able to meet the child's needs. Without exception, workers stated that the family system and environment into which a black child is being placed must be able to provide for them in a plethora of domains, including racial identity development, knowledge and acceptance of their cultural heritage, and racial socialization. All of the workers stressed the crucial importance of these dimensions of development and socialization, but the issue of racial socialization elicited the most comprehensive responses.

### Racial Identity Development

Giving that kid the right type of environments to be in and the right information in terms of history, that kid could probably grow up to be a very stable and probably a versed person in terms of who he is as well as knowing about who he's not.

I mean, are they willing to make the steps? Are they willing to visit black churches? Do they have friends or are they willing to have, say, godparents who are black?

Just in my own work, I saw families who really did reach out to other black foster parents. You know, these issues around hair care and skin care, and that just hits the surface. Those are the outside things.

They go through a lot of things. They go to black events, they go to black churches, forums, seminars, conferences, all kinds of things.

### Knowledge and Acceptance of Cultural Heritage

That family [has] to make that commitment to doing what's necessary in terms of being able to have that culturally rich environment.

They weren't trying to raise her in a all white environment but were trying to raise her in a mixed environment. She had white friends, black friends....They've taken an interest in her,...I mean in terms of her culture.

A positive experience for the children...I mean taking them into settings so that they can also have the experience of their culture and their heritage.

### Racial Socialization

On the one hand, I want to say its always optimal for a child to be in an environment with people who can identify with him, but then you have to ask yourself what is it you want them to identify with? What makes up your race?...Do I want a child's racial identity to be what I eat, what I listen to, the types of music? Or is it something that comes from that inner core of a shared experience?

Really working with families who want to adopt transracially...making sure they understand what's involved, not only with the love they give within the home but what about their community where they live? Is this child going to be accepted?...Who is their social network?

Growing up as a minority in a dominant culture, most black people know how to acclimate themselves, whereas most white people just don't have a clue.

They [Caucasians] can live their whole lives—and it can be a conscious choice or unconscious choice—and they never really come in contact with somebody different than them if they choose not to do that....People have to really go out of their way to make a conscious effort to get to know people who look different or act different than they do....Therefore, when you have a child who is black and placed in a white home...they're going to be with a white family and they're going to assume for a long time...not necessarily that they're white but that it doesn't make a difference. And then, as they start to venture out, they're going to see it makes a huge difference...in the surroundings.

It's the black foster parents who can say "Yeah, it's going to make a difference," and the white foster parents will say "Well, no, it doesn't...it shouldn't." They're still kind of idealistic....You and that child can't live in your house all the time. If you could, that'd be great, and there probably wouldn't be any problems...but how do you help that child when he or she goes outside your house?

Because unless you can understand what its like to be a minority in a dominant culture and then have to adjust everything you do to that culture, and understand that, "Hmmm, this time I'm different," you're never going to be able to help that child who is grown up with that do that.

The workers' comments quite clearly indicate their attitude that TRA/FCP is far from the ideal solution to the problem of black children lingering in the foster care system. The strategy appears to be replete with potential problems for both the adoptees and adoptive families. One of the most notable problems identified by the informants occurs when white adoptive and foster parents disregard the importance of race.

Some [Caucasian parents] just don't want to acknowledge that it's even an issue at all. That if they love and nurture the child, it just doesn't matter. I don't personally agree with that.

Sometimes that commitment might include moving out of a small little town where their child would be subject to racism...because really, when a family brings a black child into their home, guess what? They're no longer a white family. They're now themselves a multiracial family. It's not just the child who's black "but we're still white, and we're still in our white community, and we have a child who's black." They now become a mixed heritage family.

These same workers, however, clearly indicated that successful TRA is both possible and preferable to foster care drift and lingering.

I do believe that many Caucasian families can parent and love black children and can really do a good job if they have the appropriate training and support.

It...wouldn't be a good idea just to say, "Well, since we don't have black homes now, we'll just wait." I mean...we have kids who need homes now.

Am I exposing these children to the things that are going to help them with their racial identity?...To me, I guess what's connected with that is self-esteem. So for me, my question is, What am I doing as a foster parent or a parent to help my child to have the highest self-esteem? And I'm not so sure that racial identity has to be at the top of that list.

To me, there's so many kids who need homes that I just think there's more important things to worry about than are they going to feel black? Are they going to be able to identify with other black people?....it really has a lot to do with the parents and what they're exposed to.

The workers' perceptions and attitudes are congruent with empirical studies that suggest certain elements are linked to successful outcomes for these racially mixed families. For example, Kallgren and Caudill (1993) recommended two such elements: (1) placing children in TRA homes at an early age and (2) ensuring that the families have received education on issues pertaining to racial awareness.

As the workers attested and research has noted, placing black children in homes with white families who deny the child's racial identity may contribute to a diminished self-image (McRoy, Zurcher, Lauderdale, & Anderson, 1984). Conversely, when the "familial context" is aware of and acknowledges the significance of race, the TRA child appears to develop a healthy racial identity and self-esteem (Kallgren & Caudill, 1993).

### Unresponsive Child Welfare System: "The Child Welfare System Is Culturally Biased"

A majority of the workers voiced concerns that the current child welfare system is unresponsive to the black community, its children, and their families' needs. This lack of responsiveness was noted on both the institutional and the individual levels.

> Number one, I think that overall the child welfare system continues to be frankly culturally biased...The people making a lot of the administrative decisions...from what I see or what I perceive, it's still pretty much Caucasian women.

> Because of the lack of cultural knowledge, because of the people who are in control of the system...there have not been adequate attempts to really nurture more black families into adopting and into foster care.

> I frankly think it's a cop out that there's not enough black families..."Well, we've got plenty of these families already

here, so what's the difference." I do think it's a cop out to say that there are not black homes. I think it's an issue of not having sufficient efforts put into place to actually [recruit] those black homes.

Maybe the approaches that have been used to recruit black families and help prepare them are still based on a model that is more useful for middle-class white families.

In terms of times that things are offered, like the trainings, in terms of the mounds of paper work that families are expected to get through, just in terms of the trust level...to go through that whole licensing process, where you're being asked very intimate details about you're private life, your relationships, your background...If [families] don't perceive they're dealing with someone who can relate to them or can trust, there's a barrier...Part of that plays into why there are not sufficient numbers of black homes.

You rarely see a white child placed in a black home. And I've never seen any being adopted. I have never seen or heard of that in this county, and that's over 15 years...The way I feel is that they've thrown this kid away, and "Here you go, this black home is punishment."

I think that racism does play a part because...when mothers are delivering in the hospitals...a lot of who gets tested for drugs is up to the doctor's discretion, and you know black women are much more likely to get scrutinized and tested for drugs than whites are.

A pertinent example that highlights the lack of cultural awareness and responsiveness in the system is reflected in the workers' concerns about the conflict between the traditional black kinship care system and the more formal systems of adoption, structured and regulated relative foster care, and subsidized guardianship under public child welfare.

### *Kinship Systems: "The Ties That Bind"*

It wasn't called foster care, it was "you go live with who-ever." That's maybe or maybe not a family member...black people in the black community did their own kind of in-ternal foster care.

Given the...process that you have to go through to be-come a licensed foster parent....Years ago, I could have taken my sister's kids, taken them to my house, raised and fed and clothed them, and that was it...And we would have been fine. But now...you have a lot of different rules...and I can understand some of them, but...that's just tiresome.

A lot of black families say, all the time in foster care train-ing and support groups, "Why do we have to make that decision? We said we are going to keep the child. Why can't the child just stay?"

Grandmothers have raised grandchildren and great-grandchildren for years, and you didn't have to have a piece of paper stating that this kid is yours...So now, to have a system come in and say..."You need to show that you will adopt this kid and be willing to make him or her your own"..."I don't have to adopt this kid, this kid is my grandchild. I'll raise this kid...I'll do what I have to do"...and that [birth] mother is probably still going to see that child.

She's saying clearly, "He's a part of the family, he can live here as long as he wants to"...but she's constantly being asked and almost pressured to consider adoption or sub-sidized guardianship, and she doesn't want to do either. She doesn't want to adopt because, again, that would change the family dynamics...He's got permanency... she's already saying he can live here forever.

Hollingsworth (1998b) succinctly captured the culture-based belief concerning adoption this way. "The reluctance to adopt formally among African American kinship foster caregivers is based in cultural definitions of family and attitudes about family relationships" (p. 111).

Although this research focuses on the issue of TRA/FCP and MEPA-IEP, another critical social reality that dramatically affects black children and families emerged during the interviews. Some of the workers specifically identified social class as a variable that influences clients' experiences almost as much as race.

### Class Matters: "If You're Poor, That's the Strike Right There"

Certainly, poor families get scrutinized a lot more...and I would even go as far as to say poor urban families...In some of the more secluded rural areas, there's less opportunity for families to be scrutinized by child welfare systems, because they're spread out and probably aren't interacting as much with all of the major institutions that would be doing the scrutinizing.

[The major factor] would be class because the reality is probably that...the majority of them are also poor.

I notice that people who have more education and are able to afford a paid lawyer...get their kids a lot faster...The court system...If you are poor, you can forget it. They are going to do whatever they want to you and with you and your family. And you are going to be separated a lot longer. I find that to be across the board for poor people in general.

Often, workers will impose their own value system or what they've grown to believe is the best system for these children. For hundreds of years...people have raised children and done a good job, and they didn't have a bedroom for each child or...$80.00 sneakers. That's not a requirement for being a good parent...that's an American value that we're trying to impose on people...I don't think that's right. We're deciding now more than just minimum parenting standards.

The link between poverty and events that result in out-of-home placements of children has been thoroughly researched and well documented (Hollingsworth, 1998b; McRoy, Oglesby, & Grape, 1997). The multitude of problems associated with inadequate resources compounds the already vulnerable position occupied by children and youth (Jarrett, 1997b). The range of these problems varies from being at risk for child maltreatment to diminished opportunities for success and high achievement as adults (Haveman & Wolfe, 1994; Jarrett, 1997a).

The child welfare system is fundamentally charged with the responsibility of  promoting and protecting the welfare of children. According to the child welfare workers interviewed for this study, the system has failed to respond in several areas to the needs of racial and ethnic minority children and families, as well as poor families. Their sentiment is echoed in much of the research (Courtney, 1997; Hollingsworth, 1998b; Kallgren & Caudill, 1993; McRoy et al., 1997).

### Potential Harm of MEPA-IEP: "There Was No Effort to Even Look"

The literature includes many empirical studies, position papers, case studies, and reviews evaluating the efficacy of MEPA and IEP. The reaction to these laws has been observed for more than seven years. The responses of the workers to this study include the following:

> When I first started...they had a rule to first try to place kids within their own race....Three years later...they changed. You could place them really anywhere that you could find a suitable placement...whether it be black or white, so the focus changed...about 1997.

The thing that bothers me about TRA and transracial foster care…being a black foster parent, I've never had a white child placed with me or an Asian child….My thing is, you may sit there and tell me all the white kids have homes, but I know that's not true….My argument would be, don't say it's okay for a black child to live with a white parent and then for the same reason say it's not okay for a white child to live with my family because we're not white.

People are so fearful now, because of this big hand of the law. We would get drilled on how, if you dare make any decision on placement based on race, you are out of here. You could get sued personally, lose your home, everything that you own, if you're found to be in violation of that IEP.

One example that I knew…[was a] very rural, little town with no diversity, with a reputation, in fact, of being hostile toward minorities. Well now, because we have IEP…two black kids came into [the system]….The bottom line is, there was no effort to even look for a home that could have matched these children culturally. They were just immediately placed…then we found out later, on discussion, some black families were available.

I could see it setting a stage, in the sense that, if you're talking about what can be provided, probably 9 times out of 10 you will find this white home that the system would define as better…provide good education, a nice home.

I also think that particular law leads into the whole notion of bitterness between races. Obviously, you have a black family who is losing that child to these white folks. That's probably not going to create the best feelings….You probably have a white system worker who has been in court with a white attorney and white judges who are "giving my black child to this white family."

The whole effect of MEPA-IEP has yet to be witnessed. Although the statutes were passed in 1994 and 1996, respectively, it will be difficult to ascertain the full consequences of this controversial child welfare policy for several more years.

## Discussion

Three major concepts emerged from the interview data in this study. First, children requiring out-of-home placement have needs that must be prioritized. Second, the current child welfare system is unresponsive to the needs of black children and their families. Third, MEPA and IEP are potentially harmful to black families.

With regard to the importance of development of racial identity, knowledge and acceptance of cultural heritage, and racial socialization as aspects of the prioritization of children's needs, the child welfare workers in this study basically disagreed with the position presented by Hayes (1993). In this study, workers contended that minority children need and have a right to develop a distinct ethnic identity and awareness of cultural heritage. The workers indicated that those who adhere to Hayes' supposition (that racial identification and cultural heritage are neither a necessity nor a right) and who practice that belief as a childrearing strategy with black children may neglect to provide those children with adequate racial socialization (Hollingsworth, 1999).

Despite the "presumably correct...[statement] that race does not exist as a biological reality...the role that race plays in society is salient...[existing] as a social construction rather than a biological or genetic reality at the group (e.g., family) or societal level" (Helms & Talleyrand, 1997, p. 1247). Research from a variety of disciplines has extensively documented the critical significance of racial socialization (Anderson & Sabatelli, 1999; Forehand & Kotchick, 1996; Hale-Benson, 1982; Sanders, 1997). Contrary to the earlier position of the NABSW that "black children should be placed only with black families, whether in foster care or adoption" (as cited in Simon & Altstein, 1977, p. 50), the participants in this study believe that white families who are willing and able to "make that commitment" may in fact be able to raise black children and to instill in them a healthy racial identity as well as and both knowledge and acceptance of their cultural heritage.

In essence, the workers who participated in this study might applaud the idea that there are white families capable of raising emotionally healthy black children if they are realistic about both the future and "the society in which they now live" (Ladner, 1977).

The second theme that emerged from this study was that the current child welfare system is unresponsive to the needs of its clients. The experiences of the workers imply that, despite research concerning the importance of culturally aware, knowledgeable, and skilled practitioners and agencies, the system has not improved very much. The workers' comments suggest an absence of responsiveness to either black families or poor families. Several examples the workers presented illustrate this lack of responsiveness.

The first significant deficiency they identified is the failure to effectively recruit, support, and maintain sufficient numbers of black adoptive and foster families. The failure to recognize and address cultural issues in critical case decisionmaking was identified as also demonstrating the system's lack of responsiveness (e.g., "because of the lack of cultural knowledge, because of the people who are in control of the system"). The perception that the system fails to respond amenably to poor people was captured in the comment, "If you're poor, you can forget it." This shortcoming may, in part, account for the disproportionate number of black children who are placed outside of their homes and in placements of longer duration ("[they're] going to be separated a lot longer"). Finally, the systematic ignoring of traditional kinship care in the black community was identified as another example of a culturally unaware and unresponsive system. This response further exacerbates an already tenuous relationship between the black family, the larger black community, and the child welfare system in this country.

Although no strong consensus was found among them, the workers who participated in this study presented, overall, a concern for the potential harm of MEPA-IEP. Their responses generally indicate they were most concerned that the statutes may give license to less culturally aware, sensitive, or conscientious workers and agencies to abdicate their responsibility to "diligently" recruit a pool of potential foster and adoptive families who reflect the racial/ethnic diversity of the children themselves (i.e., "because of MEPA and IEP...there's not that extra effort...if a black family is available, I don't feel that there's an extra effort placed into looking [for them]").

These workers' concerns differed in some respects from the positions found in much of the literature. They did not espouse the belief that MEPA-IEP would create a legal "black market" of black babies for white families. Nor did they believe the laws would prove an opportune medium for the premature termination of parental rights. They did however, agree with the premise that, because of the unresponsiveness of the child welfare system, MEPA-IEP was potentially detrimental for poor black families, in particular, who lacked resources such as private legal counsel and other forms of recourse.

## Implications

### "When You Have a Home Like That, Maybe Transracial Adoption Is a Good Thing"

The burgeoning and disproportionate number of black children in long-term foster care has become a chronic social problem. Continued research is needed to ensure that researchers and policymakers fully understand how children and families may be inadvertently affected by adoption and permanency legislation. The effect of significant child welfare policies and procedures on this population must be thoroughly documented, and more effective "best practice" social work strategies must be established.

### Adoption and Permanency Legislation

If some aspects of MEPA-IEP are deleterious to black families and children, it is imperative that the information be disclosed, both to develop and implement appropriate safeguards and to facilitate advocacy for legislative reform of adoption and permanency placement laws.

Legislators and policymakers should restructure monitoring procedures to guarantee that agencies will develop and implement strategies that facilitate the diligent recruitment of diverse potential foster and adoptive families who resemble the children requiring placement. Similarly, administrative oversight is needed to ensure that the criteria used to approve foster care and adoptive families and homes are not biased against either racial/ethnic minorities or those who are of less than middle-class socioeconomic standing. Another strategy that would reduce bias in the placement of children is to consider placing white children in the homes of racial/ethnic minorities, when appropriate to meet the needs of the children, not because the system has given up on them (i.e., "They've thrown this kid away and...this black home is [the child's] punishment").

Finally, greater attention must be paid to the traditional black kinship care system. The placement of children with extended kin (both blood relations and fictive kin) should be encouraged and supported as much as possible. The placement process should project an awareness of and respect for the presence of strong familial ties. Recognition of existing intimate family relationships would prove much more beneficial than the formal and impersonal procedure currently in place.

### Policies and Procedures

It is extremely important to increase our knowledge concerning the assumptions, beliefs, attitudes, and perceptions that front-line workers bring to foster care and adoption services when placing black children with white families. If workers perceive certain policies and procedures as inappropriate, ineffectual, or harmful to clients, they may attempt to interfere with the exercise of those policies, only to discover that their alternative intervention may be even more harmful. When workers disagree with the organization's stated goals or policies and procedures, noncompliance may well follow.

> The policy delivered by street-level bureaucrats is most often immediate and personal. They usually make decisions on the spot...and their determinations are focused entirely on the individual. (Lipsky, 1980, p. 8).

> One can expect a distinct degree of noncompliance if lower-level workers' interests differ from the interests of those at higher levels, and the incentives and sanctions available to higher levels are not sufficient to prevail. (Lipsky, 1980, p. 17)

Therefore, the more information available regarding the beliefs, assumptions, and perceptions of direct service workers, the more likely it is that their experiential knowledge and practice wisdom will be taken into account in the development of policies and procedures. Such consideration can create partnerships between various levels of policy development, administration, and actual implementation. Furthermore, the more direct service practitioners buy into the policies and procedures, the less likely they will be to take maverick actions and "make decisions on the spot."

### Best Practices

Neither formal policy nor worker ideology is sufficient to account for the interpretation of welfare policy at the frontline level.

> Caseworkers, like other lower-level bureaucrats, do not do just what they want or just what they are told to want. They do what they can. Their capacity depends on their

professional skills, agency resources, and access to good training. (Brodkin, 1997, p. 24)

Workers' views of TRA/FCP can provide pertinent information regarding professional training needs and can direct staff training to be more efficient, effective, and beneficial.

Race remains an important issue in social work practice for several reasons, including the dramatic demographic shifts occurring in this country (Proctor & Davis, 1994). With the increased numbers of people of color, an undeniable imperative will be to learn how to recognize and accurately interpret the differences and similarities among racial, ethnic, and cultural groups. Training in understanding diverse cultural prescriptions for childrearing may greatly contribute to reduced numbers of black children in out-of-home placements.

Cultural paradigms predict how we think, feel, and make decisions. These patterns also govern our daily lives by requiring adherence to an array of expectations, including face-to-face communication (Kochman, 1981). Teaching workers about culturally based differences in communication styles will minimize some of the barriers to effective communication and interaction that currently plague the child welfare system.

Finally, studies that attempt to expose and illuminate errors in the interpretation of cultural processes (Jarrett, 1994) will further contribute to best practices in social work by aiding child welfare agencies that are currently struggling with the controversy surrounding TRA and foster care. Heightened awareness of the effects of racial and ethnic culture on groups and individuals will only enhance the development of strategies for more meaningful and productive dialogue between workers. Deficiencies in worker knowledge and skill development continue to affect negatively social services in general and child welfare in particular. Effective, efficient, best practice strategies can ameliorate the negative impact of such deficiencies.

The following excerpts summarize the varied attitudes and perceptions toward TRA/FCP and MEPA-IEP of the child welfare workers who participated in this study, and present an important point upon which the group achieved consensus:

> More recently, my view has changed…I started thinking, what's going to happen to these little black kids when they grow up to be these big black kids, especially boys?…[They] fit the description that every white police officer is looking for, or the system says he's going to be in prison….As long as it is a positive experience for the child, providing all that's needed.

> I don't agree with TRA. I think the impact could be very, very damaging to the child….When you're dealing with a child coming into the system…and then you put them in a home that's not culturally bound to their needs, I think it could be a problem….A gay white couple had adopted a black girl….This was a couple very comfortable with who they are, and I think they've given that child a very good home….They have a variety of friends, not just white friends….They had straight friends along with gay friends….When you have a home like that, maybe TRA is a good thing.

> [MEPA-IEP] may be destructive, but I think a lot of other things are destructive to the black family. If the black family was not being destroyed, we wouldn't need TRA and foster care. Obviously, other things…are affecting the black family, not just two laws. For example, poverty, inadequate housing, medical care, etc.

The experiences of the informants for this study offer a first-hand view of TRA and FCP, as well as MEPA and IEP, through the lens of black child welfare professionals. Their unique perspective has been missing from the literature for far too long. Ever increasing numbers of black children linger in foster care waiting for permanent placement. If viable solutions to this long-term problem are to be found, the concerns of frontline child welfare workers must be considered.◆

# References

Anderson, S. A., & Sabatelli, R. M. (1999). *Family interaction: A multigenerational developmental perspective* (2nd ed.). Boston: Allyn and Bacon:

Brodkin, E. Z. (1997). Inside the welfare contract: Discretion and accountability in state welfare administration. *Social Service Review, 71*(1), 1-33.

Brooks, D., Barth, R. P., Bussiere, A., & Patterson, G. (1999). Adoption and race: Implementing the multiethnic placement act and the interethnic adoption provisions. *Social Work, 44*(2), 167-177.

Charmaz, K. (1983). The grounded theory method: An explication and interpretation. In R. M. Emerson (Ed.), *Contemporary field research: A collection of readings* (pp. 109-126). Prospect Heights, Illinois: Waveland Press, Inc.

Courtney, M. E. (1997). The politics and realities of TRA. *Child Welfare, 76*(6), 749-779.

Curtis, C. M. (1996, March). The adoption of African American children by whites: A renewed conflict. *Families in Society: The Journal of Contemporary Human Services, 60,* 156-165.

Curtis, C. M., & Alexander, R. (1996). The multiethnic placement act: Implications for social work practice. *Child and Adolescent Social Work Journal, 13*(5), 401-410.

Forehand, R., & Kotchick, B. A. (1996). Cultural diversity: A wake-up call for parent training. *Behavior Therapy, 27,* 187-206.

Gaber, I., & Aldridge, J. (Eds.). (1994). *In the best interests of the child: Culture, identity and TRA.* London: Free Association Books.

Hale-Benson, J. E. (1982). *Black children: Their roots, culture, and learning styles* (Rev. ed.). Baltimore: John Hopkins University Press.

Havemen, R., & Wolfe, B. (1994). *Succeeding generations: On the effects of investments in children.* New York: Russell Sage Foundation.

Hayes, P. (1993). Transracial adoption: Politics and ideology. *Child Welfare, 72*(3), 301-310.

Helms, J. E., & Talleyrand, R. M. (1997). Race is not ethnicity. *American Psychologist, 52*(11), 1246-1247.

Hollinger, J. H. (Ed.). (1988a). *Adoption law and practice* (Rel. 9-12/97). New York: Matthew Bender & Co.

Hollinger, J. H. (Ed.). (1988b). *Adoption law and practice* (Rel. 11-12/98). New York: Matthew Bender & Co.

Hollinger, J. H. (1998). *A guide to the multiethnic placement act of 1994: As amended by the interethnic adoption provisions of 1996*. Washington, DC: ABA Center on Children and the Law, National Resource Center on Legal and Court Issues.

Hollingsworth, L. D. (1997). Effect of transracial/transethnic adoption on children's racial and ethnic identity and self-esteem: A meta-analytic review. In H. E. Gross & M. B. Sussman (Eds.), *Families and adoption* (pp. 99-130). New York: Haworth.

Hollingsworth, L. D. (1998a). Adoptee dissimilarity from the adoptive family: Clinical practice and research implications. *Child and Adolescent Social Work Journal, 15* (4), 303-319.

Hollingsworth, L. D. (1998b). Promoting same-race adoption for children of color. *Social Work, 43*(2), 104-116.

Hollingsworth, L. D. (1999). Symbolic interactionism, African American families, and the TRA controversy. *Social Work, 44*(5), 443-451.

Howard, A., Royse, D. D., & Skerl, J. A. (1977). TRA: The black community perspective. *Social Work, 22*(3), 184-189.

Jarrett, R. L. (1994). Living poor: Family life among single parent, African American women. *Social Problems, 41*(1), 30-49.

Jarrett, R. L. (1997a). African American family and parenting strategies in impoverished neighborhoods. *Qualitative Sociology, 20*(2), 275-288.

Jarrett, R. L. (1997b). Resilience among low-income African American youth: An ethnographic perspective. *Ethos, 25*(2), 218-229.

Jones, C. E., & Else, J. F. (1979). Racial and cultural issues in adoption. *Child Welfare, 58*(6), 373-382.

Kallgren, C. A., & Caudill, P. J. (1993). Current TRA practices: Racial dissonance or racial awareness? *Psychological Reports, 72*, 551-558.

Kochman, T. (1981). *Black and white styles in conflict*. Chicago: University of Chicago Press.

Ladner, J. A. (1977). *Mixed families*. Garden City, New York: Anchor Press.

Lipsky, M. (1980). *Street-level bureaucracy: Dilemmas of the individual in public services*. New York: Russell Sage Foundation.

Mannes, M. (1998). The new federal guidelines. *New Psychology and Economics of Permanency*, pp. 12-18.

McRoy, R. G. (1989). An organizational dilemma: The case of transracial adoptions. *Journal of Applied Behavioral Science, 25*(2), 145-160.

McRoy, R. G. (1994). Attachment and racial identity issues: Implications for child placement decision making. *Journal of Multicultural Social Work, 3*(3), 59-74.

McRoy, R. G., Oglesby, Z., & Grape, H. (1997). Achieving same-race adoptive placements for African American children: Culturally sensitive practice approaches. *Child Welfare, 76*(1), 85-104.

McRoy, R. G., Zurcher, L. A., Lauderdale, M. L., & Anderson, R. E. (1984). The identity of transracial adoptees. *Social Casework, 15,* 34-39.

Proctor, E. K., & Davis, L. E. (1994). The challenge of racial difference: Skills for clinical practice. *Social Work, 39*(3), 314-323.

Sanders, M. G. (1997). Overcoming obstacles: Academic achievement as a response to racism and discrimination. *Journal of Negro Education, 66*(1), 83-93.

Simon, R. J., & Altstein, H. (1977). *Transracial adoption.* New York: John Wiley & Sons.

Simon, R. J., & Altstein, H. (1987). *Transracial adoptees and their families.* New York: Praeger.

Simon, R. J., & Altstein, H. (1992). *Adoption, race, and identity: From infancy through adolescence.* New York: Praeger.

Simon, R. J., Altstein, H., & Melli, M. G. (1994). *The case for transracial adoption.* Washington, DC: American University Press.

U.S. Department of Health and Human Services, Administration for Children and Families, Administration on Children, Youth and Families, Children's Bureau. (2000, October ). *The AFCARS Report: How many children were in foster care on September 30, 1999?* Retrieved January 31, 2002, from the U.S. Department of Health and Human Services website: http://www.acf.dhhs.gov/programs/cb/publications/afcars/ar1000.htm

U.S. Department of Health and Human Services, Administration for Children and Families, Administration on Children, Youth and Families, Children's Bureau. (2000, July). *Protecting the well-being of children.* Retrieved February 5, 2002, from the U.S. Department of Health and Human Services website: http://www.acf.dhhs.gov/programs/opa/facts/chilwelf.htm

Vroegh, K. S. (1997). Transracial adoptees: Developmental status after 17 years. *American Journal of Orthopsychiatry, 67*(4), 568-575.

# Chapter 12

# Developing Collaborations Between Child Welfare Agencies and Latino Communities

*Hilda P. Rivera*

Collaborative efforts to achieve permanency planning and family stability for all children in the child welfare system are increasing. As Latino children and families constitute the fastest growing ethnic group in the child welfare system, it is important to understand how to develop culturally sensitive collaborations with their communities. The purpose of this article is to suggest helpful guidelines for developing collaborations between child welfare agencies and Latino communities.

*Hilda P. Rivera, MSW, PhD, is Assistant Professor of Social Work, Hunter College, City University of New York, New York City, NY.*

The need for communities and child welfare agencies to work together to achieve family stability and permanency planning has been well-established (Omang & Bonk, 1999; Onyskiw, Harrison, & Spady, 1999; Power & Eheart, 2000). Child welfare agencies addressing the needs of children who do not live in their own home because of neglect, abuse, or abandonment have the responsibility for either returning the child to a safe family environment or, if that is not possible, planning a permanent new home for the child. To achieve this, the federal government is increasingly mandating that agencies and state governments change from working in isolation to working collaboratively with the communities from which the children come. For instance, the New York City Administration for Children's Services, the city's public child welfare agency, is moving to a neighborhood-based service delivery system in which preventive and foster home services are focusing on community districts rather than broader geographic areas (Citizens' Committee for Children, 2001).

Achieving permanency planning and family stability is crucial for all children, but especially for children of color, who represent the great majority of children served by the child welfare system (Martin, 2000). When compared with other ethnic groups, Latino children have been found to disproportionately remain in long-term out-of-home care. In 1982, Latino children constituted 6.7% of the children in out-of-home care, and by 1993, they comprised 14% of the children in out-of-home care (Williams, 1997). As Latino children constitute one of the fastest growing ethnic groups in the child welfare system, it is critical to develop collaborative efforts that involve those children's communities (Omang & Bonk, 1999; Power & Eheart, 2000; Stehno, 1990).

Despite the importance of this topic, very little has been written about collaborative efforts between child welfare agencies and culturally diverse communities, especially those of Latino origin. The purpose of this article is to suggest guidelines for developing collaborations between child welfare agencies and Latino communities. Collaboration is described and its potential benefits are discussed, as well as the implications for involving and working with the very diverse Latino communities in the United States.

## Collaboration: What Does It Mean?

Calls have been renewed for communities and child welfare agencies to come together and work on behalf of children's safety, permanency, and well-being. As more research shows the potential benefits of developing collaborative child welfare services, the concept of collaboration has become increasingly popular among government, human service, and community organizations (Omang & Bonk, 1999; Onyskiw et al., 1999). Among the potential benefits is the development of accessible, cost-effective, and comprehensive child welfare programs and services for children and families with diverse physical, mental, emotional, cultural, and socioeconomic needs.

Nevertheless, *collaboration* can be a vague term. It has been defined in many different ways according to particular academic and professional fields. For the purpose of this article, *collaboration* is defined as a process that takes place between two or more professionals or organizations who decide to work together on behalf of children's safety, permanency, and well-being. Those involved in a collaborative effort may keep their own individual job responsibilities, but they must periodically communicate with each other and coordinate their respective services to avoid duplication and jointly work as a single, helping team.

Mattessich and Monsey (1992) added that a collaboration is a "mutually beneficial and well-defined relationship entered into by two or more organizations to achieve common goals" (p. 7). As they explained, the relationship created by the members of the collaboration should be one of commitment to: (a) the development of mutual goals, (b) jointly developed structured and shared responsibility, (c) mutual authority and accountability for success, and (d) shared resources and rewards. This definition clearly underscores four important elements that child welfare agencies must consider before they enter into a collaborative effort: (1) vision and relationships; (2) structure, responsibilities, and communication; (3) authority and accountability; and (4) resources and rewards.

The structure of collaborations varies depending on the particular needs and resources of the organizations or agencies involved. There are two common types: the interdisciplinary or interprofessional, and the interorganizational collaborations. An interdisciplinary or interprofessional collaboration involves two or more members of different professions or disciplines working together toward a common goal. For example, a child welfare agency might call on a social worker, psychologist, physician, nurse, teacher, political official, and clergy member to help a multiproblem family that requires a coordinated scope of services. Each member of this small group is trained in different professional disciplines and brings unique knowledge, skills, and work experiences that can contribute to the resolution of common problems and the achievement of common goals. For the team to work collaboratively, it is necessary that each member is committed to engaging in a continuous process of communication, examination, and evaluation of his or her individual efforts toward comprehensive planning and common goals. This type of collaboration should not be limited to members of the professional community. It should include all family and community members involved in the case.

Another type of collaboration involves different agencies or community organizations working together to provide a more extensive, comprehensive, and coordinated range of services for a child and the family. This is called interorganizational collaboration. For example, a community notices a rise in young mothers entering the child protection and welfare system. Leaders from the child welfare system, schools, youth organizations, health centers, and the community could come together to affect the identified problems. They might find that many of the agencies already provide services to teen mothers, but because those services are provided in a fragmented and uncoordinated manner, many of these young women could be falling through the cracks of the system. Respective leaders may make the decision to develop a collaborative community initiative to effectively address the problem. As discussed earlier, collaborations bring previously separated agencies or organizations into a new structure and/or relationship that allow the sharing of expertise and resources to resolve common problems and develop programs of mutual interest. Undoubtedly, the successful development of any interorganizational collaboration requires a great deal of commitment, comprehensive planning, and well-established communication mechanisms.

## Understanding Diversity Within Latino Communities

The development of any type of collaboration between communities and child welfare agencies can be very rewarding and challenging, especially if issues of diversity are taken seriously. This section focuses on the high degree of diversity within Latino communities and the importance of developing collaborative initiatives that are culturally competent.

Child welfare staff at all levels who want to engage Latino communities in their collaborative efforts should be culturally competent. As Lum (1999) described, a culturally competent practice is one that incorporates cultural self-awareness, knowledge acquisition, skill development, and inductive learning or participation in continuing discussions of multicultural practice. Lack of knowledge about the community and lack of skills to establish communication and relationships will delay any collaborative process. Moreover, unresolved issues of racism, oppression and discrimination, inequitable policies and services, misunderstanding and miscommunication from child welfare agencies and other organizations, and a hesitation to actively involve diverse communities in meaningful dialogue will severely limit the potential benefits of working in collaboration (Colon, 2001; Derezotes & Snowden, 1990; Hogan & Siu, 1988; Williams, 1997).

Therefore, it is crucial that child welfare agency staff who commit to effectively collaborating with Latino communities first reflect on their own history of individual and institutional racism, prejudice, and discrimination and their effects on professional attitude, perception, and behavior toward this population. Importantly, this reflection may lead to the reexamination and perhaps drastic revision of agency policies, procedures, practices, staff training and patterns, and organizational structures.

## Who Are Latinos?

The number of Latinos (people of Latin American descent) in the United States has significantly increased in the past several years. According to the 2000 census, the Latino population increased by 57.9%, from 22.4 million in 1990 to 35.3 million in 2000, compared with an increase of 13.2% for the total U.S. population. This population group is also incredibly diverse, with Mexicans (20.6 million), Puerto Ricans (3.4 million), and Cubans (1.2 million) as the three largest subgroups. There are also approximately 3 million Central and South Americans and nearly 1 million Dominicans. Latinos are expected to continue to grow numerically and constitute a population of 51 million people in the United States by year 2020 ("Americans," 1994).

Although Latinos share many characteristics, they are highly diverse in terms of race, language, national origin, religion, socioeconomic status, historical experience, and immigration and citizenship status (Castex, 1994; Gutierrez, Yeakley, & Ortega,

2000; Zambrana & Dorrington, 1998). Not recognizing the extraor-
dinary diversity that exists within Latino groups, and taking a
simplistic approach based on reductionistic cultural assumptions
that are not based on research, can lead to problematic practice
(Padilla, 1996).

Assumptions related to language, religious affiliation, immigration, and citizenship status are common and often wrongly
made about families of Latino origin. Very often Latinos are assumed to speak only Spanish. However, Spanish might be the
second language or only one of the many languages spoken by
some of them. In fact, many may be fluent in other European
(e.g., Portuguese, French, and English), indigenous (e.g., Quechua,
Mayan, and Guarani), or Creole dialects and languages. Latinos
are often assumed to be Roman Catholic. This assumption ig-
nores the large and growing group of Protestant Latinos and many
other Latinos who are spiritual but not religious. In addition, other
Latinos have been influenced by diverse African and indigenous
beliefs, which may be solely practiced or integrated in their Christian and/or Catholic rituals (e.g., Santeria and Espiritismo). Finally, immigration and citizenship status tend to be solely assumed by the family's appearance, language proficiency, speech
accent, and historical experiences, among other things. This assumption does not acknowledge the fact that many Latinos living in the United States are documented (have a legal right to
live and remain in the United States, including those who are
already full citizens), and those who are undocumented still have
rights, such as a child's right to schooling.

Neither prescriptions nor recipes can be given or made for
working with all Latino populations. Yet, agencies and staff seriously committed to developing a culturally competent practice
will find the process of working with and learning from Latino
communities very exciting and rewarding. In this path, the significant degree of diversity within Latino communities will be
seen not as a hurdle but as a tremendous opportunity.

## Involving Latino Communities

Communities, especially communities of color, have been historically described as having many deficits and needs rather than
many assets and resources (Kretzmann & McKnight, 1993). Latino
communities are no exception. Although social evidence and census data indicate that Latino communities are at risk of poverty,
low educational achievement, mental health disorders, and other
serious problems, these communities still have many assets and
resources that should not be underestimated (Colon, 2001;
Delgado, 1994; Derezotes & Snowden, 1990; Gutierrez & Ortega,
1991; Simoni & Perez, 1995; Zambrana & Dorrington, 1998).

The belief that Latino communities have many problems and
few resources has limited child welfare agencies and other organizations from working more closely with members of these communities. Delgado (1998) pointed out the importance of developing interorganizational collaborations based on community
assets rather than deficit models. He argued that social services
agencies should better assess existing community organizations
(e.g., bodegas, food establishments, botanical shops, and recreational
centers) that are popular among Latino community members and
that already provide them with some kind of social services.

As stated earlier, there are different types of collaborations
covering a wide range of activities that vary in structure and
membership, authority, labor intensity, and resources. The following case illustrates how collaboration can be creatively developed to use the existing resources in the community:

Restaurant "E" had been in existence three years, open six
days per week and eight hours per day. Both owners of Restaurant "E" (husband and wife) are also foster parents to a number
of children. In order for them to become foster parents, they have
had to take workshops that have increased their helping knowledge and skills. Consequently, they have a basis from which to
provide information and make referrals to social service agen-

cies. The restaurant has several bulletin boards that provide agencies or community groups with the opportunity to post information of community interest and social services available within the community. (Delgado, 1998, pp. 65-66).

This case shows how child welfare agencies and other social service organizations attempting to engage Latino communities in collaborative efforts must be open to a broader perspective of community so that they include organizations that play a meaningful role in the lives of children and families. These might include churches, businesses, and social clubs such as marketplaces, grocery stores, restaurants, botanical shops, sport leagues, and barber or beauty shops, just to name a few. Their reputation in the community, willingness to help, and access to a vast number of families can greatly contribute to the agency's outreach, program planning, and service delivery.

## Guidelines for Planning Collaborations

This section suggests some guidelines for planning collaborations between child welfare agencies and Latino communities. It is expected that the following guidelines will facilitate the development of collaborations that can effectively contribute to family stability and child permanency planning efforts.

### Organizational and Administrative Adaptations

By their very design, the friendliness and accessibility of child welfare agencies toward the community's children and families come from vary. Agencies that are attempting to make themselves accessible to Latino communities and hoping to establish collaborative relationships with these communities and organizations should take a close and critical look at their ways of conducting community outreach and planning, implementing, and delivering services. Communities and people of color often do not understand the services provided by child welfare agencies and frequently have negative opinions about them. Therefore, it is very important that the agency assesses its resources and needs, including community visibility and rapport.

In the assessment process, the agency should identify which areas need to be enhanced. Some of the organizational and administrative areas that might need to be improved are adding bilingual personnel, developing strategies and skills to conduct community outreach, and increasing expertise to develop collaborations. Besides addressing the agency limitations, it is also important to recognize its resources. Many times, child welfare agencies are not accustomed to collaboration with community members and organizations and think that they do not have anything to offer or that it is too late or difficult to initiate a relationship. This is not necessarily true. Agencies with a strong and sincere commitment to work with the community—in this case, the Latino community—will find that they may have much to contribute and that it is never too late or too difficult to involve the community in the helping process. Although the agency assessment process is a first step, it is important for staff at all levels to understand that this an ongoing process. In other words, this process will probably take time and a great deal of energy.

### Identification of Community Resources

The assessment and identification of community resources can be achieved in diverse ways. Children, families, and staff can participate in the process of gathering information about the community. Children and families can provide information about their help-seeking patterns and identify places in the community that they use for help and support. Moreover, diverse community members can serve many important functions such as members of advisory boards, recruiters of foster parents, and bridges to other organizations in the neighborhood.

Agency staff at all levels should participate in the information gathering process. They should be willing to get to know the community by walking around the community, visiting local establishments and organizations, frequenting the local library, reading local newspapers, participating in community meetings and special events, and so forth. They should take the time to talk with community members about the community's history of migration, cultural traditions, and values. Staff may be delighted to find that many community members enjoy talking about their culture when they have respectful and sympathetic listeners. In sum, it is important that agency staff raise public visibility by promoting and practicing the agency's mission and commitment to children and families.

### Relationship Building: Importance of Confianza

Relationships, especially collaborative relationships, do not occur overnight. They involve thoughtful processes in which all partners involved are flexible and willing to grow and work together. When developing collaborations with Latino communities, it is very important to maintain open channels of communication. Although technological advances to facilitate speedy information exchanges are becoming popular, frequent face-to-face interactions are essential. Written communication, such as follow-up letters or thank you notes, is also an important tool at the agency's disposal.

For collaborative relationships between agency staff and Latino communities to develop, they should be based on confianza, confidence or trust. As noted by Delgado (1998), confianza implies pure friendship that is based on mutual trust, understanding, and appreciation. This is obviously a process that involves openness among all involved parties. Staff, who are not necessarily accustomed to working outside the agency, need to feel comfortable spending time in the community, sharing information, and trusting community members. One can notice mutual confianza among both parties in the case presented earlier. The owners of Restaurant E showed their trust and satisfaction with the agency services by marketing them in their business, and the agency trusted them to post information about its services.

For the agency to connect genuinely with the community, it is crucial to establish an ongoing dialogue and address any negative opinions and concerns that are sometimes spread about child welfare agencies. The development of mechanisms such as surveys and focus groups for obtaining feedback from the community is critical. It is equally important to create systems to effectively review the feedback received from the community and to address questions and concerns in a kind and timely manner. Also, never forget to show appreciation.

Once a comfortable degree of confianza has been achieved, it is important to begin to negotiate the structure, characteristics, and extent of the collaboration. Delgado (1994) pointed out that this process might be influenced by four main factors. These are (1) the level of service provision and willingness of local community organizations to get involved, (2) agency capability (e.g., culturally competent staff), (3) relationship with the community (e.g., positive, neutral, negative), and (4) willingness to collaborate.

## Conclusion

The development of collaborations between child welfare agencies and Latino communities may be challenging and time consuming but, at the same time, such development can be very rewarding. All the work put into creating collaborations is rewarded when not only agencies but the whole community works together to achieving family stability and permanency planning for all children. This article has attempted to initiate a timely dialogue about the importance of developing collaborations between child welfare agencies and ethnically diverse communities. Although it focuses specifically on Latinos, it is hoped that this article provides useful guidelines to work with other populations.

Finally, the knowledge base for developing and implementing effective collaborations between child welfare agencies and ethnically diverse communities should be expanded. More research in the areas of community-based practice and collaboration building with Latino families and communities involved in the child welfare system is needed.◆

## References

Americans in 2020: Less white more southern. (1994, April 22). *New York Times,* 34.

Castex, G. M. (1994). Providing services to Hispanic/Latino populations: Profiles in diversity. *Social Work, 39*(3), 288–296.

Citizens' Committee for Children. (2001, April). *Closer to home: Serving children and families in neighborhoods where they live* (Interim report with support from the William T. Grant Foundation). New York: Author.

Colon, E. (2001). A multidiversity perspective on Latinos: Issues of oppression and social functioning. In G. A. Appleby, E. Colon, & J. Hamilton, (Eds.) *Diversity, oppression, and social functioning: Person in environment assessment and intervention* (pp. 92–108). Boston, MA: Allyn and Bacon.

Delgado, M. (1994). Hispanic natural support systems and the alcohol and drug abuse field: A developmental framework for collaboration. *Journal of Multicultural Social Work Practice, 3*(2), 11–37.

Delgado, M. (1998). *Social services in Latino communities: Research and strategies.* New York: Haworth Press.

Derezotes, D. S., & Snowden, L. R. (1990). Cultural factors in the intervention of child maltreatment. *Child and Adolescent Social Work Journal, 7*(2), 161–175.

Gutierrez, L., & Ortega, R. (1991). Developing methods to empower Latinos: The importance of groups. *Social Work with Groups, 14*(2), 23–43.

Gutierrez, L., Yeakley, A., & Ortega, R. (2000). Educating students for social work with Latinos: Issues for the new millennium. *Journal of Social Work Education, 36*(3), 541–557.

Hogan, P. T., & Siu, S. F. (1988). Minority children and the child welfare system: An historical perspective. *Social Work, 33*(6), 493–498.

Kretzmann, J. P., & McKnight, J. L. (1993). *Building communities from the inside out: A path toward finding and mobilizing a community's assets.* Evanston, IL: Northwestern University, Center for Urban Affairs and Policy Research.

Lum, D. (1999). *Culturally competent practice: A framework for growth and action.* Pacific Grove, CA: Brooks/Cole.

Martin, J. A. (2000). Diversity issues in foster care practice. In J. A. Martin (Ed.), *Foster family care: Theory and practice* (pp. 198–206). Boston, MA: Allyn and Bacon.

Mattessich, P. W., & Monsey, B. R. (1992). *Collaboration: What makes it work.* St. Paul, MN: Amherst H. Wilder Foundation.

Omang, J., & Bonk, K. (1999). Family to family: Building bridges for child welfare with families, neighborhoods, and communities. *Policy and Practice of Public Human Services, 57*(5), 15–20.

Onyskiw, J. E., Harrison, M., & Spady, D. (1999). Formative evaluation of collaborative community-based abuse prevention project. *Child Abuse and Neglect, 23*(11), 1069–1081.

Padilla, Y. (1996). Incorporating social science concepts in the analysis of ethnic issues in social work: The case of Latinos. *Journal of Multicultural Social Work Practice, 4*(3), 1–13.

Power, M. B., & Eheart, B. K. (2000). From foster care to fostering care: The need for community. *Sociological Quarterly, 41*(1), 85–102.

Simoni, J. M., & Perez, L. (1995). Latinos and mutual support groups: A case for considering culture. *American Journal of Orthopsychiatry, 65*(3), 440–445.

Stehno, S. (1990). The elusive continuum of child welfare services: Implications for minority children and youth. *Child Welfare, 69*(6), 551–562.

Williams, C. (1997). Personal reflections on permanency planning and cultural competency. *Journal of Multicultural Social Work Practice, 5*(1/2), 9–18.

Zambrana, R. E., & Dorrington, C. (1998). Economic and social vulnerability of Latino children and families by subgroup: Implications for child welfare. *Child Welfare, 77*(1), 5–27.

Chapter 13

# The Effect of Cross-Cultural Dialogue on Child Welfare Parenting Classes: Anecdotal Evidence in Black and White

*Suzanne M. Murphy and Doris Bryant*

The child welfare system indicates that evidence of successful completion of parenting classes is instrumental in determining whether parents are actively engaged in the process of permanency planning. Such classes vary in length and intensity with topics ranging from "How to Raise Healthy Families" to "How to Discipline Your Child." Two social workers (one white and one black), who initially disagreed about the format of a parenting class, chronicle their efforts to collaborate and create a class format that recognizes the psychosocial and, more specifically, the cultural influences inherent in facilitating these classes. The juxtaposition of the clinical concepts of projection and projective identification are evaluated against the backdrop of the social concepts of empowerment and diversity.

*Suzanne M. Murphy is President, Auburn Consulting, and Doris Bryant is Clinical Social Worker, Brooklyn, NY.*

Historically, child welfare experts have found that positive or negative parental involvement affects the behavior of children in substitute care as well as the effectiveness of service providers (Schatz & Bane, 1991). Recent trends have indicated that parent education in its various forms (parenting classes; parent self-help groups; individual, family, and group counseling; etc.) has been an integral part of permanency planning that has had a legal and a psychological agenda. According to Barth, Goodhand, and Dickinson (1999), the legal agenda "refers to the time frames, reasonable efforts requirements, and administrative procedures...[that serve] to create a secure legal status for children....Psychological permanence, referring to a feeling of belonging, was considered to bring substantial benefit to children" (p. 9).

Frequently, family court judges and child welfare personnel mandate parents of children in foster care to complete parenting skills classes as a precursor to regaining custody of their children. Dore and Lee (1999), however, found that

> maltreating parents often live in highly stressful environments plagued by poverty, family and community violence, substance use and abuse, as well as inadequate resources for housing, employment, education, recreation, and transportation. According to Azar (1989), parenting programs directed at this population must take these complexities into account. In addition to child management skills training based on behavioral principles, cognitively oriented components such as stress management, anger control, problem-solving, and developmental education are important aspects of parenting programs for maltreating parents. (p. 313)

Access to parent training is thought to empower parents to develop effective parenting skills so that they may regain and sustain custody of their children. Research indicates, however, that all training models are not created equal and that often, maltreating parents are too beleaguered by individual and societal ills to benefit from them. In addition, retention of these parents can be difficult, and retention problems may be due to the stigma that is often associated with having to attend these classes. In addition, research shows that few of the studies pertaining to parent training focus on cultural factors.

The following is anecdotal evidence of how two experienced social workers, a black (African American) woman (referred to as Ms. Black hereafter) and a white (Irish/French Canadian American) woman (referred to as Ms. White hereafter), struggled to create a parenting class that empowered participants and respected their cultural diversity. These social workers chronicle how the clinical concepts of projection and projective identification intrude on this process.

## Class History

For the past five years, every Friday morning from 10:00 A.M. to noon, there has been a parenting class offered in a conference room of a large child welfare agency. Prospective class members have been referred to the class by their caseworkers, who submit names to the agency psychologist. The psychologist had been consistently running the class, until 1999, when she hired another instructor who taught it for about a year until the instructor left due to illness. The psychologist then resumed her role as the instructor for about a month.

Late in 1999, Ms. White was approached about the possibility of running the class. Although initially hesitant, she realized that this might be an excellent opportunity to enhance her knowledge and skills in substance abuse prevention with adolescents in foster care living in congregate care facilities. She interviewed for the job, was hired as a consultant, and taught her first class in early 2000.

Ms. White used some of the material given to her by the psychologist, searched the Internet for other sources, asked colleagues, and eventually designed a curriculum that outlined a series of sessions with handouts and exercises included (Turner & Gonzalez-Rivera, 2000). She settled into the routine and enjoyed the challenge of dealing with anywhere from 6 to 26 parents in the class. The majority of class members were people of color: Approximately 60% were black, 25% Latino/Latina, 10% white, and 5% other (Asian, Eastern Indian, etc.). Some spoke little English. Others were, at times, hostile and aggressive. Others seemed fearful of saying anything. On three occasions, the psychologist took over the class while Ms. White was out of town. The psychologist reported that the class had been unhappy with her teaching, that they preferred the social worker. Both were amused by their sense of how the parents treated the psychologist like a substitute instructor; however, neither gave it much thought.

Later, Ms. White was going to be unavailable for two weeks in a row, and the psychologist found a substitute. An experienced black female social worker, who was a recent addition to the administrative staff of the agency, had agreed to cover during the two weeks. The two social workers spoke on the telephone about the coverage, then met briefly to review the curriculum and discuss the format of the class.

The black female social worker, Ms. Black, then facilitated the class for two weeks, apparently uneventfully.

When initially approached to cover the parenting class, Ms. Black was delighted to do something familiar, and to directly interact with clients. As a clinician who was now an administrator, she missed the process of facilitating and witnessing change in clients. On first meeting Ms. White, Ms. Black was impressed with her warmth and sense of organization. Ms. White supplied Ms. Black with a schedule for the class that outlined the order in which specific activities were to occur, the conditions under which clients were to be admitted, and the conditions under which they were not. Armed with this outline, Ms. Black did not anticipate any problems.

## The Awareness of Race Emerges

A small number of people attended Ms. Black's class, the majority of whom were black (of varying cultures) or Latino. One white male and one Asian female were in the minority. During the course of discussing the topic "Playing With Your Child," a black man asked why it was that the class consisted primarily of people of color. He indicated that it appears as if only children of color are in foster care. The issue of race and perceived racial inequity emerged and a brief discussion ensued. Ms. Black explored the perceptions of that class member and provided basic education to the class regarding the interaction between access to resources and child placement. At the conclusion of the two weeks, Ms. Black and class participants agreed that access to resources, which is often affected by race and socioeconomic status, impinges on the rate of child placement into foster care. Ms. Black provided little detailed feedback to Ms. White regarding the specifics of the class, noting only that things had gone well.

Privately, Ms. Black questioned the message that was being conveyed to class members about race and parenting issues. Until Ms. Black covered the class, the two previous instructors of the class were white and the students were primarily people of color. How were class members processing this?

## A Failure to Communicate

During the next several months, a degree of confusion and discomfort loomed over a planned change in classroom sites. During this period, Ms. White and the psychologist had decided that if parents called to advise that they were going to be late, they would be able to come to the class. It was later decided that if parents came late to the class and had not called, they should be allowed to come but would not receive credit for the class. This modification was not communicated to Ms. Black. When parents were late for class, Ms. Black did not allow them to come in.

At this juncture, Ms. Black felt comfortable with the class structure that had been previously outlined. It conveyed a sense of consistency, a sense of predictability, and an inherent sense of safety most often associated with structure. She, therefore, upheld it against pleas of "the other social worker lets us in" and grumblings about how difficult dealing with "your own kind" can be.

After Ms. Black taught the class, the parents were adamant in their complaints and told Ms. White that Ms. Black had been "really strict." The two social workers spoke briefly and superficially about the situation; Ms. White's conscious thought at the time was that Ms. Black was strict and Ms. White was not, and eventually this would just work itself out. Unconsciously, however, there was more at work.

On learning that the parents objected to the structure that she upheld, Ms. Black was perplexed. Ms. White and the class participants had perceived her as being a strict black woman. As a newly hired staff member, Ms. Black felt at risk because she had not as yet established herself so that others could feel comfortable with her. No one knew who she was. They did not know her temperament or her ability to judiciously exercise power. Ms. Black defended herself and her actions. She believed that the structure of the class could serve as a model for how parents might structure their interactions with their children by arriving on time and actively engaging with their children.

### Ms. Black Experiences Open Hostility

Subsequently, the class was moved to a large room in the building where Ms. Black has her office. Shortly thereafter, Ms. Black covered the class again and had difficulty with a hostile parent who was very angry about not being allowed entry into the group.

This parent arrived one hour late for class and insisted that the judge had told him to attend and, therefore, he was going to do so. He punctuated his statement with a pounding fist on the table at which Ms. Black was sitting. His fist was inches away from her face. She allowed him to sign in, but he elected to leave the class after having done so. Other class members said that they felt threatened by the actions of this parent as well as by Ms. Black's initial refusal to admit him into the class.

### Executive Power Enters

An unplanned encounter with the executive director of the agency forced Ms. Black to consider her feelings about the class. The director expressed an interest in her perspective and evaluation of the class. Specifically, the director wanted to know if the class was practical in its application of parenting principles. Ms. Black felt empowered. She also began to share her assessment of the class with Ms. White and the psychologist who had hired Ms. White.

Ms. Black determined that despite the obvious empathy that Ms. White felt towards class participants, overall her expectations of them seemed to be low. The psychologist had told Ms. Black that this might be due to the continuous arrival of new students each week, frequent absenteeism or lateness due to having to meet other responsibilities (court appearances, job interviews, housing negotiations, welfare appointments, etc.), and the great difficulty in applying newly learned parenting techniques when your children are not in your care. Despite recognizing these very real impediments, Ms. Black was disappointed that parents in general took little or no responsibility for being there; they were simply meeting the terms of mandates: "The judge told me that I have to take parenting classes." It seemed as if Ms. White could expect more from them, for example, they could show up on time and participate.

Subsequently, the two social workers met and discussed the structure of the class. Ms. Black shared her views, and Ms. White felt somewhat attacked but did not say anything. Another meeting between the two resulted in Ms. White's feeling challenged and criticized by Ms. Black. Finally, Ms. White countered the perceived attacks by citing her credentials as a white woman active in civil rights activities in the 1960s. In this discussion, Ms. White realized that this defensiveness came out of her feeling attacked as well as out of her feeling insecure about her ability to teach this class effectively.

### A Pivotal Change for Ms. White

One week, there was miscommunication regarding the agency's closing for an official holiday. Ms. Black offered to travel to the office on the holiday to meet any parents who might mistakenly come for class. To Ms. White, this was a pivotal moment, the beginning of a feeling of identification, appreciation, and bonding with Ms. Black.

### The Courage to Discuss Differences

The discussion turned to the question of structure and the value of structure itself. Ms. White outlined more fully her perception of the current structure of the class and her sense of the value of a structure that allowed for flexibility. The main point of contention seemed to be the question of parents' being allowed to join the class after the formal teaching part of the class had begun. Ms. White felt that the parents were better off attending part of the class; if they were willing to come into the class knowing that they were not going to receive credit, that reflected their commitment. There seemed to be no agreement on this question. The two workers tacitly agreed to continue to talk about this issue; a significant problem had been identified, which was an important first step in resolving conflict. Ms. White was not happy about the situation and questioned whether Ms. Black should be leading the class. She asked Ms. Black if she really wanted to do the class. As Wilson and Russell (1996) noted, there are many real tensions that exist between white and black women, and these tensions are complex and not easily resolved. The real work to be done begins with the naming of the issue, as the two workers had begun to do.

Ms. Black expressed dismay that the class ran for 2 hours per week over 12 weeks—in sum, 24 hours—a day in the life of these parents. Ms. White did not give credit when parents came late, but she did allow them to join the class. Ms. Black was upset with this. She felt that parents should be required to be in class on time and should not be allowed in when they were late. She felt that the expectations of Ms. White and the parents themselves were lower than her own. Ms. Black questioned Ms. White about other workshops that she had conducted. Specifically, Ms. Black wanted to know if she expected those participants to arrive late. Did she start workshops half an hour after the announced start time? Ms. Black indicated that she wanted to continue with the class; however, she had difficulty with what she perceived to be Ms. White's low expectations of the participants. Ms. Black noted that she would like the parents to have a goal to work on while in the class; essentially, class members should be accountable for the process, not simply be passive participants in a system that is experienced by them as "ordering them around."

After this exchange, Ms. White met with the psychologist, who mentioned the issue of race. The psychologist told Ms. White that Ms. Black thought that the parents were having difficulty accepting her because of her race, that is, she looked too much like them to be accepted by them as an instructor. This stopped Ms. White dead in her tracks, as it rang so true to her. The psychologist also suggested that the two social workers speak further to resolve the question of letting parents come into the class and stay even if they were late. Ms. White telephoned Ms. Black and attempted to reach agreement. They began to find some common ground, both recognizing the importance of these classes for the parents, particularly given their general propensity not to seek out parenting classes through child protective services (Keller & McDade, 2000).

Ms. Black and Ms. White continued to explore the issue of allowing parents to come into the class late and the issue of race as a relevant factor. Ms. White recognized what Miller (1987) said about whites being acculturated not to speak about race and how that culture of silence fosters a disconnection from the experience of racism. Energy released by the opportunity to delve into these feelings can result in a desire for more connectedness (Tatum, 1997).

Ms. Black, after what seemed to Ms. White to be a reaction of surprise, began to speak about projection and projective identification. Ms. Black spoke eloquently and passionately about her sense that the parents could not accept her because she looked too much like them. They could, however, accept Ms. White's representing authority as a white woman.

### A Pivotal Change for Ms. Black

Ms. Black was surprised and pleased that Ms. White could begin to discuss the issue of race as it affected their ability to relate to each other as well as to class participants. Ms. Black continued to explore the degree to which she felt projection—the defensive process through which an individual projects unwanted parts of the self onto another—was operating. Ms. Black noted that she had had positive feelings toward the parents in the class, and it was out of these feelings that she could expect them to become a stronger force in the class and to take responsibility for their behavior in the class. When Ms. White provided feedback regarding class members' view of her, Ms. Black was chagrined to hear how harshly she had been perceived. She realized that on some level during the struggle with Ms. White, she had begun to identify with that which had been projected. In other words, the more she opposed Ms. White's position, the more resistant Ms. Black had become.

In an e-mail to a friend the afternoon of December 8, 2000, Ms. White wrote of her excitement about this discussion with Ms. Black:

I feel like I have so much to tell you. Just got back from doing my parenting class. All kinds of good things are happening with that. I've discovered something recently about being white and what it means in a world like the child care one where the authorities are mostly white and the families are mostly black. There's a black woman who substitutes for me when I can't do the class, and the class has had a really strong reaction to her. I have experienced her as very uptight, maybe angry, etc. You know the drill. I think she has experienced me as another one of those women who comes to do something with the parents who doesn't really understand. All that is to say...we've been struggling with what to do. I have gotten to know her through this and have learned so much about this stupid black/white thing we're so saddled with. All the judgments and misconceptions that go on just based on skin color. And here we are...two educated women who care deeply about our work and how we do it. Well, we both took a chance and scratched that surface a little. The pivotal person in shifting this is the psychologist who hired me and who recommended the other woman to cover for me. She posed some questions that seemed to open up the issue...not the race one really...but just recognizing that we are different. I have been...as you know from when we last spoke...looking at issues of diversity. I did teach that class, and it was great. That work and lots of reading and thinking and opening up the concept of white privilege have led me to today's class. It was awesome. In the class itself...of course, made up of black and Latino men and women, there I am...the white woman of privilege standing there "teaching" them about parenting. And whose judgment holds as to what kind of parenting is the "right" kind of parenting? What does a black mother scared for her teenage son do to communicate to him how he should behave out there? Does a white mother understand that in the same way? Anyway...lots of stuff. I could go on about this all day, but I won't. Suffice it to say...the group today was awesome, and I'm really excited about the way this is turning out. And the psychologist wants us to write an article about this process...how we are using our differences to teach about parenting.

## The Beginning of Collaboration

Thereafter, Ms. White and Ms. Black began to talk regularly about the class, about their ideas, and about some of their feelings regarding the situation. They both recognized that there is untapped therapeutic potential for parents attending these classes. In addition, they recognized the importance of parenting skills in terms of resilience of children who are at risk (Masten, 2001).

Ms. Black felt that the clinical potential in the classes centered around the modeling that Ms. White did, the respect that she conveyed to class participants, the expectations that she relayed via the structure of the class, and her ability to facilitate open discussion around concerns that parents expressed about the inequities of the child welfare system. In addition, Ms. Black felt that her own role as the temporary teacher and Ms. White's role as the permanent teacher reflected a parallel process in relation to the birthparents and their children's foster parents. Ms. Black felt that this warranted further exploration. Through these discussions, as well as discussions pertaining to child developmental issues, Ms. Black believed that class members would take more responsibility for engaging in the class process.

Ms. White worked with the parents to outline rules for the parenting class. There were discussions about race, differences among people that go beyond color, and the importance of making this parenting class meaningful for the parents. The class had to be more than sitting in a room for 12 sessions and being given a certificate. The issue of the class and its therapeutic value was discussed. Ms. White distributed the worksheets to the class (see Figure 1).

In December, Ms. White and Ms. Black cohosted a holiday party on behalf of the parents. It was a tremendous success. After the party, and once the rules were handed out to the members of the class, Ms. White realized that something had begun to shift. She was more relaxed. There was more participation. Ms. White realized that members of the class should have an orientation packet complete with a welcome notice, the rules, and information about advocacy resources when they attend the class (see Figure 2).

Ms. Black expressed real excitement about these changes and relaxed also.

During discussions about difference, class members continued to express concern to Ms. White about Ms. Black's ability to be helpful to them. They complained that Ms. Black was not a parent and therefore could not teach a class without having had children herself. Ms. White defended Ms. Black. She asked them if she would have to have been a parent whose children were removed from her to teach the class. The discussion was quite lively, and one parent who had never met Ms. Black noted that Ms. Black was nasty. Ms. White pointed out that the parent had never met Ms. Black and asked how she could know that. The parent, a young black woman, said, "Well, she's black, isn't she?" The discussion became even more animated and was no longer about Ms. Black; it was about the parents and their feelings. In a later class, a black man spoke about taking his wife to see her regular gynecologist, an older white man. The doctor was not available, and a young black man was covering for him. This parent revealed that his immediate response was not to let her be examined by him. He questioned his credentials and wanted to be sure he was a real doctor. He explained to the class that sometimes black people take on the belief that they are not good enough. When they see a black person in a position of authority, they sometimes are unable to trust the person. The man suggested that was what was happening with Ms. Black in the class. This opened up a wonderful discussion about race and projection.

Subsequent class discussions have continued in this vein. Ms. White and Ms. Black have continued enthusiastically to collaborate on a weekly basis to deconstruct some of the cultural, devel-

## FIGURE 1
Parenting Class Rules

FRIDAYS 10 A.M.–NOON                                              6th FLOOR
12 CLASSES WITHIN 6 MONTHS
THE FOLLOWING RULES WERE WORKED OUT IN TWO PARENTING CLASSES
HELD AT THE AGENCY OFFICE IN DECEMBER, 2000. WE SPENT A GREAT DEAL
OF TIME TALKING THROUGH THE VARIOUS ISSUES AND FEEL THAT, TOGETHER,
WE CAME UP WITH RULES THAT WE WERE ALL COMFORTABLE WITH.

THE PARENTING CLASS IS A CLASS, AND IT IS NOT THERAPY. THERE WILL BE
TIMES, HOWEVER, WHEN SOMEONE MAY BRING UP AN ISSUE THAT IS SENSI-
TIVE AND MUST BE ADDRESSED AT THE TIME. THE GROUP AGREED WE
SHOULD TAKE TIME FROM THE CLASS IN THOSE CASES SO THAT WE COULD
TALK ABOUT THE ISSUE IN A THERAPEUTIC MANNER.
AGENCY TELEPHONE NUMBER 000/000-0000
THE FOLLOWING WERE AGREED UPON:

- LATENESS: AFTER 10:30 A.M., PARENT MAY JOIN THE CLASS BUT WILL
  RECEIVE NO CREDIT It was agreed upon that a parent who comes late should
  join the class with the understanding that no credit can be given. It was further
  stressed that even though a parent is late, there is much to learn from the class,
  and the parent's name will still be on the list that s/he attended the class even
  without credit. This is a good thing to do to show your interest and commitment. In
  addition, a parent who is late and remains for the rest of the class will be given a
  MetroCard.
- CALL: If you think you might be late, call before 10:00 A.M. and leave a message
  at the desk on the 6th floor. If you call before 10:00 A.M., you will receive credit for
  the class unless this becomes a regular occurrence. Then it will be up to the
  Parenting Class instructor to decide about credit. It was stressed that you should
  be sure to leave your name and that you should get the name of the person you
  spoke with. It was also noted that you should be sure to check that the person you
  are speaking to is on the 6th floor because sometimes calls can get transferred
  around the building. You want to be sure that your message gets to the Parenting
  Class instructor.
- 10:00-10:30 A.M.: TALKING TIME This is the time when we take care of letters
  parents might need for court or for their caseworkers, when we review the previous week's class and also when we bring up issues of concern that someone
  might need to talk about.
- 10:30 A.M.-NOON: CLASS Class begins at 10:30. As noted above, anyone arriving after that time may join the class but will not receive credit.
- MUTUAL RESPECT Everyone was very clear that there should always be respect
  for each other. There will be no rudeness or judgments about people and what
  they say.
* ONE PERSON TALKING AT A TIME It was agreed that sometimes there is an issue
  being talked about which gets people excited and involved. This is a good thing,

## Figure 1 (continued)
Parenting Class Rules

but it is important that everyone wait for their turn and respect the person who is
speaking.

* PRIVACY This is also a part of respect. It was agreed that we should respect a
person's privacy by not talking to other people about something personal that a
parent might have said in the class.
* COMING TO CLASS HIGH Everyone recognized that there are parents coming to
the class who are struggling with alcohol and substance abuse problems. It was
agreed that when a parent comes to the class under the influence of any substances, it is very disruptive to the class. It will be the determination of the instructor as to whether or not the parent will be allowed to remain in the class.
* LETTERS The instructor can give you a letter outlining the number of classes you
have attended and the number you have remaining until graduation. If you need a
letter which has more detail, you must make that request the week before you
need the letter.
* HOMEWORK When you begin the series of parenting classes, you will be given a
folder with a homework sheet. This is a list of questions for you to think about and
to answer about your child/ren. It is your choice to do this homework or not. If you
do the homework, you will be given credit for one class.
* GRADUATION After having completed 12 sessions, you will be given a certificate
that you have completed the Parenting Class.
* PERSONAL PROBLEMS As noted above, we all agreed that this is a parenting
class, not group therapy. We also agreed that if a parent has a personal problem
and feels comfortable bringing it up, then we could spend some class time discussing that problem. We recognized that an important part of the class is the
ability of the members to help each other. Help can come in many forms. It can be
by listening and respecting each other as well as by providing information and
offering support.

PARENTING CLASS TOPICS
RAISING A HEALTHY FAMILY
COMMUNICATION
ANGER MANAGEMENT
PROBLEM SOLVING
HEALTH AND SAFETY
SELF-ESTEEM
AGE APPROPRIATE EXPECTATIONS/SCHOOL
PREVENTING DISCIPLINE PROBLEMS
POSITIVE DISCIPLINE
PLAYING WITH YOUR CHILD/DURING VISITS AND AT HOME
BUDGETING TIME
SUBSTANCE ABUSE

## FIGURE 2
### Welcome to Parenting Class

**WELCOME,**

Parenting classes are held on Fridays from 10:00 A.M. to noon. You are expected to attend 12 classes within 6 months. When you begin the series of Parenting Classes, you will be given a folder with this sheet, a homework sheet (your choice to complete), the class rules and a list of places you may call for help. At each class there will be handouts, so please try to bring your folder and a pen or pencil every week. It will be helpful if you could answer these questions. Please be sure to ask the instructor if you have any questions.

YOUR NAME: _____ TODAY'S DATE: _____

FULL NAME OF EACH CHILD; DATE OF BIRTH; DATE & LOCATION OF PLACE-MENT: _____
_____
_____

CASEWORKER'S NAME: _____ TELEPHONE: _____

WERE YOU ABLE TO ATTEND YOUR 72-HOUR CONFERENCE?
    YES_____ NO_____

WERE YOU ABLE TO ATTEND YOUR 30-DAY CONFERENCE?
    YES_____ NO_____

HOW MANY SERVICE PLAN REVIEWS (SPRs) HAVE YOU BEEN ABLE TO ATTEND? _____ (These important case conferences are held every 6 months)

PERMANENCY PLANNING GOAL (PPG): (Please check one)

BACK TO YOU: _____
TO OTHER FAMILY MEMBERS: _____
TO INDEPENDENT LIVING: _____
TO ADOPTION: _____
TO A HIGHER LEVEL OF CARE: _____

FAMILY GOALS: (Please list the goals which you and your family are expected to meet) _____
_____

OTHER COMMENTS OR QUESTIONS: _____
_____

THANK YOU.

opmental, and societal issues that impinge on the class. Class attendance and involvement improved; previous members of the class referred others. Since mid-December, the class discussions have been so lively that they went without the usual 10-minute break.

In many ways, the class has been a microcosm of recent permanency planning initiatives (through the Adoption and Safe Families Act) that have focused on actively engaging parents in the process of planning for their children from the moment that they are placed into care. Initially, the goal for the class was to impart information to those who were perceived to lack it; the goal now focuses on empowering members to become more reflective of their roles in relation to the parenting class instructors, to their own children, as well as to the child welfare system itself. In addition, the members are encouraged to be more proactive and less besieged by the stigma of being in a parenting class.

Although many of the parents remain suspicious of Ms. Black, they exhibit incredible courage in exploring and sharing their feelings. They continue to struggle toward accepting her...and themselves.

## Deconstruction of Psychological and Cultural Influences

Many of the maltreating parents in this parenting class indicated that they had histories of having been abused and or neglected by their parents. Some acknowledged having substance abuse histories as well. Their early object relationships, therefore, are thought to have been inconsistent. Their tendency to view Ms. Black as strict and/or distant may need to be assessed within this context. Unconsciously, they may have collectively projected unwanted parts of themselves onto her. Ms. Black's recalcitrance in not allowing latecomers into the class may have exemplified her (projective) identification with the role of the persecuting, rejecting, or unavailable parent. Ogden (1982) described projective identification as an interpersonal interaction and intrapsy-

chic process through which one of the projector's aims is to communicate a feeling state:

> First, there is the unconscious fantasy of projecting a part
> of oneself into another person and of that part taking over
> the person from within. Then, there is a pressure exerted
> through the interpersonal interacting such that the recipi-
> ent of the projection experiences pressure to think, feel,
> and behave in a manner congruent with the projection.
> Finally, after being "psychologically processed" by the
> recipient, the projected feelings are reinternalized by the
> projector. (p. 12)

The parents were, therefore, able to distance themselves from
that which was projected onto the black worker and respond to
it, while simultaneously provoking her to experience it. The following factors may have contributed to her ability to experience
projective identification: Her educational background and status
as a clinician may have conveyed a sense of being separate, her
status as someone who is not a parent may have qualified her as
different, and her skin color may have offered a sense of oneness.
The black worker's experience of her role as the bad parent, fil-
tered through the lens of an African American clinician who is
not a parent, allowed her to process how it felt to be ostracized
and alienated from those whom she sought to engage.

By employing the above, class members appeared to be making an unconscious effort to communicate with Ms. Black in an
effort to be responded to and understood. What, however, were
they saying?

Perhaps, these parents perceived Ms. Black (an administrator) as an extension of the child welfare system that had obtained
and retained custody of their children. Did they want her to understand how humiliating the removal of a child could be—how
humiliating it could be to be deemed not good enough? Perhaps
they saw her as akin to a modern day Uncle Tom—someone who
does the bidding of an oppressive system that colonizes children

of color. Or perhaps they were afraid that the judgment of a black woman who had achieved middle class status would highlight their perceived inadequacies.

Unfortunately, due to her role as substitute instructor, Ms. Black could not consistently be available to explore these issues with a population of constantly changing parents. This has placed Ms. White in the position of verbally presenting a balanced view of Ms. Black. In general, Ms. White has had to conceptualize and present Ms. Black as a teacher of the class who is equally invested in the growth potential of class members.

Ms. Black reiterates this whenever she conducts the class. It is hoped that these actions will encourage class participants to begin to accept the idea that Ms. Black can be benevolent. This is seen by both Ms. Black and Ms. White as a precursor to the eventual self-acceptance that these parents appear to be striving toward.

## Summary and Conclusions

Two social workers, one white and the other black, have struggled to create a parenting class format that is inclusive of the clinical concepts of projection and projective identification within a backdrop of cultural diversity and empowerment. Through anecdotal evidence, they find that their commitment to collaborate (as evidenced by sustained dialogue) has resulted in class participants' increased engagement as signified by a decrease in absenteeism and lateness and the near disappearance of requests for break times. In addition, class participants have been more vocal in stating their expectations of themselves and others within the child welfare system.

The process of creating this class format is continuing, and the class may evolve into another format as cross-cultural dialogue continues between Ms. White and Ms. Black. One outgrowth of this experience has been an increased awareness of parenting resources that speak to the issue of cultural difference in rearing children. Beal, Villarosa, and Abner (1999) have written about black parenting and addressed a range of issues that encompass health, nutrition, self-esteem, and cultural pride. Hewlett and West (1998) chronicled their literary partnership (a white woman and a black man) and suggested ways that society can redress the inadequate support that many parents receive. Perhaps resources such as these will serve to enlighten birthparents of children in foster care that parenting authority figures of color do exist.

The foster parent and the birthparent must struggle to achieve balance in sharing parenting responsibilities, just as Ms. Black and Ms. White have worked at finding their own equilibrium. The workers' journey in recognizing, identifying, and building on their differences offers hope that foster parents and birthparents can effectively bridge their differences, thereby supporting the goals of permanency for families.◆

## References

Barth, R., Goodhand, J., & Dickinson, N. (1999). Reconciling competing values in the delivery of child welfare services under ASFA, MEPA, and community-based child protection. In *Changing paradigms of child welfare practice: Responding to opportunities and challenges*. Rockville, MD: U.S. Department of Health and Human Services.

Beal, A., Villarosa, L., & Abner, A. (1999). *The black parenting book*. New York: Random House.

Dore, M., & Lee, J. (1999, July). The role of parent training with abusive and neglectful parents. *Family Relations, 48*(3), 313-325.

Hewlett, S., & West, C. (1998). *The war against parents: What can we do for America's beleaguered moms and dads*. New York: Houghton Mifflin.

Keller, J., & McDade, K. (2000, May/June). Attitudes of low-income parents toward seeking help with parenting: Implications for practice. *Child Welfare, 79*(3), 285-312.

Masten, A. (2001, March). Ordinary magic: Resilience processes in development. *American Psychologist, 56*(3), 227-238.

Miller, J. (1987, November). *Connections, disconnections and violations*. Presented at a Stone Center colloquium, Wellesley, MA.

Ogden, T. (1982). *Projective identification and psychotherapeutic technique*. New York: Jason Aronson.

Schatz, M., & Bane, W. (1991, November/December). Empowering the parents of children in substitute care: A training model. *Child Welfare, 70*(6), 665-678.

Tatum, B. (1997). *Why are all the black kids sitting together in the cafeteria?* New York: Basic Books.

Turner, S., & Gonzalez-Rivera, L. (2000). *Growing stronger families*. San Diego, CA: Children's Hospital and Health Center Press.

Wilson, M., & Russell, K. (1996). *Divided sisters: Bridging the gap between black women and white women*. New York: Anchor Books Doubleday.

# Chapter 14

# There's No Place Like Home: Achieving Safety, Permanency, and Well-Being for Lesbian and Gay Adolescents in Out-of-Home Care Settings

*Gerald P. Mallon, Nina Aledort, and Michael Ferrera*

A study was conducted with 45 self-identified gay, lesbian, bisexual, transgendered, and questioning (GLBTQ) youth and agency staff at the two known gay-affirming child welfare agencies in the United States: Green Chimneys GLBTQ Programs in New York City and Gay and Lesbian Social Services in Los Angeles, California. The study examined the question, "What are the challenges presented in ensuring permanency, safety, and well-being for gay and lesbian youth in a gay-affirming child welfare environment?" Guided by the framework outlined in the Child and Family Services Reviews National Standards, which support better outcomes for children and youth, the investigators sought to explore the challenges of ensuring permanency, safety, and well-being for this population, as these challenges were identified by the agency staff and youth who live and work in either of these two gay-affirming programs.

*Gerald P. Mallon, DSW, is Associate Professor, Hunter College School of Social Work, New York City, NY. Nina Aledort, MSW, is Director of Community Initiatives, Hunter*

D espite the emphasis on permanency and other child welfare reforms of the U.S. Adoption Assistance and Child Welfare Act of 1980 (P.L. 96-272) and the more recent Adoption and Safe Families Act of 1997 (ASFA), a dramatic increase has continued in the number of children requiring out-of-home care. According the most recent statistics from data submitted from states over a six-month period from October 1, 1999, to March 31, 2000, there were 588,000 children residing in foster care nationwide (www.acf.dhhs.gov/programs/cb/publications/afgars/apr2001.htm). In addition, many children in care have serious emotional needs and come from families experiencing persistent poverty, racism, homelessness, unemployment, substance abuse, domestic and community violence, neglect, and chronic mental illness. Too often, even before children enter out-of-home care, they have experienced the traumatic effects of relationship disruptions and violence and have struggled with medical and behavioral difficulties. Some may require specialized care and support from a mix of foster families and community health, education, and mental health treatment programs. In special circumstances, some may require group or residential treatment, preferably in community-based settings, to assist them in coping with their life circumstances. A great need exists to find and support diverse foster families in the same neighborhoods from which foster children come, so that whenever it is in their best interest, children can stay in their communities. This need for stability is particularly true for the overrepresented populations of children of color (Billingsley & Giovannoni, 1972) and for lesbian and gay youth (Mallon, 1992, 1997b, 1998, 2000a).

*College Center on AIDS, Drugs, and Community, and Doctoral Student, Hunter College School of Social Work, New York, NY. Michael Ferrera is Director of Public Policy, Gay and Lesbian Social Services, Los Angeles, CA. Ms. Aledort acknowledges the assistance and support of Dr. Mallon and Doug O'Dell in the writing of this article.*

Nearly two-thirds of children entering out-of-home care return to their families within two years. It is estimated, however, that one-fourth of the children in care—many of whom entered as infants—have no plans for either being reunited with their birthfamilies or adopted by relatives or other families. This population of children—with deeply rooted behavior problems resulting from child abuse or neglect and intensified by separation, loss, and unresolved grief—poses the greatest challenge today to timely permanency planning for children in out-of-home care.

It is widely acknowledged that all children and youth require security, love, acceptance, connectedness, a moral/spiritual framework, and lifetime families for their healthy growth and development. They also need stable families and supportive communities, especially in the early years of life, to form the secure attachments so vital to positive self-esteem, meaningful relationships, positive school achievement, and success in the adult world of family and work (Fanshel, 1982; Fanshel & Shinn, 1978; Maas & Engler, 1959). Sadly, child welfare systems and the professionals who work in them have had an uneven history of meeting the developmental needs of youth for stability and continuity in their family relationships.

Self-identified lesbian and gay youth who are in state custody are a little-known, not well-recognized, and generally invisible population in child welfare. In recent years, however, the needs of gay and lesbian youth have been more recognized through the development of several specialized out-of-home care programs in New York and Los Angeles. The emergence of these programs reflects changing standards in the child welfare and legal systems (Mallon, 1998, 2000a). Mallon (2000a) described the evolution of care for this unique population as a necessity for the permanency, safety, and well-being of these youth in systems that are predominantly hostile to the existence of these youth.

Caring for lesbian and gay youth is fundamentally different from traditional foster care for adolescents. In out-of-home care settings, the needs of this group of youth are complex and present a unique set of challenges. Child welfare professionals are often unprepared for the particular challenges of caring for these youth and working toward permanency by ensuring their safety and establishing their well-being.

For example, Mallon (1998) found that lesbian and gay youth in out-of-home care settings receive fewer services than do non–gay identified youth. Lesbian and gay youth are generally at high risk for verbal harassment and physical violence (Mallon, 2001; Savin-Williams, 1994). They experience multiple placements and are often separated from their siblings (Mallon, 1998). They have experienced a high incidence of homelessness (Bucy & Able-Peterson, 1993; Fitzgerald, 1996; Kruks, 1991; Luna, 1991). Often, they are not reunified with their families (Sullivan, 1994). In addition, they have a difficult time attending community-based educational programs (Mallon, 1999) and accessing physical or mental health services that are affirming of their identity and adequate to meet their needs (Ryan & Futterman, 1998).

This article presents findings from a study conducted with 45 self-identified gay, lesbian, bisexual, transgendered, and questioning youth (GLBTQ; for the purposes of simplicity, they are referred to as lesbian and gay in this article) and agency staff at the two known gay-affirming child welfare agencies in the United States: Green Chimneys GLBTQ Programs, in New York City, and the Gay and Lesbian Social Services (GLASS), in Los Angeles. The study examined the question, "What are the challenges presented in ensuring permanency, safety, and well-being for gay and lesbian youth in a gay-affirming child welfare environment?" Using the framework outlined in the Child and Family Services Reviews National Standards (Children's Bureau website, http://www. acf.dhhs.gov/programs/cb), which supports better outcomes for children and youth as a guide, the investigators sought to explore the challenges of ensuring permanency, safety, and well-being for this population, as identified by the agency staff and youth who live and work in either of these two gay-affirming programs.

## Child and Family Services Reviews

The final rule, published in the *Federal Register* (65 F.R. 4019-4093) on January 25, 2000, sets forth the requirements for child and family service reviews, as required by ASFA, including the establishment of national standards for certain statewide data indicators that will be used, in part, to determine a state's substantial conformity under Titles IV-B and IV-E of the Social Security Act. The determination of a state's substantial conformity is based on a review of certain outcomes and systemic factors using quantitative and qualitative data. A state that is found not to be operating in substantial conformity, based on a Child and Family Services review, has an opportunity for program improvement prior to the withholding of any federal funds.

The national standards are based on information that is reported by states to the Detailed Case Data Component of the National Child Abuse and Neglect Data System and the Adoption and Foster Care Analysis and Reporting System.

## Setting

Both Green Chimneys' GLBTQ Programs and GLASS are voluntary, nonsectarian, multiservice agencies dedicated to the development of safe and affirming environments that focus on basic education and life skills for self-identified GLBTQ youth and their families to restore and strengthen their emotional health and promote safety, permanency, and well-being. Green Chimneys' New York City headquarters is located in Harlem; GLASS is headquartered in West Hollywood, California.

Green Chimneys GLBTQ Programs are home for 12 young women and 49 young men, ages 12 to 20. Self-identified lesbian and gay youth at Green Chimneys are typically experiencing significant academic and family issues to the extent that they are not able to be productive in their previous community-based environments. Four distinct programs serve lesbian and gay youth in Green Chimneys' programs base in New York City. Three are community-based in Harlem, and one is located in East Midtown Manhattan.

GLASS is home to 36 GLBTQ youth, ages 12 to 18. Self-identified GLBTQ youth are placed in one of five different community-based group homes situated in the West Hollywood area of Los Angeles. Youth are placed in the program either by the Los Angeles County court system or by voluntary agreement between their parents and the Los Angeles Department of Social Services. Youth are placed in specific group homes according to their age and program needs. Within the past decade, GLASS has expanded its mission to include foster care and has initiated a program that recruited, screened, trained, certified, and supervised foster parents.

A central theme in the GLASS and Green Chimneys programs is that the agencies are first and foremost child welfare organizations developed specifically for GLBTQ children, youth, and affected families. They are organizations that as their central mission, work with GLBTQ adolescents and their families within the context of a child welfare environment. The ultimate objective for youth at GLASS or Green Chimneys is for each youth to return to his or her own family community or to assist the youth in identifying another permanent arrangement, such as adoption or the development of close, lasting relationships with caring adults.

Both agencies' programs are specifically designed for gay and lesbian as well as HIV-affected children but have served (and continue to serve) all youngsters in need, regardless of sexual orientation.

## Permanency Planning

A literature search for articles on permanency planning for adolescents revealed few sources specifically addressing the challenges that adolescents face. This lack of information reflects the generally held belief that the best child welfare can offer to adolescents is a goal of independent living.

In the past few years, practitioners have begun to question this assumption, particularly in light of the pervasiveness of former child welfare youth in the homeless population. Although often considered to be separate populations, in policy and practice, the overlap between street  youth and foster care youth is quite large (Holdway & Ray, 1992). The prevalence of a history of child welfare involvement for street-involved and homeless youth is significant (Bass, 1992; Clatts, Davis, Sotheran, & Atillasoy, 1998; Jonson-Reid & Barth, 2000; O'Brien, 1993). O'Brien (1993) found that 28% to 43% of youth interviewed in a shelter had a history of child welfare involvement. One large-scale study of youth exiting foster care in California reported that 16.8% of the adolescents in care had "unsuccessful" exits, such as running away, refusal of service, incarceration, hospitalization, abduction, or death (Jonson-Reid & Barth, 2000, p. 464). Bradley (1997) discussed residential instability as an important factor correlating to youth homelessness. He stated, "Youth leaving institutional settings or foster care often become homeless due to poor discharge planning and follow up" (p. 169).

Child welfare professionals often label lesbian and gay youth in foster care as "difficult." Due to systemic and philosophical barriers, youth who are perceived as difficult may receive less responsive care than they require from systems. A child may be discharged from care at age 18 due to "noncompliance," with little or no real planning in place to ensure against the youth's joining the ranks of the homeless.

In a study of more than 900 homeless and/or street-involved youth, Clatts and colleagues (1998) reported that "one-third (35%) self-identified as gay, lesbian, or bisexual" (p. 199), and that youth older than the age of 18 were more at risk for entrenchment in the street. This is a large overrepresentation of lesbian and gay youth, as conventional wisdom holds that approximately 10% of any population is lesbian or gay. No conventional statistics are available on the prevalence of people of transgender experience in the general population. The history of a lack of affirming/appropriate placements for GLBTQ youth may have either passively encouraged them to leave placements through neglect or may have actively engaged in discriminatory behavior against these youth. Given the high risk of homelessness to which GLBTQ youth are prone, an innovative, culturally appropriate effort in permanency might significantly deflect that risk.

O'Brien (1993) and Lewis and Heffernan (2000) urged practitioners to create permanency plans for older adolescents. O'Brien stated, "Let's take the 20 year old foster care youth discharged from foster care—possibly with a high school diploma but probably not—and having *no relationship in his life....These* children are not faring well, because the child welfare system had not taken it upon itself to help these children develop a lasting relationship in their life while they were in foster care" (p. 10). He emphatically argued that adolescents should be freed for adoption and that the goal of independent living should be abolished. Lewis and Heffernan, 10 years later, stated, "The structure dictates that adolescents cannot be successfully connected to healthy parenting adults. Consequently, adolescents bear the label of 'unadoptable;' they have been found unsuitable for family life" (p. ii). All of the above authors recognize the difficulty of approaching adolescent permanency in a new manner, and Lewis and Heffernan acknowledge that adolescents themselves must be brought into the process if there is to be any hope for success. Although there continues to be a great deal of debate about this issue, many child welfare practitioners are questioning the suitability of the focus on independent living services versus a focus on youth permanency. This study looks at attitudes of GLBTQ adolescents in care toward adoption and permanency, as well as some of the systems in place that encourage or hinder this process.

## Method

This exploratory study, documenting the permanency experience of youth in two gay-affirming agencies, is an effort to uncover clues about how professionals and the young people themselves perceive the experience. Given the paucity of conceptualization and theory building regarding this phenomenon, the use of qualitative methods seems warranted. Qualitative methods are generally more suited to the study of relatively uncharted social circumstances and lend themselves to the description of complex social realities. Such descriptions can serve as "ends-in-themselves or they may be useful in generating hypotheses that can be tested at a later date by quantitative methods" (Epstein, 1988, p. 188). This study uses methods drawn from a mixed design approach. Both qualitative data derived from interviews and quantitative data derived from survey responses were collected for analysis.

## Subjects

Six youth (two from GLASS and four from Green Chimneys) were randomly selected to participate in qualitative, in-depth interviews. The interviews were conducted by using an open-ended interview guide combined with probes to elicit further data. In addition, 45 youth volunteered to participate in this study by completing an anonymous, self-administered questionnaire.

## Procedure

The questionnaire consisted of a series of open-ended questions and five-point, Likert-type scale questions about the young person's experiences with permanency. In New York, 34 of the 46 eligible self-identified gay and lesbian youth responded to the questionnaire, with responses from each of the three program sites. In Los Angeles, 11 of the 36 eligible youth responded to the questionnaire. Heterosexually oriented youth and youth in the runaway and homeless program were not asked to complete survey instruments.

## Sample

The study population comprised foster care program youth from Green Chimneys and GLASS who self-identified as lesbian, gay, bisexual, or transgendered ($N$ = 45). All but three of the subjects were male ($n$ = 42). The overwhelming majority were young people of color (95.5%), reflecting the disproportionate representation of children of color in the U.S. child welfare system (www.acf.dhhs.gov/programs/cb/publications/afcars/apr2001.htm). Of the total subjects, 58% ($n$ = 26) identified as having a gay sexual orientation, 20% identified as bisexual, 7% ($n$ = 3) identified as lesbian, and transgendered youth were 13% ($n$ = 6) of the sample. One youth identified as questioning (see Table 1).

## Findings

Several themes emerged from analysis of the qualitative data. Quantitative data were analyzed using simple statistical tests. Findings were organized into the three major areas explored by the Child and Family Services Review: (1) safety, (2) permanency, and (3) well-being.

### Safety

In the Child and Family Service Review process, two outcomes are expected from this variable: (1) Children and youth are, first and foremost, protected from abuse and neglect, and (2) children are safely maintained in their own homes whenever possible.

GLBTQ youth are particularly attuned to issues of personal safety. Although the investigators of this study did not assess these specific standards, clear anecdotal evidence from interviews conducted and questionnaires gathered suggests strong evidence of abuse and maltreatment for self-identified gay and lesbian youth, both in out-of-home placements and in their family systems.

Mallon's (1998) study of these youth in out-of-home care provides ample evidence that they were at-risk at home, in their communities, and in foster care placements. Youth interviewed for this study also noted that they have experienced abuse and maltreatment in these same milieus.

TABLE 1
Sexual Orientation by Race and Ethnicity

| Race/Ethnicity | % (n) | Gay | Lesbian | Bi-sexual | Trans-gender | Ques-tioning |
|---|---|---|---|---|---|---|
| African American | 42 (19) | 7 | | 7 | 6 | 1 |
| Latino | 29 (13) | 10 | 2 | 1 | | |
| Multiracial | 22 (10) | 7 | 1 | 2 | | |
| White | 4 (2) | 2 | | | | |
| Caribbean | 2 (1) | 1 | | | | |
| Total %(n) | 100 (45) | 58(27) | 7(3) | 20(10) | 13(06) | 2(1) |

Many young people, including lesbian and gay youth, enter the foster care system because it offers sanctuary from abusive family relationships and violence in their homes. Rindfleisch (1993) observed, "Once in placement, children and youth are presumed to be in an environment superior to that from which they were removed. So they are not thought to need protection beyond that provided by state licensing activities" (p. 265). For many youth interviewed for this study, however, the brutality they experienced before entering a child welfare placement did not stop after they entered the system.

Lesbian and gay young people, unlike their heterosexual counterparts, are targeted for attack specifically because of their sexual orientation (Comstock, 1991; Garnets, Herek, & Levy, 1992; Herek, 1990; Herek & Berrill, 1992). North American culture, pervaded by a heterocentric ideological system that denies, denigrates, and stigmatizes gays and lesbians, simultaneously makes lesbians and gay men invisible and legitimizes hostility, discrimination, and even violence against them. Thus, safety has always been an issue for gays and lesbians. Gay and lesbian youth, both inside and outside child welfare systems, must assess safety issues in their lives every day. When gay or lesbian people engage in behaviors permissible for heterosexuals (such as walking down a street holding hands or kissing), they make public what Western society has prescribed as private. They are accused of flaunting their sexuality and are, thereby, perceived as deserving of or even asking for retribution, harassment, or assault.

## Lack of Safety in the Family System

The 45 persons in this study reported that verbal harassment and, at times, physical violence was often inaugurated at home within their own family systems. Many of these young people reported that relatives, and sometimes citizens in their community, increased the momentum of this violence by joining in the harassment. The extent to which gay and lesbian young people experienced verbal harassment and physical violence—in foster care placements, by their peers, and in some cases by staff charged with caring for them—is astonishing. The stigma attached to being gay or lesbian often prevented them from reporting their victimization (Goffman, 1963). Many young people reported that when the abuse was acknowledged, the victims themselves were blamed. Consequently, more than one-half of the youth in this study chose, at some point, the apparent safety of the streets rather than the foster care system.

Tirades from family members, peers, and even staff members that began with denigrating verbal taunts in some cases escalated into physical violence. Gay and lesbian young people deemed to be disposable individuals, deserving of being jostled into line or kept in the closet, frequently found that environments were so poor and the fit was so bad that many felt they literally had to flee for their lives. Some who migrated to a safer environment found the safety and fit that they sought. Others found an even less favorable fit.

## Lack of Safety in Foster Care Systems

Seventy-eight percent of young people and 88% of child welfare professionals interviewed for this study reported that it was not safe for gay and lesbian adolescents in group homes or congregate care settings to self-identify as gay or lesbian. One professional from New York, who was interviewed for this study, linked the issue of safety with the phenomenon of hiding:

> In most agencies, it is just not safe for a gay or lesbian young person to be identified. In our agency, clearly it is safe because we are gay-affirming, but this has not been the case for many youth who come to us from other child welfare agencies. Youth report that, when staff find out, they either treat the young person differently or close their eyes to some of the negative situations that emerge. It is just not safe for them to be out and because they are not out, the staff think that they do not exist.

Clearly, in a gay-affirming placement, the issue of lack of safety because of one's sexual orientation is diminished. When youth in this study were asked to describe their experiences in their current placement, one young woman noted:

> At least you don't always have to watch your back. I can be myself. No one is telling me to be more like a girl or to stop acting "that way." I'm not going to tell you there are no problems. I'd be lying. There are problems here, too, but I never have any problems about being gay. It's really the first place I have ever felt safe.

One additional indicator of safety is whether or not the youth feels safe in coming out, as suggested by the individual above. This study found that the age when youth first came out to themselves ranged from 6 to 18 years, with a mean of 12.9 years. These findings are consistent with findings made by D'Augelli and Hershberger (1993).

Youth in this study came out to their parents almost one year, on average, after coming out to themselves (see Table 2). Among the respondents of this study, age at first disclosure to family ranged from 8 to 19 years, with a mean age of 13.7.

*Permanency*

In the Child and Family Service Review process, two outcomes are expected from this variable: (1) Children will have permanency and stability in their living situations, and (2) the continuity of family relationships and connections will be preserved for children and youth.

Several areas related to the first permanency outcome, evaluated as part of the Child and Family Service Reviews process, were explored in depth. The second outcome area was less fully explored. The following areas were explored: (a) foster care reentries; (b) stability of foster care placements, with a goal of no more than two placement settings; (c) length of time to achieve reunification, with a goal of reunifying children and youth with families in less than 12 months from the time of the latest removal from the home; (d) length of time to achieve adoption, with a goal of less than 24 months from the time of the latest removal from the home; and (e) preserving connections and developing relationships.

Specific questions were asked about each of these five areas. Using the questionnaire, the authors found that youth interviewed ranged in age from 2 to 18 years at their first placement; the average age at first placement was 11.8 years. Their initial placement age was younger than when they came out (12.9 years). This fact dispels the myth that gay youth first enter placement after they initially come out.

Despite permanency mandates for youth to remain in care for shorter periods of time, the overall mean length of time spent in placement for youth in the study sample was 4.2 years. Most of these youth (65%, $n = 33$) spent more than one year in care. The present investigators decided to use this variable, even though federal officials determined that it was impossible to use "length of stay in foster care" as a statewide data indicator for determining substantial conformity. One finding of this study that is of great concern is that the respondents experienced multiple placements

TABLE 2
**Age of Coming Out to Self (in years)**

|                      | Range | M     | Mode |
|----------------------|-------|-------|------|
| Coming Out to Self   | 6-18  | 12.9  | 15   |
| Coming Out to Family | 9-19  | 13.66 | 14.5 |
| First Placement      | 2-18  | 11.75 | 13.1 |

(range, 1–40 placements). The average number of placements for the overall sample was 6.35.

Clearly, youth interviewed for this study had experienced multiple placements; had reentered foster care (in some cases, several times); were not frequently reunified with their families, as evidenced by their long lengths of stays in foster care settings; and lacked permanent connections to their communities and families of origin.

The narratives of these 45 youth also reflected these findings, particularly in three areas: placement stability, length of time in foster care placements, and adoption issues.

## Placement Stability

Youth interviewed for this study experienced significant placement instability; 80% ($n = 36$) experienced multiple placements within the child welfare system. Some youth had as many as 40 different foster care placements. Gay and lesbian youth are frequently seen as a problem by many untrained out-of-home care systems. The youth themselves note that they leave placements where they have found a "poor fit" and search for a program where the fit is more natural. One youth in California noted the following about his placement instability:

> It gets really hard to keep track of your things and yourself when you move from place to place. I have been in so many different placements that I can't remember. If I try to count them, I get lost when I get to about 30. Most were terrible. In most, it was not said out loud, but you knew

that you couldn't tell them you were gay. In some, I didn't even have a chance to say good-bye. A social worker just met me at school with all my clothes in one of those big black plastic garbage bags. Whenever someone met me at school, I knew it was over. Some places were not so bad. GLASS is the best. At least here I can be myself and no one tries to make me change. I am with my own people here.

## Length of Time in Placement

Youth interviewed for this study spent an average of 4.2 years in foster care, well beyond the 15 to 22 months suggested by ASFA legislation. The longer children remain in care, the less likely is their reunification with their family of origin (Hess & Proch, 1993). Youth in this study had been in care for 1 to 14 years. As she discusses her estrangement from her mother, this young woman from New York expresses heartrending pain:

I have been in foster care for more than nine years. I have had 10 different placements. At first, the social workers arranged for my mother to visit me and for me to visit her, but as time went on, those visits were fewer and fewer. My mother had real problems with my being a lesbian, but no one ever talked to her about that. I haven't seen or heard from my mother in more than five years. Sometimes I think maybe she is looking for me and can't find me. But then I remember that she knows the address of the agency and could have contacted them if she wanted to. I have two younger sisters, and I have lost them too. It's hard to lose your whole family. Even all these years later, and even though I am now 19 years old and getting ready to go out on my own, it still hurts.

## Creation of Relationships

Youth in this study, in many cases estranged from their own families of origin, still sought out adult role models, mentors, and fictive kin (Weston, 1991). In addition to adoption, many viable means exist to achieve permanency for youth. Fictive kinship relationships, intimate lasting bonds with adult role models and mentors, and relationships with agency staff members were all permanency options referred to by the youth we interviewed.

Many non-Eurocentric cultures have the concept of *comadres, compadrazos*, godsisters, and othermothers (Collins, 1986). Gay fictive kinship, a similar concept, has been fully explored by scholar Kath Weston (1991). Youth interviewed for this study spoke about the importance of these fictive kinship networks as communities of mutual support. One youth, in New York, spoke at length about the importance of his "house"—the House of Extravaganza. He spoke about his "house mother" and "house father" and their importance in his life. The New York Ball Scene is an extensive network of houses where youth and adults come together to "walk a ball." One young man described walking a ball as "like participating in a beauty contest…but there are many different categories not found in traditional beauty contests." Young people who are members of houses are mentored by older adults, cared for by the house community, sometimes given housing and finances, and helped toward self-sufficiency and independence.

Many youth also spoke about the importance of staff members in their lives. They view these staff as permanent connections, not just temporary links. In reflecting about his relationship with a staff member in his group home, one youth remarked:

> I don't know where I would be without John [a social worker in the group home]. He is always there for me. I can call him when I need to talk, he helped me get a job, and he is always working with me to help me become independent. I know this is his job, but I know that what he does with me is more than what most people do at their jobs. When I leave in six months, I know that we will continue to be connected. I guess you could say we have a bond.

## Adoption Issues

A time-honored myth in the field of services for children, youth, and families is that most adolescents do not want to be adopted. In this study, only 8% of the respondents were in fact adopted at some point in their lives. Nevertheless, more than one-third of the youth surveyed (34%) indicated that, if they could be adopted, they would like to be adopted. Although adoption may not be the primary permanency plan for all youth, clearly, it is an option that many youth in this study do not want to overlook. Despite the fact that some social workers may not have explored adoption as a viable permanency option, interviews with youth suggested that adoption should be investigated as an option. One young woman in New York remarked:

> I don't think I am too old to be adopted. I would really like a family. It would be nice and I think I am pretty adoptable. My social worker never even asked me if I would like to explore adoption. I think they mostly think that it's only little kids that people want to adopt, but I would like my social worker to see if she could find a family for me.

## Well-Being

Several areas related to well-being are evaluated as part of the Child and Family Service Reviews process: (a) Families have enhanced capacity to provide for their children's needs, (b) children and youth must receive appropriate services to meet their educational needs, and (c) children and youth must receive adequate services to meet their physical and mental health needs.

Respondents were not queried directly in this area in the survey instrument, but interviews with youth revealed important data in these three areas.

## Enhanced Capacity of Families

Visitation with parents while youth are in out-of-home care settings and involvement of youth and families in service planning are two key issues in exploring this outcome area. Both Green Chimneys and GLASS have very liberal visiting policies, which actually went exceed the mandated requirements for worker visitation and for establishing youth/family visitation. One youth summarized the reports of most others:

> For the most part, I can visit my family whenever I want. In fact, I can visit every weekend. The problem is, though, I don't visit. Every time I go, they are always trying to get me to change. My mother will say, "You can come home, but you can't wear those clothes that you wear, and you have to toughen up a bit." I'd rather not go, if I have to change. But I can go. Same thing with inviting her for meetings. She is always invited, but she never comes. She says she feels uncomfortable around "those people." She means gay people.

When asked what his family would need to permit more frequent visits, he added this honest, but self-deprecating, remark: "They would have to accept the fact that I am a faggot."

### Educational Placements

Unfortunately, many educational placements are not safe environments for GLBTQ youth (Mallon, 1997, 2000b). Therefore, many of these youth drop out of traditional school settings or focus on acquiring a general equivalency diploma. Youth in foster care may experience even greater difficulty in school because their sense of impermanence extends to school placements as well as foster care placements. Interviews conducted with GLBTQ adolescents in this study help to identify and explore the reasons why some youth may leave school before graduation.

Several prominent themes emerged in the interviews with youth at Green Chimneys and at GLASS: verbal harassment, physical harassment and violence, and the unresponsiveness of school personnel. One youth in Los Angeles summarized these factors:

I had lots of problems being gay and being in high school. It was a nightmare. First it was the constant taunting— "hey homo, hey fag"—day in and day out. It was so exhausting. Then came the shoving, the physical stuff, all the fights. The staff were absolutely no help. When you went to them, they said, "If you didn't tell people all your business, you wouldn't have to deal with this." The whole thing was terrible. One day I just decided that I couldn't take it anymore, and I left. I never went back.

### Health and Mental Health Services

GLBTQ youth in foster care have health and mental health needs typical of their status as adolescents, but they also have needs unique to their status as sexual minority persons.

**Physical Health Care Issues.** The youth interviewed noted that GLBTQ youth have health-related issues in several key areas: reproductive health and parenting, trauma and sexual assault, eating disorders, substance abuse, suicidal ideation, and sexually transmitted diseases. Access to preventive and restorative health care services may also pose special difficulties for GLBTQ youth, especially those in the foster care system.

Transgender youth have unique health-related concerns. Many noted that they faced discrimination in health care settings because they are gender variant. Fearing rejection, ridicule, and harassment, many transgender youth reported not seeking the services of mainstream health care systems. Youth with gender identity issues are reported to experiment frequently with hormones, usually obtained illegally on the streets. Injecting unprescribed hormones is, in itself, high risk. Many, however, also share needles, thus placing themselves at higher risk for HIV transmission. Although not all transgender persons opt for genital reassignment surgery, some do. Genital reassignment surgery is not an option during adolescence; however, medically supervised hormonal therapy and ongoing counseling are options that can and should be explored.

More than 30% of the youth interviewed for this study said that they had lived on the streets for some period of time. Living on the streets puts the health of some GLBTQ youth at constant risk (Zide & Cherry, 1992). Runaway and homeless GLBTQ youths typically do not have ready access to health care that recognizes and addresses sexual concerns. In addition to the life-threatening consequences of HIV infection, substance abuse, and street violence, street youth often suffer from upper respiratory infection, body and pubic lice, burns, numerous injuries, sexually transmitted diseases, dermatological problems, and mental health problems. The extremes of temperatures, irregular sleep in exposed places, poor diet, a propensity toward smoking cigarettes, and the lack of hygiene opportunities for regular showers exacerbates these problems. Hunger is also a serious problem for street youth. Several studies from Seattle, Los Angeles, and New York (Mallon, 1998; Seattle Commission on Children, 1988; Victim Services/Traveler's Aid, 1991) have suggested that more than 33% of the runaway and homeless youth populations surveyed in those cities identified themselves as lesbian, gay, bisexual, or transgendered.

Homeless lesbian, gay, and bisexual youth are also at risk for severe mental health problems. Street youth suffer primarily from anxiety and depression. Many have also suffered from childhood sexual, physical, or emotional abuse or other trauma related to family violence. A young white lesbian in Los Angeles described her home situation:

> My family was always a mess. My mom's boyfriends were always disgusting. Most times they beat her. Sometimes, they beat my brothers and me. One of them molested me for years, starting when I turned 11. I didn't tell my mother. I mean, she couldn't even help herself. How was she go-

ing to help me? My life was a nightmare from the time I was 5 until the time I left home at 15. Believe it or not, running away from home was the best thing that ever happened to me. But I still have a lot that haunts me about all the stuff that happened to me.

At times, the psychological stress, as exemplified in the above description, is more than many young persons can endure. Some GLBTQ questioning youths report suicide attempts to escape from the isolation and estrangement from their pain.

**Mental Health Issues.** Although homosexuality was deleted in 1972 from the American Psychiatric Association's *Diagnostic and Statistical Assessment Manual II* (1974), youth report that some mental health professionals still act as though a gay, lesbian, or transgender identity is curable. Indeed, some clinicians claim to be able to cure homosexuality through reparative or aversion therapies. Research has shown that these efforts have been unsuccessful; although one's sexual behavior is changed, one's sense of internal "goodness of fit" remains gay or lesbian. Contemporary clinical approaches to working with GLBTQ youth do not attempt to change the young person's sexual orientation; instead, the approach is to work with youth from a GLBTQ-affirming perspective (Gonsiorek, 1988; Ryan & Futterman, 1998).

Mental health practitioners most often see GLBTQ youth for the same presenting problems as other adolescents, such as, depression, anxiety, suicidal behavior, somatic disorders, chronic stress, and gender identity issues (Remafedi, 1994).

Chronic stress from verbal harassment is a common theme identified by researchers investigating the experiences of GLBTQ youth (Hunter & Schaecher, 1987). Coming out to family, the fear of being found out, negotiating safety, and managing one's GLBTQ identity are additional stressors that these youth face. These factors can contribute to eroding a GLBTQ youth's sense of self-worth, self-esteem, and confidence and can lead to youth needing treatment. In addition, the need to hide distorts almost everything about a young GLBTQ person's life, promotes dysfunction, and can cause a youth to seek help (Martin, 1982).

**Psychiatric Hospitalizations.** Like heterosexual youth who suffer from severe psychiatric disorders, some GLBTQ youth may require psychiatric hospitalization. Historically, inpatient mental health settings either have ignored sexual identity issues or have made them the inappropriate focus of treatment.

Many issues present a challenge to adolescent treatment facilities, including the availability of mental health services that are friendly to adolescents. A self-identified GLBTQ youth may present a particular challenge for staff in out-of-home care. Many GLBTQ youth who are hospitalized remain long after they need to stay, simply because appropriate residential programs cannot be found. One young person in New York recalled:

> I was in Kings County for five months. I was initially admitted because of depression, but once I came out as gay, that became the big focus of my treatment. In fact, almost every session focused on that issue. I went on several interviews for placement in group homes, but somehow I never got accepted. I heard later from one worker that it was because I was gay. When I was accepted by Green Chimneys, lots of things changed. I could finally be myself, and then I got better.

## Discussion

Permanency planning involves a mix of family-centered casework and legal strategies designed to ensure that children and youth have safe, caring, stable, and lifetime families in which to grow up. Lesbian and gay youth in out-of-home care need exactly the same things. They need targeted and appropriate efforts to protect safety, achieve permanence, and strengthen the family and the youth's well-being. They also need early intervention and prevention, with reasonable efforts to prevent unnecessary out-of-home care when safety can be assured. Safety must remain a paramount concern throughout the life of the case.

Gay and lesbian youth need appropriate, least restrictive out-of-home placements—if possible, within their family (relatives as the preferred placement/permanency option), culture, and community. They need comprehensive family and child assessments, written case plans, goal-oriented practice, frequent case reviews, and concurrent permanency plans. These youth also need reasonable efforts to reunify families and to maintain family connections and continuity in children's relationships when safety can be assured. They need time-limited reunification services and reasonable efforts to find alternative permanency options outside the child welfare system when children cannot return to parents. These options may include adoption, legal guardianship, or in special circumstances, other planned alternative permanent living arrangements. Lesbian and gay youth need expedited filing of a petition for termination of parental rights at 15 months after placement—when it is in their best interests and services to promote adoption and postpermanency services, if required. These youth need collaborative case planning—partnerships among birthparents, foster parents, agency staff, court and legal staff, and community service providers, as well as frequent and quality parent–child visitations. Finally, gay and lesbian youth in out-of-home care also need 6-month case reviews, 12-month permanency hearings, and timely decisionmaking about where children will grow up. The timelines must be based on the children's sense of time (National Resource Center, 2000).

Although these principles seem rational for youth in out-of-home care, the data gathered in this study suggest that very few of these areas have been explored by child welfare professionals who work with lesbian and gay young people. These young people experienced very long lengths of stay, multiple placements, serious concerns about personal safety, and a lack of appropriate school and health/mental health services. In essence, they seemed to have needs in almost every area explored by the Child and Family Service Review process.

We would, however, like to point to several areas where there is the greatest hope to enhance services for GLBTQ youth in out-of-home care.

First, lesbian and gay youth need to remain with their families of origin when it is safe to do so. Therefore, family support and preservationists need to work on developing their own competencies and skills in the area of understanding and affirming youth who self-identify as lesbian or gay. These professionals must also be able to work intimately with the parents of these young people, not only to keep the children at home but to help the parents deal with their own feelings about having a child who identifies as lesbian or gay (see Berzon, 1992; Dew, 1994; Fairchild & Hayward, 1989; Griffin, Wirth, & Wirth, 1986; Strommen, 1989). Professionals need a great deal of training as well as opportunities to process their feelings regarding this population of young people (Mallon, 1997c, 1999). Organizations like Parents and Friends of Lesbians and Gays can be very helpful partners in this effort.

When and if lesbian and gay youth have to be separated from their families, gay-affirming placements with trained staff clearly are safer and better places than regular foster care placements for GLBTQ youth who require placement in out-of-home care. Prior research (Mallon, 1998, 1999) has clearly demonstrated the deleterious effects of a hostile environment on lesbian or gay youth in foster care. Youth in this study remarked overwhelmingly that living at Green Chimneys or GLASS was a very positive experience for them. Not surprisingly, their most common comment about the best aspect of being in a gay-affirming placement was: "You are safe here, and you don't have to hide."

States and local districts around the country should explore these two models for GLBTQ youth. The models are replicable and cost-effective, because placements can be stable and youth can move toward permanency when they feel that their needs are being met. If lesbian- and gay-affirming programs cannot be developed, child welfare organizations must, at the very least, ensure safety for all youth and must work toward developing niches of safety for youth who identify as other than heterosexually oriented.

The parents of lesbian and gay youth who are in out-of-home settings also deserve to have child welfare professionals who know how to help them process what it means to have a child who is not heterosexually oriented. Too often, child welfare professionals erroneously assume that parents cannot or refuse to deal with the issue of their child's sexual orientation. This refusal might be true for some parents, but it is not a correct assumption about all parents of a lesbian or gay youngster. Child welfare professionals, especially those who work with families toward reunification, need to become more comfortable and knowledgeable about talking with parents about sexual orientation and sexual identity issues. Reunification is possible, is desired by many youth and families, and must be explored for every lesbian and gay youth in out-of-home placement. This goal requires workers to increase their knowledge, skills, and abilities in working with the population and to gain greater comfort in dealing with families about sensitive issues like religion, stigma, culturally sanctioned anti-gay and lesbian sentiments, and embarrassment. Ongoing, regularly scheduled sensitivity training and adequate supervision by a skilled supervisor can enhance workers' skills in these areas.

Our attention was also drawn to the area of youth permanency and adoption as a permanency option. Adoption is clearly one direct route to permanency, and it is one that seems not to have been adequately explored by some social workers who worked with 34% of the youth in this study. Exploration and work toward an array of permanency options for lesbian and gay youth are needed. Assisting youth in the transition from foster care to self-sufficiency is a clear and necessary goal for all youth in care. Even as youth are being prepared for self-sufficiency, workers should concurrently explore an array of permanency options, for example, adoption, mentoring relationships, self-sufficiency, and development of fictive kinship networks of mutual support. Youth permanency can be achieved in many ways, but adoption and the development of specific families for lesbian and gay youth—including gay and lesbian resource families (foster and adoptive parents)—should also be investigated as permanency options (Mallon, 2000c; Ricketts, 1991).

The lesbian and gay youth in this study had suffered a great deal from the traumatic effects of verbal harassment and the threat of physical violence directed at them because of their gay or lesbian orientation. When the youth is lesbian or gay, safety is clearly a paramount concern throughout the life of the case. Further work is needed to focus on helping youth process these feelings and assist them in developing adaptive strategies to cope with hostility. Youth workers will need training to assist them in this process (Mallon, 2001a).

## Conclusions

All children and youth, including those who self-identify as GLBTQ youth, need loving, stable homes. ASFA requires child welfare agencies to work with children and families quicker and better—a challenge that, many believe, depends on the capacity of child welfare agencies to be more family-centered and child-focused, community-based, open and inclusive, culturally relevant, nonadversarial, and concurrent in the consideration of the range of permanency options for children. And, we would add, more sensitive to the unique needs of GLBTQ youth.

Although more and larger child welfare programs for lesbian and gay youth exist throughout the country than existed five years ago, a need remains to develop practice principles and guidelines specific to working toward permanency for these youth. Current child welfare practice models are based on foster care and adoption services for heterosexually oriented youth and are framed in a heterocentric social context (Mallon, 2000a). To assist gay and lesbian adolescents to create viable long-term family structures that will help to create stability and family structure, workers and administrators must begin to look beyond tradition-ally understood concepts of permanence. Given the overrepresentation of ethnic minority children in foster care, also reflected in this sample population of gay and lesbian adoles-cents, these models must be culturally sensitive and build on the inherent strengths of extended families (Hegar & Scannapieco, 1995). Services must also be made available to the families of gay and lesbian youth who are in care, many of whom have been largely neglected by the system. Finally, continued research is needed on the significance of a gay-affirming environment for lesbian and gay youth as well as on the needs and desires of vul-nerable adolescents in long-term placement.

Recent research into the attributes of successful child welfare programs suggests that to achieve positive outcomes for children, agencies need to be comprehensive, flexible, responsive, and per-severing; see children in the context of their families and deal with these families as part of neighborhoods and communities; have a long-term, prevention orientation with a clear mission; continue to evolve over time; be well-managed by competent and committed and skilled individuals; have well-trained and sup-ported staff to provide high-quality services; and encourage prac-titioners to build strong relationships based on mutual trust and respect (Schorr, 1997).

It is critical that child welfare agency efforts to become effec-tive and efficient be linked to children's urgent developmental needs for emotional and legal permanence. To do this, child wel-fare agencies must be representative of a diverse mix of family-centered, child-focused, and culturally relevant philosophies, program components, and practice strategies to help children live in families that offer continuity of relationships with nurturing parents or caretakers and the opportunity to establish lifetime relationships (Maluccio, Fein, & Olmstead, 1986). This process is intended to safely limit both entry into placement and the time

children spend in out-of-home care, because it is widely acknowledged that the uncertain and long-term nature of the foster care
experience has a negative affect on children's overall sense of
belonging and emotional well-being (Sudia, 1986).◆

## References

American Psychiatric Association. (1974). *Diagnostic and statistical manual of mental disorders* (2nd ed.). Washington, DC: Author.

Bass, D. (1992). *Helping vulnerable youths: Runaway and homeless adolescents in the United States*. Washington, DC: National Association of Social Workers Press.

Berzon, B. (1992). Telling your family you're gay. In B. Berzon (Ed.), *Positively gay: New approaches to gay and lesbian life* (pp. 67–78). Berkeley, CA: Celestial Arts.

Billingsley, A., & Giovannoni, J. M. (1972). *Children of the storm*. New York: Harcourt Brace Jovanovich.

Bradley, J. (1997). Runaway youth: Stress, social support and adjustment. New York: Garland.

Bucy, J., & Able-Peterson, T. (1993). *The street outreach training manual*. Washington, DC: U.S. Department of Health and Human Services.

Clatts, M. C., Davis, W. R., Sotheran, J. L., & Atillasoy, A. (1998). Correlates and distribution of HIV risk behaviors among homeless youths in New York City: Implications for prevention and policy. *Child Welfare, 77*(2), 195–207.

Collins, P. H. (1986). Learning from the outsider within: The sociological significance of black feminist thought. *Social Problems, 3*(6), 22–31.

Comstock, G. D. (1991). *Violence against lesbians and gay men*. New York: Columbia University Press.

D'Augelli, A. R., & Hershberger, S. L. (1993). Lesbian, gay, and bisexual youth in community settings: Personal challenges and mental health problems. *American Journal of Community Psychology, 21*(4), 421–448.

Dew, R. F. (1994). *The family heart: A memoir of when our son came out*. Reading, MA: Addison-Wesley.

Epstein, I. (1988). Quantitative and qualitative methods. In R. M. Grinell (Ed.), *Social work research and evaluation* (3rd ed., pp. 185–198). Itasca, IL: F. E. Peacock.

Fairchild, B., & Hayward, N. (1989). *Now that you know: What every parent should know about homosexuality.* New York: Harcourt Brace Jovanovich.

Fanshel, D. (1982). *On the road to permanency: An expanded data base for children in foster care.* New York: Child Welfare League of America.

Fanshel, D., & Shinn, E. (1978). *Children in foster care: A longitudinal investigation.* New York: Columbia University Press.

Fitzgerald, M. D. (1996). Homeless youths and the child welfare system: Implications for policy and service. *Child Welfare, 75*(3), 717–730.

Garnets, L., Herek, G. M., & Levy, B. (1992). Violence and victimization of lesbians and gay men: Mental health consequences. In G. M. Herek & K. T. Berrill (Eds.), *Hate crimes* (pp. 207–226). Newbury Park, CA: Sage.

Goffman, E. (1963). *Stigma: Notes of the management of a spoiled identity.* Englewood Cliffs, NJ: Prentice-Hall.

Gonsiorek, J. C. (1988). Mental health issues of gay and lesbian adolescents. *Journal of Adolescent Health Care, 9*(2), 114–122.

Griffin, C., Wirth, M. J., & Wirth, A. G. (1986). *Beyond acceptance.* Englewood Cliffs, NJ: Prentice-Hall.

Hegar, R. L., & Scannapieco, M. (1995). From family duty to family policy: The evolution of kinship care. *Child Welfare, 74*, 200–216.

Herek, G. M. (1990). The context of anti-gay violence: Notes on cultural psychological heterosexism. *Journal of Interpersonal Violence, 5*(3), 316-333.

Herek, G. M., & Berrill, K. T. (Eds.). (1992). *Hate crimes: Confronting violence against lesbians and gay men.* Newbury Park, CA: Sage.

Hess, P., & Proch, K. O. (1993). The heart of reunification. In B. A. Pine, R. Krieger, & A. N. Maluccio (Eds.), *Together again: Family reunification care* (pp. 519–527). Washington, DC: Child Welfare League of America.

Holdway, D. M., & Ray, J. (1992). Attitudes of street kids toward foster care. *Child and Adolescent Social Work, 9*(4), 307–317.

Hunter, J., & Schaecher, R. (1987). Stresses on lesbian and gay adolescents in schools. *Social Work in Education, 9*(3), 180-188.

Jonson-Reid, M., & Barth, R. P. (2000). From placement to prison: The path to adolescent incarceration from child welfare supervised foster or group care. *Social Service Review, 22*(7), 493–516.

Kruks, G. (1991). Gay and lesbian homeless/street youth: Special issues and concerns. *Journal Adolescent Health, 12*(7), 515–518.

Lewis, R. G., & Heffernan, M. S. (2000). *Adolescents and families for life: A toolkit for supervisors.* Boston, MA: High Popples Press.

Luna, G. C. (1991). Street youth: Adaptation and survival in the AIDS decade. *Journal of Adolescent Health, 12*(7), 511–514.

Maas, H. S., & Engler, R. E. (1959). *Children in need of parents.* New York: Columbia University Press.

Mallon, G. P. (1992). Gay and no place to go: Serving the needs of gay and lesbian youth in out-of-home care settings. *Child Welfare, 71*(6), 547–557.

Mallon, G. P. (1997a). Entering into a collaborative search for meaning with gay and lesbian youths in out-of-home care: An empowerment-based model for training child welfare professionals. *Child and Adolescent Social Work Journal, 14*(6), 427-444.

Mallon, G. P. (1997b). Toward a competent welfare service delivery system for gay and lesbian adolescents and their families. *Journal of Multicultural Social Work, 5*(3/4), 177–194.

Mallon, G. P. (1997c). When schools are not safe places: Gay, lesbian, bisexual, and transgendered young people in educational settings. *Reaching Today's Youth, 2*(1), 41–45.

Mallon, G. P. (1998). *We don't exactly get the welcome wagon: The experience of gay and lesbian adolescents in child welfare systems.* New York: Columbia University Press.

Mallon, G. P. (1999). Gay and lesbian adolescents and their families. *Journal of Gay and Lesbian Social Services, 11*(1/2), 23–33.

Mallon, G. P. (2000a). Gay men and lesbians as adoptive parents. *Journal of Gay and Lesbian Social Services, 11*(4), 1–21.

Mallon, G. P. (2000b). *Let's get this straight: A gay and lesbian affirming approach to child welfare*. New York: Columbia University Press.

Mallon, G. P. (2000c). Your silence will not protect you: Helping schools to retain gay, lesbian, bisexual, and transgendered young people in educational settings. *Reaching Today's Youth, 5*(1), 22-26.

Mallon, G. P. (2001a). *Lesbian and gay youth issues: A youth worker's perspective*. Washington, DC: Child Welfare League of America.

Mallon, G. P. (2001b). Sticks and stones can break your bones: Violence and verbal harassment in the lives of gay and lesbian adolescents in child welfare settings. *Journal of Gay and Lesbian Social Services, 13*(1/2), 65-81.

Maluccio, A. N., Fein, E., & Olmstead, K. A. (1986). *Permanency planning for children: Concepts and methods*. New York: Tavistock.

Martin, A. D. (1982). Learning to hide: The socialization of the gay adolescent. In S. C. Feinstein, J. G. Looney, A. Schartzberg, & A. Sorosky (Eds.), *Adolescent psychiatry: Developmental and clinical studies* (Vol. 10). Chicago: University of Chicago Press.

National Resource Center for Foster Care and Permanency Planning at the Hunter College School of Social Work. (1999). *Handouts on concurrent permanency planning*. New York: Author.

O'Brien, P. (1993). Youth homelessness and the lack of adoption planning for older foster children: Are they related? *Adoptalk*, 10-11.

Remafedi, G. (Ed.). (1994). *The denial of death*. Boston: Alyson.

Ricketts, W. (1991). *Lesbians and gay men as foster parents*. Portland: University of Southern Maine.

Rindfleisch, N. (1993). Combating institutional abuse. In C. E. Schaefer & A. Swanson (Eds.), *Children in residential care: Critical issues in treatment* (pp. 263–283). Northvale, NJ: Jason Aronson.

Ryan, K., & Futterman, D. (1998). *Lesbian and gay youth: Care and counseling*. New York: Columbia University Press.

Savin-Williams, R. C. (1994). Verbal and physical abuse as stressors in the lives of lesbian, gay male, and bisexual youths: Associations with school problems, running away, substance abuse, prostitution, suicide. *Journal of Consulting and Clinical Practice, 62*, 261-269.

Schorr, L. B. (1997). *Common purpose: Strengthening families and neighborhoods to rebuild America*. New York: Doubleday.

Seattle Commission on Children and Youth. (1988). *Report on gay and lesbian youth in Seattle*. Seattle, WA: Seattle Commission on Children and Youth.

Strommen, E. F. (1989). "You're a what?" Family member reactions to the disclosure of homosexuality. *Journal of Homosexuality, 18*(1/2), 37–58.

Sudia, C. (1986). Preventing out-of-home care placement of children: The first steps to permanency planning. *Children Today, 15*(6), 49.

Sullivan, T. (1994). Obstacles to effective child welfare service with gay and lesbian youths. *Child Welfare, 73*(4), 291-304.

Victim Services/Traveler's Aid. (1991). *Streetwork project study*. New York: Victim Services.

Weston, K. (1991). *Families we choose: Gay and lesbian kinship*. New York: Columbia University Press.

Zide, M. R., & Cherry, A. L. (1992). A typology of runaway youths: An empirically based definition. *Child and Adolescent Social Work, 9*(2), 155–168.